HERE'S WHAT SOME FOLKS SAID
ABOUT *HEE HAW*

"*Hee Haw* was more than a TV show, it was an American institution."

—Roy Clark

"I thought they were crazy having little pigs dance across the screen."

—Hank Williams, Jr.

"It's merely foolish!"

—Grandpa Jones

"There were so many negative reviews, people began tuning in to see how bad we were."

—Sam Lovullo,
producer of *Hee Haw*

"Thank you for giving me the opportunity to show the world I'm black."

—Charley Pride

"Hey, this isn't a show, this is a place to come over and have a good old time!"

—Roger Miller

"That's all!"

—Cathy Baker,
Hee Haw regular, at the end of
every show

LIFE
IN THE
KORNFIELD
MY 25 YEARS
AT *HEE HAW*

Sam Lovullo
and *Marc Eliot*

BOULEVARD BOOKS, NEW YORK

Photographs courtesy of Gaylord Program Services, Inc.,
a *Gaylord Entertainment*℠ Company.

Grateful acknowledgment is made for permission to reprint
photographs found on pages 176 & 241 by Dean Dixon.

Grateful acknowledgment is made to Judy Mock for use of her photo of
Sam Lovullo with George and Nancy Jones, which appears on page 115.

Grateful acknowledgment is made to Mamy Music for permission to
reprint lyrics from "Pffft You're Gone."

LIFE IN THE KORNFIELD

A Boulevard Book / published by arrangement with
the authors

PRINTING HISTORY
Boulevard trade paperback edition / December 1996

The Putnam Berkley World Wide Web site address is
http://www.berkley.com/berkley

ISBN: 1-57297-028-6

BOULEVARD
Boulevard Books are published by The Berkley Publishing Group,
200 Madison Avenue, New York, New York 10016.
BOULEVARD and its logo are trademarks belonging to
Berkley Publishing Corporation.

PRINTED IN THE UNITED STATES OF AMERICA

10 9 8 7 6 5 4 3 2 1

INTRODUCTION

by Marc Eliot

MY INITIAL encounter with the inestimable Sam
Lovullo came about as the result of working with
Roy Clark on the writing of his memoirs. At one point,
I needed some information about *Hee Haw*, which Roy hosted
for a quarter-century. He suggested I call Sam in L.A. "Don't
worry," Roy said, smiling that great crinkly-eyed, closer-than-
a-brother grin as he gripped my shoulder, "Sam has all the
answers. To everything. He's an experience you won't soon
forget, Hoss."

Roy was right. Not long after, on a hot July night I called
Sam from my home in New York and explained what I needed.
Over the phone, he proved a font of information, endlessly
fascinating as he verbally rowed through the endless tribu-
taries of his reservoir of memories.

I wound up faxing Sam the entire chapter of Roy's book on
Hee Haw, so he could check the facts. Although he said he
would be happy to, it wasn't until later on I discovered there
had been a part of him that didn't want to read it at all, did-
n't want to bother with it, didn't want to sit down in those so-
called glory days of retirement to do what amounted to a hell
of a lot of work.

Fortunately for all of us, it was the other part of Sam that
prevailed. Opening up the pages of a chapter in Roy's book
was like reading a chapter in his own life. Like any great event

in the days we like to lump together and label our "past," the danger of looking back is the realization of time gone by that will never come this way again.

From there it was but a short leap to my asking Sam to think about working with me on a book about the legendary TV show, and an even shorter one for him to say no. He didn't want to do it. He didn't want to look back. He didn't want to get caught up in all of it again. He didn't want to live in the past. He didn't want to work that hard. He didn't have the time. He was too busy. He had too many new things going. He wasn't sentimental.

You know what they say, the difficult takes time, the impossible a little longer. In the fall of 1993, at Sam's California estate, we sat down and began the work at hand: to compile the history of one of the most popular and enduring electronic artifacts of modern American popular culture.

I've always have been a city-boy, born, raised, educated and, except for periodic, extended visits to the West Coast, a lifelong resident of New York. I was lucky to have had the opportunity to spend the best days of my youth in the musical back alleys of folk-rock-pop Greenwich Village.

Ironically, it was Phil Ochs who, in the early sixties, first turned me on to the glory and thrill of country music. I'll never forget my urban, protest-singing pal raving over the sound of Hank Williams's voice. Indeed, the break in his throat on the opening wail of "Your Cheatin' Heart" became one of the defining moments of my musical life. I've never heard anything like it before or since. Sure, I'd had a taste of so-called "country," or Southern music, as we city kids called it. I'd been around long enough to remember when Buddy Holly helped crash through the barriers of boredom that had imprisoned the fifties. I knew Marty Robbins's "El Paso" by heart. Everyone my age did. The Everly Brothers were heroes to every New York kid who listened to "77-W-A-BEEE-CEEEE!" Jerry Lee Lewis, Johnny Cash, Conway Twitty, Sonny James, Ferlin Husky, and George Hamilton IV were all a part of country's first crossover into rock and roll, and what can there possibly be left for anybody to say about Elvis?

Still, although his music led to all that followed, because Hank Williams never slipped into the commercial mainstream (he was almost completely unknown outside of the south), I came to him relatively late in my musical formation. When Phil turned me on to Hank Williams, I had no idea of the enormity and power of his work, or that he had already been dead for a decade.

Phil taught me how to avoid the hip prejudice most of my peers had when it came to rock and roll. I didn't, couldn't, look down at country music. Quite the opposite. By the time Dylan showed up and rescued my generation from the potbelly pabulum of post-payola pop, most of what passed for rock and roll was no longer very compelling. The action was definitely in country. Dylan knew it, and his public embrace allowed a lot of other Johnny Horton-come-latelys in Tin Pan Alley to take an unashamed first-look at their musical country cousins.

Something was happening out there in the hinterlands, Mr. Jones told us, and *Hee Haw* helped put a face to it.

One of the most pleasant surprises I had working with Sam Lovullo was the discovery that like me, Sam was not a native Nashvillian, but a born-and-raised New Yorker. This Italian-American California-based family man went to Nashville for the first time in 1969, as *Hee Haw*'s producer.

Nor, as I found out, were John Aylsworth and Frank Peppiatt, the show's creators and writers, good old country boys. They were (and still are) a couple of urbane, witty, New York/Hollywood pros whose primary goal in creating and writing *Hee Haw* was to actually go to Nashville as little as possible. Bernie Brillstein, another key player in the formation of *Hee Haw*, was far more comfortable putting together *Saturday Night Live*, a witty, youthful, rock-oriented comedy variety show that became a staple of NBC's Saturday night lineup. And certainly no one from the corporate offices of CBS ever entertained any idea of actually *going* to Nashville to live among the natives for the run of the show.

As a result of this, one of those unique, happy accidents that rarely occurs in television, an *original* concept, was allowed to remain just that. No one at a level of corporate power had the inclination to step in and "fix" *Hee Haw*. Because TV's so-called "rural" sitcoms had proved to the network brass that "country" could draw ratings—although you can be sure none of them ever watched a minute of them—the boys in charge believed there was a huge audience for that kind of "stuff." Therefore, as long as *Hee Haw* brought in stations and ratings, and won its time-slot, which it consistently did, Sam Lovullo remained the sole proprietor of Kornfield Kounty, the mythical home of *Hee Haw*, USA.

Every week for a quarter of a century, *Hee Haw* delivered the best in both classic country music (Johnny Cash, Bill Monroe, Loretta Lynn, Roy Clark, Buck Owens, Roy Acuff and George Jones for openers) and classic country variety/comedy (Minnie Pearl, Grandpa Jones, Archie Campbell, Junior Samples, Pat Buttram, George "Goober" Lindsey, Kenny Price, etc.). As legitimate a form of American entertainment as vaudeville, burlesque, Broadway or Hollywood, *Hee Haw*'s hillbilly humor showed off an otherwise overlooked aspect of our endlessly diverse popular culture, and in doing so helped provide the impetus for the Garth Brooks generation of country, by far the most commercially viable form of popular music in America today.

Many of my friends and associates have long ago stopped trying to figure out where the buoys are in the stream of my career. However, among the many unexpected and often turbulent rivulets I have traveled, none seems to have caused more brows to raise than my recent writings on country music. This reaction always brings a smile to my face. I usually say nothing, preferring instead to turn in the direction of some good old boy's voice ringing like a golden cracked bell somewhere further down the road, wailing a heartbreakingly beautiful version of "I Saw the Light," and wait for all my urban popsters-disguised-as-hipsters up there ahead of me to catch up.

When they do, I'll be waiting with a stack of Hank Williams CDs to lead them on the long and fabulous journey that awaits. And the *Hee Haw*, of course, will be on all of us.

April 18, 1996
Hollywood, California

This book is dedicated to my wife, Grace, my children, Linda, Lisa, Tony, Torey, and family and friends, and to God, who gave me the wisdom, support and love to make this book happen.

—SAM LOVULLO

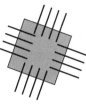

PART ONE

THE STORY OF HEE HAW

"It's merely foolish!"

—GRANDPA JONES

Before Hee Haw, *I produced* The Jonathan Winters Show. *Jonathan was a frequent* Hee Haw *guest*

T HE TOUGHEST day of my life was June 30, 1993, when I had to close down my *Hee Haw* office at the Grand Ole Opry complex in Nashville, get on a plane and fly home to Los Angeles for the last time. I'd spent so much time in that office, it was more like my home than a place of business. How, I wondered, as I packed the last of my things, do you put twenty-five seasons' worth of memories, friendships, births, marriages, divorces, deaths and celebrations into cardboard boxes?

I had been with *Hee Haw* from the start, part of the show's creative nucleus that had first come together in the sixties on *The Jonathan Winters Show.*

I joined Jonathan's show as an associate producer in its second season, and a year later I met two Canadian writer/producers, John Aylesworth and Frank Peppiatt, when they were brought on board by the CBS network. Along with their manager, Bernie Brillstein, Frank and John had compiled a very successful track record of network TV variety shows: *The Perry Como Show, The Judy Garland Show,* and *The Jackie Gleason Variety Hour.*

The Jonathan Winters Show had debuted on CBS in the fall of '66, and it had done well enough, but the feeling among the network boys upstairs was that Jonathan's quirky brand of fringy, improvisational humor had too narrow an appeal to reach a broad-based audience, particularly in the South. In an attempt to improve the show's ratings in its second season, Perry Lafferty, then the West Coast vice president of programming for CBS, decided to bring in Peppiatt and Aylesworth as writer/producers.

In truth, they were primarily writers, which left Perry still in need of someone to handle the actual business of "producing," someone to make sure the trains ran on time. That someone turned out to be me.

No one was more surprised by Perry's decision than I was. The farthest thing from my mind was producing a major network television show. I was a born-and-bred Italian New Yorker, transplanted to the West Coast to attend UCLA where I majored in accounting in the School of Business Administration. Upon graduation in 1954, I hoped to be hired by a Wall Street corporation and work my way up the legendary ladder of success. I never dreamed my future would be in television.

Meanwhile, though, I secured a job in the accounting department at CBS-Television and, once there, determined to carve a niche out for myself. I made it my goal to learn the language of show business, and I used this to develop an especially valuable skill—the ability to read a script and determine what it would take in dollars to produce it. I soon found myself advising others how to negotiate a deal and how to work with outside writers, producers, lawyers and talent.

As a result, I was assigned to supervise the financial administration of several of the network's most successful programs, including *Lassie*, *The Judy Garland Show*, and *The Beverly Hillbillies*. Over the next twelve years, I worked my way up to the position of West Coast manager for Business Affairs.

In 1967, a contract for a fellow by the name of Bill Larsen, a production manager and associate producer on *The Jonathan Winters* and *The Danny Kaye* shows, came up for renewal. Bill wanted a huge raise in salary, and Perry, through our Business Affairs department, requested that I negotiate the deal. During our talks, Bill threatened to walk if he didn't get everything he wanted. There was a showdown, and when it was over, he was out, and somehow I found myself in. Perry assigned me the suddenly vacant position as associate producer for what was supposed to have been Bill's next project, *The Jonathan Winters Show*.

Don Sipes, the vice president of my division, gave his okay, with the proviso that I continue to fulfill my duties in Business Affairs. I now had a chance to make a major career leap, and it might be jeopardized by the very thing that had made it possible—my ability to do my original job!

I knew this was a once-in-a-lifetime chance, and was determined to come up with a plan to make it happen. I knew *Jonathan Winters* was going to be rehearsing Thursdays, blocking Fridays and taping Saturday nights. I told Don I was prepared to split my week. Monday through Wednesday and part of Thursday I would devote my time to Business Affairs. From Thursday afternoon through Saturday night, I would work on *The Jonathan Winters Show*.

Don thought I was crazy, that I could never pull it off, but he agreed to let me give it a try. For the next year, the only sleep I got was the few moments I could find during each day when I lay down on my office sofa and caught a nap. I almost never made it home.

There's no question it was a struggle and put a heavy strain on my personal life. I was married with four small children—Linda, Lisa, Tony and Torey—and I was almost never available to share the responsibilities of raising them with my wife, Grace. Thankfully, when we first discussed what I should do, she agreed I had been given a major career opportunity and had to go for it.

Moreover, because no one else was as sure as I was that I could pull it off, I declined any fee for my work on *The Jonathan Winters Show*. I insisted I receive only my regular Business Affairs salary. Also, as I was involved in Bill Larsen's departure, I didn't want it to look as if I had gotten rid of him just to take his job. I felt I had something to prove on two fronts, and didn't want to do it on company time. Occasionally, to demonstrate the organization's appreciation, Anne Nelson, my Business Affairs associate who was in charge of the show, would send me a check for a few hundred dollars for my work—money which kept me going at the time.

I maintained that schedule through the end of my first season with the show, after which the original producer and his entire staff were let go. It was thereafter that Perry Lafferty brought in the creative team of Peppiatt and Aylesworth and put us all together. This marked the formation of a team that would stay together for nearly twenty years.

In the fall of 1968, just before production on the third season began, Perry called me back into his office. "Sam," he said, "I just don't think you can keep doing both jobs." He was right. At the age of thirty-nine I definitely needed to make a decision about the direction of my career. Either I was going back into the Business Affairs department or I was staying in programming. After much soul-searching and many a sleepless night, I decided to opt for the latter.

Having committed myself, I worked as hard as I could with Frank and John to try and turn the show around. We were able to keep it going through all of the 1968-69 season. There's no question that Jonathan was and is a great talent, with an ingenious comic mind. However, for one reason or another, his particular brand of humor attracted a mostly urban, eastern audience. As a result, we always had trouble reaching the rural south, which seriously affected our ratings. During the show's third—and what would prove to be its final—season, we decided to take a chance and attempt to broaden the show's appeal to the South by booking "country" performers.

We quickly discovered there were remarkably few country acts with any prior national exposure. Among the few was Minnie Pearl, a bona fide country legend whose long association with the Grand Ole Opry radio broadcasts had earned her a national following. We knew of Jimmy Dean, who'd gained network exposure with his CBS morning show in the early sixties, and Roy Clark, who'd recently done well in a recurring role on *The Beverly Hillbillies*.

We also knew of George "Goober" Lindsey, because of the popularity he'd gained as a regular on the *The Andy Griffith Show*, and Buck Owens, then the number one hit-maker in country music. Although Buck's network exposure was limited, he did have a very popular syndicated TV show that aired throughout the South. Finally, we booked perhaps the greatest living country legends of them all, Roy Rogers and Dale Evans.

Sure enough, each and every time we had one of these five country acts on, we experienced an immediate jump in ratings—primarily because of the South. That told us something no one else in network programming had realized. There was a vast, largely untapped southern audience for network television.

Still, near the end of our third season, it became clear that no matter what we did, the numbers just weren't there consistently enough to justify renewal, and we were canceled.

At the same time, ABC announced it had signed Johnny Cash to host his own network variety show, to be broadcast out of Nashville, Tennessee's, legendary Ryman Hall, the home of the Grand Ole Opry. I found this notable for two reasons. First, Johnny Cash was the only country singer ever to host a regularly scheduled, prime-time, one-hour network variety show, and, second, that show was the first to be broadcast out of Nashville.

I believe it was no accident that ABC had suddenly decided to take a chance on a country-music variety show. CBS had already experienced great success with a slew of so-called "rural" situation comedies—*The Beverly Hillbillies, The Andy Griffith Show, Green Acres*, and *Petticoat Junction*—all highly rated. It had finally become obvious to all of us that there was a definite and sizable nationwide audience for country-style entertainment.

CBS was also experiencing a limited degree of "country" success with *The Glen Campbell Show*, its 1968 summer replacement for the Sunday night *Smothers Brothers Comedy Hour*. In the sixties, the producer of a successful television show "owned" his time slot and controlled the summer replacement programming. Glen Campbell's show, which the network loved, was owned by Tommy and Dick Smothers, whose show the network hated.

Although *The Smothers Brothers Comedy Hour* was very strong, CBS was having problems with Tommy Smothers. They didn't quite understand or appreciate his political satire and kept trying to rein him in, which only made him more outspoken. After repeated warnings, early in 1969, the network canceled their show.

That infamous incident occurred just as the regular broadcast season was coming to an end. Because the Smothers brothers were also the producers of Glen's show, CBS had to let it go as well. Now, with the popular Sunday-night, 8:00 P.M. time slot suddenly available, Mike Dann, CBS's East-Coast head of programming, instructed Perry Lafferty to quickly come up with a country variety show to replace Glen's.

As it happened, Perry knew that Frank and John had been trying to develop a country variety show ever since the cancellation of *The Jonathan Winters Show*—something their personal manager, Bernie Brillstein, called *Hee Haw*.

When production had ended on Jonathan's show, I figured my short but illustrious career as a network producer had come to an end, and I decided to return to my full-time position in Business Affairs. No sooner had I settled in, though, than I received a call from Perry Lafferty, who said he wanted to see me in his office immediately. When I arrived, he nodded for me to take a seat. "Are you settled into your office yet, Lovullo?"

"Just about."

"Well, I've got something I want to talk to you about. I just got word from Mike Dann, head of CBS programming. We've decided to do a one-hour special called *Hee Haw*, based on Frank and John's concept."

"Hey," I said. "That's great."

"Do you know where they are right now? I've been trying to reach them. I want a production meeting in my office at five this afternoon."

I said, "I really don't know. I'll find them." Perry's office was on the third highest level of the building. I remember getting up, looking out his window at the cars going down Beverly Boulevard and Fairfax, and knowing I had just lied. I knew exactly where they were: Across the street at the Farmer's Daughter, a local CBS hangout, drowning their sorrows in gin and tonics over losing *The Jonathan Winters Show*.

"Furthermore," Perry said, "You're going to produce the special in Nashville, Tennessee."

I couldn't believe my ears! I almost jumped out that window!

"Understand, you'll still be an employee of the network, just like before. I want you to go to Nashville and, you know, watch over our interest."

I was back in business! I thanked Perry, left his office, and went directly to Farmer's Daughter, where I found Frank and John feeling no pain. I walked in and they slurred a greeting my way, adding, "You have any work for two guys who are unemployed?"

"Frank, John, I want to tell you something. *Hee Haw*'s been picked up by the network. Perry wants to see you in his office at five this afternoon."

Well, you never saw two guys sober up so fast! They ran out of the place, went to their respective homes, got cleaned up, shaved, showered, and were ready for that meeting.

And that's how it all began.

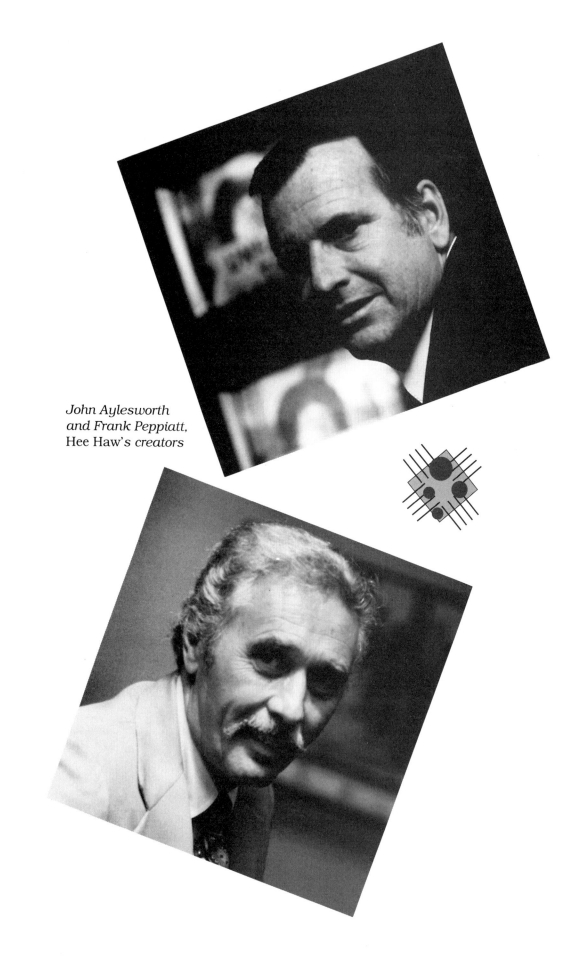

*John Aylesworth
and Frank Peppiatt,
Hee Haw's creators*

IN JANUARY 1968, *Laugh-In*, a midseason replacement variety program hosted by the comedy team of Dan Rowan and Dick Martin, made its debut on NBC. *Laugh-In* proved to be one of those rare programs which introduced something fresh that hadn't been seen before on television— a whole new style of comedy. Before, TV comedy/variety had always been presented the same way: a big opening number, a couple of comedy skits, one or two musical segments, a guest star, and a splashy close. *Laugh-In* dragged network television kicking and screaming into the so-called "psyche-delic '60s" with an endless barrage of one-liners and nonstop comic moments, none of which lasted more than a sentence or two.

Laugh-In debuted during the third season of *The Jonathan Winters Show*, and in truth, we tried to emulate some of their comedy stylings. We noticed, for example, that Jonathan got a better response from the audience when he delivered one-liners than he did acting in comedy sketches. As a result, we cut way back on the sketches and increased the one-liners. This was a style we would continue and develop with *Hee Haw*. However, unlike *Laugh-In*, which was hip, urban, cerebral and timely, we gave our show a southern twist, including a stable of rural "characters" as unlike *Laugh-In* stars Judy Carne and Goldie Hawn as possible. Also, whereas *Laugh-In* offered fifty-two minutes of nonstop one-liners, we did sketches, and every eight or ten minutes we interrupted the comedy with a straight musical number, performed by top country stars.

Frank, John, and Bernie Brillstein, who helped realize the

physical "look" of *Hee Haw*, developed the show under the umbrella of their newly formed Yongestreet Productions (named after a famous Canadian boulevard). The idea was to reflect the lifestyle of moonshiners, straw hats, overalls and lots of Daisy Mae–type country gals. All the other current variety shows, except for *Laugh-In*, dressed their stars in tuxedos.

We were given the official go-ahead for the special the first week in May of 1969, with a directive to finish by June 19. That gave us about five and a half weeks from start-up to air!

The initial success of *The Johnny Cash Show* had convinced the powers at CBS that producing *Hee Haw* in Nashville was the way to go. As I flew down to Tennessee with our director, Bill Davis, who'd helmed *The Jonathan Winters Show*, and John Aylesworth (Frank hung back in Los Angeles), I thought about how none of us had ever even been to Nashville before. We were about as far from Tennesseans as you could get. I was born and bred an Italian-American New Yorker, and Bill, John, and Frank were Canadian! Not one of us could have picked out a country singer from a band of angels if our lives depended on it!

Before our departure, CBS announced to its affiliates that *Hee Haw* was coming in as a midseason replacement for *The Glen Campbell Show*. The Nashville affiliate, WLAC, happened to have a sales representative in Los Angeles who came by to let us know he wanted our production business. We arranged to meet him in Nashville.

However, our first choice for a stage was the obvious one, the Ryman Auditorium, the home of the Grand Ole Opry. The only problem was at that time the Ryman's TV facilities were owned by the NBC network, and we were on CBS. Besides, *The Johnny Cash Show* was already taping there. Nowadays, shows from one network often rent out the facilities of another, but in those days it was akin to having Gimbel's rent window space at Macy's. It just wasn't done.

We looked at several other facilities before finally settling on the CBS affiliated studio, Channel 5—WLAC-TV—with a small production studio operated by 20th Century

Productions, headed by WLAC Vice President Roy Smith. We liked what we saw at Channel 5 and were eager to strike a deal with Smith, who was just as anxious to get the show. He was hoping to create a niche for himself in the growing field of country-oriented programming. Elsewhere, Porter Wagoner and Dolly Parton were doing a successful regional television show out of Nashville, and Buck Owens had one out of Oklahoma City. Smith was looking to make a connection to the network, and believed having a CBS show coming from his studio was the best way to do it. I, on the other hand, had no grander dreams than negotiating a good price.

After touring the facility, I told Roy Smith I was prepared to make a deal on the spot. Even though it was small as a matchbox (which in fact became its nickname) and not at all equipped for the size of our operation, there was something about the intimate feel I liked. I figured putting on a show in a place this size would bring everyone closer together and make us, by necessity, more like a family than a "cast and crew." The boys would all share one dressing room, as would the girls. I hoped if we all worked together and dressed together, we'd all wind up laughing together.

At the time, we thought we were just going to do the special. However, even before we finished it, the network decided to keep us on the air for the remainder of the summer and ordered twelve additional shows. So, instead of having to do just one *Hee Haw* show, we now had to come up with twelve, *all in that same five and a half weeks*!

The first thing we needed to do was to supplement our writing team. We signed Jack Burns, a comedy writer from the West Coast and one half of the stand-up team of Burns and Schreiber. We felt Jack understood the type of humor we were after from his years writing and acting on *The Andy Griffith Show* (years later, Jack would join *Hee Haw* as a performer). We also brought in George Yanok, a solid sketch writer; Gordie Tapp, a Canadian comedian; and Archie Campbell, a regular comic on the Grand Ole Opry who introduced us to

Buck and Roy, doing what they do best

the ins and outs of country-style comedy and music. Together, they dreamt up many of the early, rural-based comedy routines that became so much a part of our show, including "The General Store," "The Moonshiners," "The Barber Shop" and "The Kornfield." There's no question they were instrumental to the success story of *Hee Haw*.

We also decided to go after those country acts that had worked so well for us on *The Jonathan Winters Show*. We wanted Roy Clark and Buck Owens to be our weekly cohosts. Everyone knew Roy was a great instrumentalist, but we also wanted him for his comedic abilities, which we knew from *The Jonathan Winters Show*. Perry Lafferty had had a relationship with Roy from the time he'd appeared on *The Beverly Hillbillies*, and that made things a lot easier, although in truth, it didn't take much to convince Roy to sign on to a show that could give him additional national TV exposure.

We hoped to rely on Buck to carry the show's musical load. I first became friendly with his manager, Jack McFadden, when Buck appeared on Jonathan's show, and I called to ask him if Buck would consider being one of our cohosts. What I didn't know at the time was that Buck was actively looking for a way to move himself out of regional syndication TV and onto a network. After working out a few last-minute hitches having to do with, of all things, billing (whose name came first—I'll tell you more about it later on), Buck signed on, and we were off and running. Within a matter of days, we had assembled our first cast of "regulars."

During that first five-week production period, no one seemed to "get" what Frank and John were going for, though after a few days of taping, I began to "see" it. We'd go in and tell our actors, "Today we've got to change this, don't ask any questions, just do it this way." Although I had an idea in my head of what we wanted, we were, in reality, a bunch of performers, a couple of writers, and a crew of technicians thrown together inside a studio the size of a matchbox with no one really knowing exactly what the hell he or she was supposed to do. So we frantically taped a series of bits and sketches and a bunch of musical numbers, then took it all into the editing room to try to find a way to make some sense of it all.

At the time, everyone's input was welcome, although quite honestly there weren't very many people around who seemed to have any understanding at all of what we were (or should be) after. Ironically, someone who seemed to "get it" was a young, smart, very aware woman who had no direct connection to the show. She was, rather, a switchboard operator at Channel 5. I used to talk to her about what we were attempting, and she always seemed to focus right onto the concept. I found her quite interesting, and helpful. She was a smart young lady with an eye on the future, and it wasn't long before she landed a job in the local news department. Then, one day, she disappeared. I had no idea what happened to her, until a few years later she reemerged as the host of her own TV talk show. Does the name Oprah Winfrey sound familiar?

To help realize my vision, I brought to Nashville some of the best technicians in the business whom I'd worked with in Los Angeles. Audio people, quality control people, and Leard Davis, the extremely talented lighting director of *The Jonathan Winters Show*. I've always considered lighting in television at least as important as (if not more so than) set design, and in my opinion, Leard was the best in the business. He gave the show a special look that stood out. He worked with us for sixteen years, until his unfortunate early death from cancer. I can still see Leard standing there, always with a lit cigarette in his hand, poor nervous genius that he was.

For our first shows, we used two main sets—the barn and the porch—and superimposed a lot of barnyard animation. The animation was created jointly by Frank and John, and Herb Klynn. Herb had done a lot of animation for ABC before starting his own company, Format Films, supervised by his right-hand person, Hank Jordan. Together, they produced the *Alvin and The Chipmunks* TV cartoon show. Along with Leard's lighting, Herb's animation gave *Hee Haw* a definite physical "look." Herb created our famous donkey and the dancing pigs. His work carried over into our set design. The brilliant colors, the board fence, and the hayfield all reflected his "animated" style. The show's sound effects were by Joe Siracusa, who'd worked with Spike Jones, and was responsible for all the crazy noises the band made.

Even with the best talent and technicians, those five and a half weeks proved a very rough haul. Among many problems we encountered, we discovered that the Nashville-based crew had no experience building sets. They tended to build them as if they were building houses, gigantic, fortresslike constructions. I saw one carpenter bang a nail into a flat and then start to putty and paint it. I went over and explained to him that wasn't necessary in television, that TV cameras could never pick up that kind of detail. Well, the fellow up and quit right then and there, saying he couldn't work for a TV producer who tried to tell him how to practice his craft.

When they finally finished building what would become our home-base set, the living room, it was so gigantic they couldn't get it from the studio's basement shop up and onto the stage. They wound up having to cut the thing in half, and reassemble it on stage.

Somehow, by June 10, we'd managed to tape enough material for twelve shows. I then had to lug the raw footage back to Los Angeles with me for postproduction, because editing facilities didn't exist in Nashville.

Editing, of course, was the key to *Hee Haw*. From the first day we went into production until the end, twenty-five seasons later, we always did our shows the same way—in bits and pieces, like movies, rather than in the chronological order of the finished product. We would tape enough material for thirteen shows in June and another thirteen in October. The shows that we did in June would start airing in the fall. By January of the following year we would run the shows produced the previous October. Once we ran all twenty-six shows, we would rerun them until the next fall season began.

We'd tape so many one-liners, "The Kornfield," "Picket Fences," "Empty Arms Hotels," "The Barber Shop," and musical numbers, and then we'd patch them together later. The June/October split-taping schedules afforded us several creative advantages. For example, if a recording artist's new record hit big in the fall, we'd be able to get him on that season during the October production period.

Often, our best creative ideas surfaced while the cameras were running, and so we discovered the most effective way to plan our days. For example, we learned the best time to tape "The Kornfield" was the middle of the day, because not every regular cast member was required in every segment. However, usually by the afternoon, they all would have shown up to be in our famous full-cast "*Hee Haw* Sa-loot!"

Incidentally, taping "The Kornfield" was a difficult, often chaotic process. I always felt sorry for our assistant producer, Sandy Liles, whose job it was to constantly monitor and catalog everything. Bear in mind we didn't have the advantage of computerized technology. In those days, everything was still done by hand.

The lack of technology also affected the "style" of the show. For example, wireless microphones, or "Lavaleers," weren't yet available. Because we had to use an overhead "boom" mike for musical numbers, it was difficult to go to a "wide" shot that would also show the artist within the set. As a result, all our early performances were shot "tight," or in medium close-up.

It wasn't until we completed editing the first show that original cast member Grandpa Jones "got" what we were trying to do, turned to me, smiled and said, "It's merely foolish!"

Exactly!

We were still editing the twelve additional shows when the first *Hee Haw* aired. The date was June 15, 1969. Some of the first sponsors on the show were Kool cigarettes, Honda motorbike, Dristan, Silva Thins, Quiet World, Reynolds Wrap, and Procter & Gamble. Their commercials were sold by the CBS network.

Loretta Lynn and Charley Pride were our very first guests, both suggested by Buck Owens. In those early years, we depended a great deal upon Buck to deliver the best country music acts in the business. Loretta Lynn appeared in a cowboy outfit, long skirt, big boots, and a guitar that looked bigger than she was. She stood on our porch, played her guitar, and sang, accompanied by the unseen Buckaroos. Charley Pride did his song standing on the barn set, in front of a couple of bales of hay. So much for production values!

The day after we debuted, I remember sitting in the editing room reading the reviews and being horrified by the negative critical reaction. Each was worse than the one before it. When Frank Peppiatt saw me sitting there looking a bit despondent, he came over and said, "What's the matter, Sam?"

"I don't know, Frank." I didn't want to tell him I was thinking about the future of the show, and my own as well. I was still technically employed by CBS, "on loan," so I could maintain my family medical benefits, but that didn't stop me from wondering who was doing my old job, and how well? I was sure now that *Hee Haw* couldn't possibly last, there'd be nothing for me to do at the network, and I'd be let go. I was a young man with a wife and family, and, brother, let me tell you, I was scared.

As if he could read my mind, Frank put his hands on my

shoulders and said, "Don't worry, Sam, we've got a winner. Those critics are doing us the biggest favor in the world."

He was right, of course. There were so many negative articles about the show, people began tuning in to just see how bad we were, and once they found us, they were surprised that they liked what they saw and they tended to stay for the whole ride. Sure, we were cornball, but *hilarious* cornball, good old-fashioned country humor, much of which was brand-new and quite refreshing to the folks up in New York and out in Los Angeles, and other sophisticated cities across the nation. By our fifth broadcast, we were a bona fide hit.

In fact, our ratings proved so consistently strong that after our summer run ended, CBS decided it wanted to keep us on the air. However, because its fall schedule was already in place, the network positioned us as the first midseason replacement. Anticipating a January airdate, I returned to Nashville on November 3, 1969, and in the next twenty-six days we taped enough material for ten new shows.

The first casualty of the '69–'70 season was *The Leslie Uggams Show*, which premiered on September 28 and went off the air December 21. We replaced it the following week, December 29, 1969, and stayed on the air without missing a single week's telecast for the next twenty-four years.

THREE

RETURNED once again to Nashville in May of 1970 to tape enough material for thirteen new episodes, and again the following October for nine more. We were a hit show with high ratings, and the future couldn't have looked brighter. In the spring of 1971, I received two phone calls from New York. The first was from an executive at CBS who wanted to congratulate us for having the twelfth highest rated prime-time network show in the nation that week. The second was from another executive, calling to inform us that we were canceled.

To fully understand why and how such a seemingly incomprehensible thing could have happened when we were flying so high, it's necessary to understand how the business of television operates. The industry is essentially cyclical in nature, rising and falling in waves of similar types of programming. In the '50s, quiz shows dominated prime-time programming. In the '60s it was Westerns, such as *Gunsmoke* and *The Virginian*. The '70s gave us the golden age of sitcoms, led by *The Mary Tyler Moore Show*, *Bob Newhart* and *All in the Family*. By the mid-'80s, the sitcom was declared brain-dead and virtually disappeared from the airwaves, until *The Cosby Show* restored the genre to the front ranks. Currently, the trend seems to be back to one-hour medical and police dramas.

One of the reasons CBS gave us the original go-ahead in 1969 to do *Hee Haw* was the success it had experienced not only with Glen Campbell's summer replacement show, but with rural comedies in general. At the time, the most popular shows on TV were the half-hour sitcoms *The Beverly*

Hillbillies, *The Andy Griffith Show*, *Petticoat Junction*, *Gomer Pyle USMC*, and *Green Acres*.

These shows had been developed during the regime of James Aubrey, the vice president of CBS programming until 1967, when he was replaced by Mike Dann. Dann decided to continue capitalizing on the network's successful string of rural programs, and he green-lighted *Hee Haw*.

In 1970, he was replaced by his assistant, Fred Silverman, who decided he wanted to change the image of the network. He canceled every one of its rural programs, including *Hee Haw*. (Incidentally, CBS wasn't the only network intent upon changing its image. Considering the cyclical nature of TV, it isn't surprising that ABC followed Silverman's example. They decided that Lawrence Welk, who had been on their network since 1955, no longer fit the network's "image," and they canceled his show.)

What was behind Silverman's actions? Television networks are made up of several hundred affiliates, a small number of which the network are legally allowed to own. These are called O and O's—owned and operated (by the network). The three majors—ABC, CBS and NBC—own and operate affiliate stations in New York City; Chicago; Los Angeles; Washington, D.C.; Philadelphia; and San Francisco. Television advertising is sold on the basis of "cost-per-thousand." In 1971, CBS's O and O's informed Silverman they were no longer willing to carry *Hee Haw* because the advertisers' "cost-per-thousand" fees were too low to be profitable.

Everybody always talks about ratings (the relative popularity of all network shows), but in truth they really don't mean all that much. It's the *audience share* that counts: what share a program gets of all viewers who are watching television during a *specific time period*. The show with the greatest share, meaning that it has more people watching it than anything else at the time, "wins" its hour. *That's* what counts to advertisers. Homes are counted in multiples of a thousand, a figure upon which the cost for advertising is calculated. The problem Freddy Silverman faced when he took over CBS was that even though his network's programs were rating high, the cost-per-thousand was quite low because the audiences were primarily rural. As a result, the network couldn't demand the big dollars from the so-called urban cosmetics and appliance sponsors.

To improve the network's profit margin, Silverman knew he had to win a greater share of urban viewers, particularly at CBS's O and O's. A lot of people have written about the "cultural" changes Silverman brought to CBS, but in truth his actions were done for strictly financial reasons.

Hee Haw was a typical case in point. At the time of our cancellation we were reaching about twenty million people, one out of eight in the country. Those are pretty great numbers. The problem was, many viewers were in the economically depressed South. Because we—like the rest of CBS's rural programs—couldn't deliver a high enough cost-per-thousand rate for the network's O and O's, we faced cancellation.

Incidentally, years later, I happened to be at an industry luncheon where Fred Silverman was scheduled to speak about his experiences as a programmer for three networks. By this time he had left CBS, gone to NBC, left there, did a stint at ABC, left there, and essentially was looking for a job. I'll never forget his opening remarks. "I guess you all know I'm unemployed," he began. "I was the one responsible for kicking *Hee Haw* off the network. Is it any wonder I'm unemployed and they're still going strong?"

After the show's cancellation, I was preparing to return to Los Angeles, hoping to get my old job back in Business Affairs. As I was packing my bags, I got a call from a very dear friend of mine at CBS, Mike Donohew, director of Business Affairs on the West Coast. "Sam," he said, "you're a damn fool if you come back to the company."

"Mike, I have no choice. I've got a family to support."

He brushed that aside. "My friend, there's a gold mine in country music and you ought to stick with it."

What I didn't know at the time was that Frank, John, and a new partner, Nick Vanoff, were about to launch a daring plan to save the show by attempting something that had never been done before. Some called it desperate, others plain crazy. Because they held the show's syndication rights, they decided to move *Hee Haw* into first-run syndication—*without the support, production facilities, or blessing of the network!* Although I didn't know it at the time, that's what Mike's call to me was all about. He'd heard rumors that the network had no interest in continuing with *Hee Haw*, syndicated or otherwise, and wanted to tell me to stick with Frank, John, and Nick.

From the time CBS first produced the show, Yongestreet had had the benefit of the services of Nick Vanoff. He was a very successful and respected TV producer. Among his many hit shows were *The Hollywood Palace*, *The Steve Allen* and *The Perry Como* shows. When *Hee Haw* was first given the green light by CBS to go into regular weekly production, Frank and John had offered Nick and his partner, Bill Harbach, fifty percent ownership of the show. Most first-run television programming is produced either close to breakeven, or at a deficit. The real money is in syndicated reruns. Nick and Bill helped strengthen Yongestreet's financial viability and assure the stations it could afford to deliver a new show every week in the meantime.

To make the deal, Nick Vanoff insisted upon and received fifty-one percent of Yongestreet's stock, which gave him control of the company. I have to confess when I first heard about it, young and inexperienced as I was, I felt offended. I went to Frank and John and said, "Why the hell did you guys do that for? There's no way I would have let the show go over budget. You didn't have to worry about that!"

As I would come to understand, Frank and John really had no choice but to sell. If something unforeseen happened and the show did go over budget, they were personally liable according to the terms of their contract with CBS. Later on, of course, they regretted having sold off any portion of *Hee Haw*. Not only did the show never go over budget, but over the years it proved to be an extremely profitable venture. However, at the time it was something that had to be done.

Several unrelated events had taken place around the time of *Hee Haw*'s cancellation that made the notion of moving to syndication seem possible. One of the most significant was a series of Federal Communications Commission changes in broadcasting regulations that required all the networks to divest themselves of their wholly owned syndication subsidiaries. (CBS, for instance, was forced to sell its syndication subsidiary, which changed its name to Viacom and became one of the major independent syndicators in the business today.) The reason for the ruling was simply that if a network controlled the programming that appeared on independent, competing stations, it might find itself in violation of fair trade and antimonopolistic regulations. For example, if a network wanted to ensure a high rating for its own program, it could schedule something at the same time on its syndicates that it knew no one would watch. In any case, the ruling meant that even if CBS had wanted to continue with *Hee Haw* in syndication, it couldn't have.

During the attempted transition to syndication, to express their ongoing confidence in my ability to produce the show, Frank, John and Nick offered to let me buy into the show. After all, I had produced all fifty-one network programs, and I was the one spending all the time in Nashville. They had the title of executive producers, but in reality they mostly concentrated on the writing. I felt gratified by their acknowledgment of my contributions, and would have loved to buy in, but unfortunately for me at the time, I just didn't have that kind of money.

A crucial meeting took place late one morning at the show's Beverly Hills office to figure out how to effectively make the move into syndication. At the meeting were the show's owners, Peppiatt and Aylesworth, their manager Bernie Brillstein, and Nick Vanoff and Bill Harback.

Although I wasn't a principal, I was asked to come in and talk a bit about my experiences in Nashville and my thoughts about the ongoing popularity of country music. There was some concern because following our cancellation, it appeared that over at ABC, Johnny Cash's ratings had fallen off and he was also about to get the axe (remember, TV programming comes in waves).

I was asked by Nick Vanoff what I knew about syndication and to speculate about the future of country on television in general, and *Hee Haw* in particular. "Let me tell you something, Nick," I said. "In my opinion, Nashville is going to develop into a major television center, mainly due to what I see as a coming boom in country music. If you want to know what I think, we pushed too much comedy at the expense of music."

It was true. The fifty-one shows I'd produced for the network were made up mostly of one-liners and sketches, with two, maybe three songs at the most, in a show.

Still, I wasn't sure what Nick's reaction was going to be. I could tell immediately that Bernie Brillstein didn't like what I was saying. He dismissed my ideas as the ravings of an amateur. Partially because of Johnny Cash's cancellation, he had begun to change his thinking about trying to save the show. As he put it at the meeting, he thought we were crazy— "trying to beat a dead donkey."

At this point I stood up and said, "Okay, guys, you do what you want to do." I headed for the door, opened it, then turned around and, in a booming voice, stated what has since become known as one of my best "Samisms": "I don't think you understand! Either way, you're going to win or lose!"

I stormed out and returned to my own office. A few minutes later, Bernie Brillstein swung open my door, pointed a finger at me, and shouted, "I don't want you telling my clients what to do! That stupid donkey is dead! I want Frank and John to forget about shitkicking and move on!"

In a quiet voice, I said, "I don't think you understand, Bernie." He left, and I sat down at my desk. A few minutes later I heard a knock on my door. It was Nick Vanoff. He walked in laughing. "Do you realize what you said when you left that office?"

"I don't know what I said, Nick."

"'Either way you win or lose.' What the hell did you

mean by that?" I shrugged my shoulders. Nick looked at me and said, "You believe in this show, don't you?"

"Yes I do." I said. "I've been to Nashville. I've seen what's happening. We're at the start of something that could really make history."

I went on to tell Nick about the very first song that Roy Clark had performed on *Hee Haw*—"Yesterday When I Was Young." I told him how impressed I'd been, not only by the song, but by Roy's performance of it—how it reminded me of when I was a kid and my daddy used to take me to the opera, how I'd sit there with my mother and him and read the story lines. To me, country music was the same thing. Great stories, all about love, hate, life, death, all of it. "Nick," I said, "as far as I'm concerned, if I had the money, I would buy you and your partners out right now, and do the damn thing on my own."

He looked at me, said nothing and walked out of my office. Five minutes later he returned and said, "Pack your things. We're going to do this, Sam."

I looked at him in disbelief, speechless for one of the very few times in my life.

"By the way, I assume with your background in the 'Business Affairs' department you understand how barter works?"

"I certainly do."

"Good. Because I want you to get on a plane and fly to Chicago, to the NATPE convention. Get yourself a suite at the Ambassador, start talking to people and see how many stations you can convince to take *Hee Haw* on a barter plan."

NATPE (The National Association of Television Producers and Executives) was then in its fourth year of existence. The primary purpose of *the* annual convention was to give independent television producers an opportunity to meet the sales representatives of syndication distributors and individual station programmers. The convention was attended by every syndicator looking to buy programming to sell to stations and every producer with a show for sale.

The NATPE convention was undergoing a tremendous growth period, as was syndicated programming, following yet another FCC ruling (which would prove favorable to *Hee Haw*) that required individual stations to devote the hours between six and eight P.M. to local news or local programming, a time period the Commission defined as "prime access." As a result, stations which didn't have the money or the expertise to produce their own programming had to find prepackaged syndicated programming to fill those hours. *Hee Haw* happened to fall perfectly within the acceptable definition of programming for prime access. Knowing that, Nick hoped I might be able to line up enough stations at the convention to keep us alive.

The standard commercial breakdown for one hour of syndicated programming was eight positions, known as "four and four"—four commercial spots for the producers, four for the local station, plus mid-breaks, and so forth. Our plan was to offer each station's sales representative the show for free, including four commercial positions, then take the remaining four positions to New York and line up sponsors on a cost-per-thousand basis, based on the total number of stations we signed. This was the "barter" plan that Nick had devised. The key to the whole thing was the sale of those four spots, which would be our only source of income. Out of that revenue, we'd have to pay the production costs of the show, with enough left over to show a profit.

Whatever fears I had on the flight to Chicago, and believe me I had many, disappeared as soon as I hit the convention floor. I was immediately overwhelmed by distributors who'd heard the show was available. The crush was so great, the first chance I got I grabbed the phone and called Lisa Todd, one of our *Hee Haw* Honeys. I asked her if she could fly in to help me, which she was more than happy to do. By the end of the second day, every major distribution company wanted to make a deal to handle *Hee Haw*.

That night, I called Nick. "Look," I said, "you're the owner of the show. I'm just a producer. Some major decisions have to be made. I think you ought to get on a plane and fly here as soon as possible."

The next morning, Nick arrived with a new member of the Yongestreet team, Alan Courtney. Alan was the former president of Four Star Productions, former film executive at MGM, and former programmer for NBC and CBS. He was a smart salesman and knew every advertiser and media buyer in the business. He had also just produced a movie in England for Yongestreet, and Nick figured he would make a valuable addition to our organization. In the ensuing years, during which Yongestreet produced a number of specials—among them "The Nashville Palace" and shows starring John Wayne, Don Knotts and Herb Alpert—Alan's contributions would indeed prove invaluable.

We spent the rest of that day analyzing the situation. Every distributor had put essentially the same deal on the table. Their organization would handle the selling of the program to individual stations for forty percent off the top. It didn't take Nick, Alan and myself long to figure out that the distributor would wind up making all the money. Out of the sixty percent left, we'd have to pay our production costs and make our profit.

So in spite of all the enthusiasm at the convention, we returned to Los Angeles without a distribution deal. At our next meeting, Nick said to me, "Well, Sam, what do you think we ought to do now?"

I was prepared with an answer. Although we had been canceled by CBS, we were still on the air, in reruns. I knew that the stars of the show wanted to continue doing it. I also knew that the record labels all wanted us to stay on the air, because we had proven we could sell records. And I had the support of Nashville's community leaders, who were eager to keep a major TV operation in their city.

"Simply this," I said. "Wire all of the CBS stations we're currently on, and offer the show and the same barter plan on a *station-by-station basis*." This had never been done this way before.

Nick looked at me and smiled. "What are you waiting for?" I went back to my office, and instructed Marcia Minor, my associate producer, to gather a list of every individual CBS affiliate station that was carrying *Hee Haw*, as well as a second list of the remaining independent stations, 748 in all. This was before computers, printouts and faxes, and it took two days to compile the lists. Once the task was completed, the ladies who worked in our office—Carol Warrian, Dottie Delaplain, and Marcia—spent the next day and night sending out wires that told CBS affiliates that _Hee Haw_ was available in their markets on the barter plan and that the show would continue with the _Hee Haw_ gang.

We sent 748 wires and got back more than 400 positive responses. Everybody wanted the show. The reaction was so overwhelming that by evening the Western Union offices in Beverly Hills, Van Nuys and Culver City were completely jammed. In many instances we had two or more stations competing in the same city, and had to decide which one to give the show to. Nick's feeling was that if a CBS station in a particular market was ranked number three, and an ABC station was stronger, we should go with the stronger station.

I disagreed. "Nick," I said, "if a CBS station agrees to run _Hee Haw_ in the same time slot when it was on the network, we should stay with them. The audience doesn't know or care about whether we're on the network or syndicated. Wherever possible, we should stick with the audience that's gotten us this far."

Which is exactly what we did.

Shortly after we had lined up our "network," Nick instructed me to "get on your horse and go back to Nashville." The plan was that I would resume production, while he and Alan went to New York and lined up sponsors for our four spots. The next hurdle was to find a way to finance the transitional production period. To do so, Nick, Frank and John took second mortgages on their homes. I admired their courage. These were men willing to put everything they had on the line.

Meanwhile, I was still on loan to the show from CBS, and was now being pressed to make a choice—either stay with _Hee Haw_ or go back to the network. I was finally able to negotiate a deal with Perry Lafferty to go on an extended leave of absence (without pay) so that I could continue my medical benefits and protect my family until the show went back on the air.

By May 1971 I was back at Channel 5, in production to tape thirteen new shows. I insisted we make no compromises in our style or the quality of talent. To ensure the latter, I continued to pay our talent the same amount we had paid while on the network. Whoever came in to do the show was paid by check before he or she left the studio that day. The set fee for a guest performer was a thousand dollars. It was a thousand dollars when we debuted in 1969, and a thousand dollars when we finally left the air nearly twenty-five years later.

Between May 25 and June 23, I taped enough material for thirteen new shows, which we had to have ready for air by September 18, 1971, the day we made our syndicated debut. We "premiered" on 227 stations, 152 of which were CBS affiliates. This meant that a lot of people never knew we'd made the switch from the network to syndication. Our ratings remained as high as ever.

However, we were still struggling financially, because when we went back on the air we had only secured one paid, or "cash" advertiser, Procter & Gamble. The rest of our spots were "exchanges," promotions for books and records. For instance, if someone was selling an album, we'd give free time on our show in exchange for a percentage of the sales.

At the end of our first year in syndication, I got the call I knew was coming. Perry Lafferty decided the time had come for me to resign. "Sam," he said, "I hope you're making out financially."

"Of course I am," I said. But it was a lie. Because we were still operating at a huge deficit, I was making only five hundred dollars a week. By comparison, Buck and Roy were making several thousand dollars a show, for two skits. All I really had in the way of security was Nick, Frank, John and Alan's assurance that somewhere down the line they would take care of me.

When I came home to Los Angeles that December, Nick called me into his office and said, "We're having a Christmas luncheon tomorrow for everybody who's worked on the show." It was really nice of him, but as I prepared to leave, I could tell Nick had something on his mind that he wanted to talk to me about. Sure enough, he asked me to stay.

Frank and John were sitting on the couch, and Nick, who never liked to sit at meetings because he was on the short side, was standing by his desk. "Merry Christmas, Sam," he said and handed me an envelope. I figured he was giving me a little bonus, and started to put it in my coat pocket.

He said, "Aren't you going to open that?"

My first thought was, Not really, I'll take it home to my wife. Then I realized, He wants me to open it now, so, okay, I will. Inside was a check for fifty thousand dollars! I couldn't believe it!

"Merry Christmas, Sam," Nick said. "That's a little something for all the hard work you've done for all of us and the show."

Grace never saw the money. I went right out and bought some real estate, on which our new home sits today.

Buck and Roy klowning in the Kornfield

FOUR

I'M FOREVER being asked what the secret of *Hee Haw*'s success was and my answer is always the same. *Hee Haw* was the Grand Ole Opry of television, with a little bit of something for everybody.

Over the years, *Hee Haw* established a style of television all its own, both on and off the screen. Because we taped all the material for a full season's worth in two production periods a year, the regular cast only had to spend a small amount of time actually working on the show.

We'd designate certain days for taping our music segments with Buck, the Buckaroos, Roy, and our guest performers. Other days would be set aside for comedy. "The Kornfield," for instance, where we saluted a different hometown each week, became one of our signature pieces. Everybody who came on the show went into the Kornfield and "*sa-looted*" their hometown. Some of the other sketches that became reg-ular parts of the show were Gordie Tapp as The Old Philosopher; "The Culhanes," which featured Grandpa Jones, Junior Samples, Gordie Tapp and Lulu Roman; "The Moonshiners," our country "soap opera" with all our pretty girls in the background; "The Naggers"; "The Board Fence" that would swing up and swat someone in the butt; "The KORN Newsroom" featuring Don Harron; "The Haystack," which was our corner "love spot"; Grandpa's "What's For Supper" routine; "The Barbershop"; "The Singalong"; and "The General Store." "Pickin' and Grinnin' " started out as a duo with Buck and Roy, but soon expanded to include the en-tire cast. Besides all this, we borrowed the concept of the old Burma Shave signs to use as bumpers—a series of rhyming one-liners along the roadside that led into commercials.

They say imitation is the sincerest form of flattery. If that's the case, then I guess we had reason to feel very flattered when a lot of what we originated on *Hee Haw* began showing up in one or another form on other shows. On-camera "break-ups" became a regular part of the show, and proved such a popular idea that it was stolen by a lot of other shows and producers. Dick Clark once said, "The break-ups made *Hee Haw* the funniest damn show on television."

On *Hee Haw*, we used jokes you could hear anywhere, and sometimes that's exactly what would happen. Around the time *Hee Haw* went on the air, I remember seeing a show on Broadway—*Sugar Babies* with Mickey Rooney and Ann Miller—and it seemed very much a takeoff of what we did. They had a schoolhouse similar to Minnie Pearl's, and like hers, it was filled with adults dressed as children. There was a lot of music, and of course a bevy of scantily clad beau-ties. All they were missing, I thought at the time, was a don-key!

Hee Haw is also responsible for a lot of the "live" comedy you see on television today. *Saturday Night Live* is a good ex-ample. Just think about it: the show has a regular cast, guest stars, and short comedy bits intermixed with live perfor-mances by rock-and-roll artists. Incidentally, many of

Saturday Night Live's original cast of regulars just happened to be managed by Bernie Brillstein.

A country act couldn't get on our show unless it had a song on *Billboard* magazine's country charts. After all, I could get all the "novelty" and traditional music the show needed from the cast sing-alongs, the fiddles, and Roy and Buck's banjo songs. If I was going to buy outside talent, the smart money said I should get those artists who had something on the charts. It proved one of the key elements to the ongoing success of the show.

We also presented what were, in reality, the first musical videos. In the beginning, we'd go out to the countryside and shoot videos of animals and farmers and then edit them to fit the story line of a song. One of our writers, George Yanok, appeared in them along with Pat McCormick, a brilliant stand-up comedian, actor, and writer for the *Tonight Show*; "little person" Felix Silla; "Giant" Mickey Morton (who went on to play the Jolly Green Giant in all those TV commercials); Billy Beck; and later on, Gunilla Hutton, who became a regular on *Hee Haw* in 1971.

The video material was a very workable production item for the show. It provided picture stories for songs. However, some of our guests felt the videos took attention away from their live performances, which they hoped would promote record sales. If they had a hit song, they didn't want to play it under comic barnyard footage. In particular, Buck Owens and Chet Atkins didn't want us cutting away from them. After awhile, because several performers were against it, and because the expense of shooting on location kept mounting, we did away with the concept.

Today, of course, performers would do anything to get a video on the air, and the average cost of one is more than we'd spend on five complete shows!

Guest performers were always dropping by, eager to be on the show. If we used them, they'd always come up to me before leaving, and say, "Hey, since I'm already here, why don't you tape some sketches?" They knew, of course, that each time we used a song or comedy bit of theirs on a different show meant another "fee," plus repeat money.

For our regular cast members, working those couple of weeks a year was worth about $50,000. For Buck and Roy, for three days' work each production period earned them two hundred fifty to three hundred thousand dollars a year. In addition, the show helped their record sales, fair dates and other bookings. They always toured to sold-out crowds.

Buck was a total professional about fulfilling his side of the contract. If he had to be at the studio at nine o'clock in the morning, he was there nine o'clock sharp. Roy, on other hand, was nearly always late. Finally, one day I said to Roy, "You know every hour that goes by costs me twenty-five thousand dollars . . ."

He looked at me, smiled and said, "Sam, every time I see you, all you do is talk about money . . ."

People used to come to me and say, "Damn it, Lovullo, you have to get on Roy. We have to start on time!"

Then one day, he certainly surprised us: he came in and boy, I tell you, he flew through his numbers and bits. After, he came up to me and said, "You know, chief, I saved you three hours today. Where's my seventy-five thousand bucks?"

We were becoming a force, not only in syndicated television where we had rewritten the rule book, but in country music and the city of Nashville. Before we'd brought the show there, its leading industries were the publishing of religious books and Bibles, the baking of Eucharistic hosts, and the manufacturing of coffins. It wasn't until after *Hee Haw* established itself as a hit show that Nashville became recognized as a *recording* center of country music. The city fathers and politicians hoped we would prove the springboard to making Nashville a center of television production as well.

There was the money factor too. When we first began on the network, each show was budgeted at $150,000 to $175,000. Twenty-five seasons and 585 shows later, the budget was the same. During the time the show was in production, we pumped fifty-eight million dollars into the local Nashville economy. And, at its peak, *Hee Haw* generated upwards of eight million dollars a year in advertising revenues. It doesn't take a rocket scientist to realize the kind of profits we generated, both for Yongestreet and Nashville.

It should come as no surprise, then, that the city welcomed us with open arms. Civic leaders were always coming by, treating us as if we were official dignitaries. At one time or another we also had the police chief of Nashville, the sheriff, the mayor, and the governor visit our studio. Every week, it seemed, we were receiving another award. We worked closely with the chamber of commerce and played a lot of charity events. We even had our own softball team that competed with the fire department and the police department.

Each production period, the local fire department would invite the entire cast and some city officials over for a cookout. First, speeches would be made, and then, right next to the fire trucks, they'd lay out tables and chairs where we would lunch on some of their local "Dago cabbage!" Just divine!

Minnie Pearl entertaining the Hee Haw Honeys

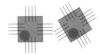

Minnie Pearl's house was located next to the governor's mansion. She always had a neighbor-to-neighbor relationship with whoever the governor of Tennessee was. Governor Blatton, for instance, made an appearance on the tenth anniversary celebration show, in 1979. His successor, Governor Dunn, also appeared as a guest, and did a little storytelling.

However, the politician who was everybody's favorite was Secretary of Education for President Bush, Lamar Alexander. He was a terrific fellow and a not bad piano player either. One time he performed a duet with Minnie Pearl on the show.

Skull Schulman, a Nashville nightclub owner, became an unofficial member of our family. He operated the Rainbow Lounge in Printer's Alley, near the Ryman, where everybody from the Grand Ole Opry hung out. Skull knew everybody in Nashville. I first got to know him just after I chose the Channel 5 "matchbox" as our studio. He called each and every struggling country singer in Nashville and told them to try to get to meet us, because we were important Los Angeles-based show business people and could showcase them on *Hee Haw.*

Among the many talented, still unknown artists we found through Skull was Mel Tillis, who came down to audition with his guitar slung over his back. I remember he was so nervous, he stuttered a mile a minute. It wasn't until he started singing that I realized how good he was, and what a gold mine of untapped talent there was in Nashville.

Skull became a great friend of the show. He'd get the *Hee Haw* gang to agree to visit kids in hospitals, then go out and buy gifts for the cast members to give to the sick children. He was so much a part of the scenery that a number of times, during "Pickin' and Grinnin' " taping sessions, Skull would be on the set, dressed in *Hee Haw* overalls.

One time, a few days before we were scheduled for a backstage party, Skull asked me if he could have some of the raw fabric with which we made our *Hee Haw* overalls and costumes. I told him he could have all he wanted. He then took it to a local seamstress who made him a *Hee Haw* tuxedo, which he wore to the party. Later on, when we went into the merchandising business, Skull's club in Printer's Alley became our primary retail outlet.

One of the things I am most proud of are the many artists whose careers either began or were immeasurably boosted by their appearance on *Hee Haw*. Most often I'd book a new act after hearing them perform in a local club, reading about them in *Billboard*, or after I heard about them from people in the record industry. I booked Sammi Smith after she recorded Kris Kristofferson's "Help Me Make It Through The Night," which I had first heard on an advance copy from the record label. She performed it on *Hee Haw* and it did indeed become a huge hit.

Showcasing country's newest rising "stars" helped our ratings, and it didn't take long before we'd exceeded our highest network ratings. By the start of the 1972–1973 season, we had become the number one syndicated show, not only in ratings, but in audience share as well. Ironically, our chief competition for the top syndicated spot was *The Lawrence Welk Show*.

Back then the A. C. Nielsen Company didn't include syndicated programs in their ratings system as they now do. Lucky for CBS they didn't, because we would have embarrassed the hell out of the network with the kind of numbers we knew we were pulling.

As the years passed, we kept up with all the technical innovations being made. We may have looked like we were a bunch of hayseeds, but behind the scenes we were quite progressive. In 1973 we were the first TV program to switch to totally electronic editing. This was one of the few times the industry noticed that we existed, and nominated us for an Emmy Award in Best Editing. Much to my amazement, we actually won!

The content of our show also continued to evolve. During the '70s, Chuck Barris's *The Gong Show* was a very popular program, and Frank and John decided to do a country version of it on *Hee Haw,* "The Country Dong Show." Our host was Junior Samples. In reality, he was the whole "show." The original *Gong Show* used a gong to eliminate bad acts. In our version, Junior Samples chased bad acts off the stage with a hook. He was so funny introducing the people in the segment, people hardly paid any attention to the acts themselves!

The "Thompson Brothers," were a singing duo who used to walk around the streets of Nashville in search of a record label. To draw attention to themselves they'd wear bathing suit trunks in the summer under fur coats, with Russian fur hats on their heads. George Lindsey happened to spot them one day, and without telling me anything about them, suggested we book their act on the show. The day they showed up to tape their segment, they wore their fur coats with nothing on underneath!

Toward the end of the '70s, I started getting pressure to use "cloggers" on the show. It was the kind of act I had always tried to avoid, simply because we didn't have any time for them. We already had a large cast, which meant our regulars were always angling for airtime. When we were on the network, the show had six commercial spots. In syndication that number had gone up to eight, eventually to twelve. That meant twelve full minutes out of every sixty were commercials. To make up for the lost time, we had to delete some things. We couldn't cut out the music, because we were essentially a music show, so we cut down on comedy. The last thing I needed was a clogging act with eight to sixteen people that required a lot of rehearsal and many camera setups. Plus, you have to mike the floor to get that tapping sound.

Because of the continuing demand, I finally gave in and decided to try to use the same cloggers who played the Grand Ole Opry, the Stoney Mountain Cloggers. They made their first appearance on the show March 17, 1979, and caught on. From then on, during every production period, we'd tape two or three clogger spots.

We also used another Grand Ole Opry group, the Ralph Sloane Cloggers. I'd been asked to book Ralph many times and never did. Then, one time I had an unexpected cancellation and decided to give his group a a try. I got him on the phone and told him that if his troupe showed up the next morning at nine I'd put them on.

Sure enough, the next morning, there they were. All except one young girl who'd gotten lost trying to find the studio. We were on a tight schedule, and had to go without her. In spite of the missing member, the group did a great job. Ralph was very appreciative of my giving him this kind of national exposure. We taped the spot in November 1979. What I didn't know at the time was that Ralph was dying of cancer. Two months later, in January, he was in the hospital, and died a couple of weeks before the show was due to air.

Six years ago I ran into Ralph's brother Melvin at the Opry, and during our conversation I told him that I'd never forgiven myself for not waiting for that last dancer to show up, and that I was still sorry Ralph had never gotten to see the show.

He looked at me for a long time and finally said, "He did see it."

I was surprised. "He did?"

"Yes. One week before he died, I went to the TV station. Everyone was afraid to tell you, they weren't sure what you'd say, but I asked them if they'd send a special video machine and a copy of the show to the hospital." (This was in the days before home VCRs.)

That made me feel better, for a number of reasons. First, because I was happy that Ralph got to see his group on TV, and second, because the incident served as a solid reminder to me that *Hee Haw*'s first priority was people, not schedules.

IN 1980, after ten years of production at the Channel 5, WLAC "matchbox"—our home from the very first *Hee Haw*—we moved the production of the show to the Opryland complex. In some ways, the move made everyone connected with the show quite happy. We were moving from the least modern, least spacious facilities in Nashville to a sprawling, state-of-the-art TV complex. In other ways, it made many of us sad. Being forced to work under such cramped quarters had brought us all together in a very special way and kept us close, like a large family living in a too small house.

It was in December 1979 that I first found out we would have to move. At the time, I was a board member on the radio and television committee of the Country Music Association (the CMA). I was attending one of their seminars in Jamaica, when I received a message to call the home office immediately.

I knew something important was up, but had no idea what. My first thought was, oh Lord, I'm so far from home, I hope nothing's happened to my family. My wife, Grace, was in Jamaica with me, and we'd left our young children back in Los Angeles with family members.

I excused myself and went to the nearest phone, praying no one had died. If you've ever tried to call the United States from Jamaica you know it's easier to reach the pope. Finally, I got Tom Irwin, WLAC's assistant general manager, and Harold Crump, the general manager, on the line. "Sam," Harold said, "We've made a decision you need to hear from us before it hits the press. We no longer want *Hee Haw* produced at our facilities."

I was of course relieved to find out nothing had happened to my real family, and switched my thinking to my adopted one. My God, I thought, what had happened? We were totally set up at Channel 5, and had been for ten years. We only used the facilities twice a year, always paid our bills on time, and never had a problem with anyone. What had gone wrong?

I tried to discuss the situation with Tom and Harold, but they weren't going to budge. They assured me we'd done nothing wrong, that the station was simply no longer interested in having any outside productions using its facilities. They said they were sorry, but the decision was irrevocable. *Hee Haw* had to find a new home.

I just couldn't understand it. I asked if they'd be kind enough to hold off making their decision at least until I returned from Jamaica. They said no, they couldn't, that I needn't bother coming to Nashville, to go ahead and continue with my meeting and have a good time. With that, they hung up.

Nevertheless, I hopped on the next plane for the States, and as soon as I got to Nashville, I went to see Tom and Harold. As I feared, there was no moving them. We were out. I had until our next scheduled production period, June 1980, to find new facilities.

I began searching for new facilities and learned the Opryland complex was available, having opened their doors only three years earlier. I went over to inspect the facilities and liked what I saw; the place had more lights, individual dressing rooms, individual parking, a whole lot of space and comfort. But I was hesitant anyway. My main concern was preserving the look, feel, and spirit of our little show. What if we lost the natural intimacy we'd developed through the years, and which showed up so vividly on the tube?

Just before we actually made the move, my lighting man, Leard Davis, echoed my concerns: "Sam, once you're at the Opryland studios, *Hee Haw* is going to go downhill. You and I were at CBS when they moved Climax and Playhouse 90 from their tiny New York studios to Television City in Hollywood. Remember what happened? The budgets went up, there was more lighting, more people, more stagehands, bigger sets. The same thing is going to happen to *Hee Haw.*"

He was right. Opryland's gigantic studios would require bigger staff, more sets, and fancier lighting. We would acquire a new formality I didn't want and the show didn't need.

As a result, I did keep searching for something smaller, which upset the Opryland people. They couldn't understand why I didn't jump at the opportunity to use what were without question the best facilities in town. Finally, unable to replace the matchbox, I reluctantly agreed to make the move.

My new office was in a trailer just behind the backstage area of the Grand Ole Opry. We moved in time to resume production in June 1980. As I feared, the show became a costlier operation. On the plus side, the Opryland facilities made it easier to attract a greater number of Hollywood-based acts whose performers wouldn't be caught dead in the old matchbox.

Right up until the end of *Hee Haw*'s run, I was constantly on the lookout for new talent. There wasn't a letter that went unanswered or a person who came into my office with whom I didn't eventually meet. I never turned people away without at least hearing their demo or watching their video.

I remember one series of letters I received from a young lady in Mississippi who wanted to be a country singer. But she was married and had two young kids, which unfortunately is an obstacle to the kind of single-minded dedication it takes to make it in the music business, especially when you're just starting out.

One of her letters said she was coming to Nashville, and she asked for an appointment to see me. I set it up for a Friday afternoon. As soon as she came into my office I felt a good vibe. She was real homespun, obviously a dedicated wife and mother. I asked her if she'd ever been to the Grand Ole Opry. She said when she was a child she'd visited the old Ryman Auditorium, but never the new Opryland complex. Since I was going to be backstage that afternoon, I invited her to join me.

We entered the stage area just as they were finishing

setting up for the Friday night show. The house was still empty, and I told her it would be all right if she went and stood on the stage. She did, and tears started rolling down her face when she asked me if I'd let her sing a song.

I told her I couldn't find an accompanist that fast. She said that was all right, she'd do it a capella. She was standing in the center of the stage, on a floor circle that refers to the song "Will the Circle Be Unbroken." It's part of the original Ryman stage, cut out and transplanted, for the sake of remembrance and continuity. The young lady began singing Patsy Cline's "Crazy."

And I was blown away! It was so beautiful, I trembled. I had never heard anything like it before. The more she got into it, the more I could appreciate what she was all about. When she finished, she broke into a terrible crying jag. She then asked if she could bring her parents by some time, to show them the actual spot on the Opry stage where she had sung. Unfortunately, because she was an unsigned, unknown, and inexperienced performer, I didn't want to book her.

About a month later, Tony Bennett came to Nashville to appear at the Opry for a fund-raiser to benefit a local charity. Tony has always been an idol of mine, so that evening I decided to stand backstage to watch and listen to his performance. When he was through with one number, he came over to where I was standing. "Tony," I said, "that was sensational."

He looked at me, as if to say thanks, and who exactly are you? I said, "I'm Sam Lovullo, from *Hee Haw*." He remembered me from a luncheon in Los Angeles. We got to talking and I told him how great I thought he sounded, and how wonderful the acoustics at the Opry were. That reminded me of the young lady who'd sung a capella for me, and I told Tony about her. He went back on stage for his finale and announced that he was going to sing the next song a capella. He asked for a single spotlight, and went into "Fly Me To the Moon," without any musical accompaniment. It was just outstanding. The whole thing struck me as an amazing chain of events, typical of the kind of thing that the public never finds out about, yet accounts for so much of the magic of the business that I'm in.

I continued to get mail asking for, of all things, more cloggers. I went into my files and came up with Debbie Austin and Diane Hicks, two lovely young ladies from Knoxville, Tennessee, who called themselves The Moonshining Cloggers. I had first come across them when the show was still at Channel 5. Closely guarded by their husbands, these two cute little gals, a brunette and a redhead, had auditioned for me, and I'd put their photos in my talent file, where they stayed for the next six years. Now, in 1980, they finally made their first *Hee Haw* appearance.

When I called that June to book them, I spoke to Debbie. At first she didn't believe it was really me. It took a good half hour to convince her I was on the level. In fact, I had to tell her to hang up, call the Opryland complex and ask for Sam Lovullo. She did exactly that, dialed information, got the Opryland complex's number, called and asked for me. Then and only then did she admit she was actually talking to Mr. Sam.

They came to the studio a week later. Diane brought her two girls, both of whom were also cloggers. During rehearsal, the kids joined in with the mother. I thought to myself, this is great, and taped two numbers with just the adults and then one with the children. We aired the three segments on separate shows. The one with the kids really caught on, which was great. However, from then on, I was constantly inundated with kids wanting to be on the show.

I got together with Debbie and Diane and we came up with a project called the *Hee Haw* International Clogging Contest. We organized it as an annual event, with the winners promised an appearance on *Hee Haw*. We ran it for three years, and it really gave our ratings a boost. Clog dancing, which we helped popularize on *Hee Haw*, anticipated country line dancing, so very much in vogue today.

In 1981, to update the show, I decided to introduce "The Songwriter's Segment." I wanted to show the faces of the people who wrote the great country hits. The way the segment worked, I'd book a songwriter such as Curly Putman to work with his buddy, Roy Clark. Roy would kick it off by performing one of Curly's songs on the guitar, then the two would talk about when, how and why it was written. Roy would then segue into another song of Curly's, and so on. It was an informal three-and-a-half, four-minute spot, a way of paying tribute to many of country's greatest songwriters.

One of the best songwriter segments we ever did was with the legendary Felice and Boudleaux Bryant. These two legends performed "Rocky Top," one of their biggest, most covered hits. The number of letters that poured in afterward was unbelievable!

The songwriting segment lasted for about two years and then faded. The up-and-coming composers were not writing traditional country music, which was what our viewers were into. We simply ran out of legends!

When we were at Channel 5, we didn't have room for live audiences during the taping of musical numbers. Usually the only people in the studio besides those working on the show were friends of the performers. I'm a believer that you need that intimacy; the artist can relate and work better and do a better job before a live audience. But it wasn't until we moved to Opryland that we had ample seating facilities to accommodate the public.

Requests to view a *Hee Haw* taping were always coming in. Although we never advertised for an audience, people always found a way into the studio to watch the musical numbers.

We seated the audience on a first-come basis in a special bleacher section. I would chose about a hundred to come down to the ground level and sit right under the performers' noses. This drove the insurance people crazy, because audience members were constantly tripping over cables. And, because they were technically "on the set," a lot of them would just get up and go over to Roy and start talking to him. Guess what? He and the other cast members loved it! The only problem we ever really had with this policy was the song pluggers, who were forever trying to get a new song to Roy, or Buck, or into some guest artist's hands!

Archie Campbell giving Roy a clip job

SIX

I N 1981, after thirteen years and 312 shows, Yongestreet Productions sold *Hee Haw* to the Gaylord family of Oklahoma City.

The Gaylords' involvement with *Hee Haw* had actually begun two years earlier, when they became interested in a film Yongestreet had in development, "365 Days with *Hee Haw*." The idea was to do a movie feature about Buck Owens and Roy Clark in search of Kornfield Kounty. In their travels they would run into other cast members who would join the search. Frank Peppiatt, John Aylesworth, Jack Burns and I worked on the script. When it was completed, I worked up a budget for it of $5.5 million.

At the time, the Gaylord family was looking to get into the film business. The family had made its fortune in the newspaper-publishing business and then acquired a great deal of valuable Oklahoma and Texas property. When Ed Gaylord,

Sr. died at the age of 100, the family business was passed to Ed Gaylord, II.

In the late '70s, the family had launched a production company in Los Angeles and talked film producer Elmo Williams (of *Cleopatra* and *Tora Tora Tora* among many others) out of retirement to become president of Gaylord Film Productions. Elmo was aware of the Yongestreet movie project, figured it was perfect for his new production company, and arranged with the Gaylord Group to meet Frank, John, Nick and Alan.

After several meetings, when it became clear to all involved that the film wasn't going to happen, Ed Gaylord brought up the possibility of buying *Hee Haw*. Nick Vanoff's first reaction was simply, "I don't think you-all have the money to buy the show."

After he'd named his price, though, it didn't take much convincing from the Gaylord's chief executive, Jim Terrell, and their secretary-treasurer, Glen Stinchcomb, that they were serious.

I was in Nashville at the time. I got a call from Nick's office, asking me to come to L.A. for the weekend. I had no idea what was going on. I thought to myself, here we go again, the show is aging, they want me to make some changes. Maybe more cloggers, fresh comedy bits or new talent.

I flew back and met with Nick, who took me into his confidence and told me the show had been sold to the Gaylord company. The reason Nick wanted me to know before almost anyone else was that my current contract as *Hee Haw*'s producer was about to expire and he wanted to extend it. Actually, he told me that this was one of the Gaylords' conditions for purchasing Yongestreet.

So, in the meantime, I was offered a contract extension with a hefty raise, which I accepted. I was then asked to have breakfast that Sunday morning at the Century Plaza Hotel with Ed Gaylord and Glen Stinchcomb. When I arrived at the hotel for breakfast, I was met by my Yongestreet associates. They wanted to be sure that I completely understood that the show was sold, I was going to be dealing with some wonderful new people, and that from this point on I was on my own.

My first reaction was that I was being sized up. The Gaylords wanted to make sure I wasn't one of those Hollywood producers who smoked big cigars and drank martinis, which isn't the Gaylord image. No problem. There was, however, one question they wanted me to answer more than any other. At one point, Ed looked me in the eye and said, "Sam, how much longer do you think *Hee Haw* will stay on the air?"

"Mr. Gaylord," I replied, "it will stay on the air as long as you want it to. And that all depends on how much money you want to make."

Not long after, the Gaylords expanded their physical presence in Nashville. Ed began visiting the show at the Opryland complex and liked what he saw. On weekends I'd often take him around the city to look at available real estate. I didn't know it at the time, but he had already begun thinking about investing in Nashville and possibly building a brand-new, Nashville state–of–the–art studio complex.

It was during this same period of time that the American General Insurance Company of Texas had attempted a hostile takeover of the National Life Assurance Company of Nashville. Part of National Life's assets were the Grand Ole Opry, the Opryland Park, The Nashville Network and the Opryland Hotel, a beautiful traditional colonial structure (one of the finest in the country).

Because we were now based at the Opryland studio complex, I followed the situation very closely and came to the conclusion that for American General to effect the takeover without acquiring a huge amount of debt, they would probably have to sell the Opryland complex.

Which is exactly what happened. Once American General gained control of National, it put the complex up for sale. There was no shortage of buyers: Kroegers Marketing Company was very much interested, as was the Marriott Hotel Corporation, primarily because of the Opryland Hotel.

Budweiser beer also expressed some interest, as did the Ingram shipbuilding corporation.

One afternoon when Ed Gaylord and his wife, Thelma, were in the studio to watch a taping of Roy Acuff and Minnie Pearl, I went to them and said, "Have you been following what's been going on with American General? This entire entertainment center, the park—everything associated with the Opry might go up for sale. It's something you might want to investigate."

He looked at me and said, "Who do I need to talk to?"

The answer was Bud Wendell, once a principal of National Life Assurance. I offered to feel him out since he and I were friends, having both served on the CMA board and having socialized together many times with our families. I went to Bud's office and told him my feeling about what I believed was the impending sale of Opryland. Bud said he didn't know anything about it.

I figured that's what he would say, what he would have to say. I said, "Bud, I think I know what's going on. You need to talk to the Gaylords. You don't have to say anything. Let them ask you and you can answer any way you want. We owe it to these people. After all, they do own *Hee Haw* and pay the rent here." Bud agreed to meet with Ed, Jim Terrell and me, as long as the meeting was held in my office trailer.

I wish I'd had a photographer for the occasion. Here were Ed Gaylord, Bud Wendell and Jim sitting on a milk crates. Ed Gaylord didn't smoke but Bud and Jim did, like chimneys, and the tiny office was soon fogged up like a backroom poker game, which, in many ways, the meeting sort of resembled. At one point, Bud admitted that American General was entertaining a possible sale of certain divisions, and he referred the Gaylords to Boston Investment.

Not long after, the Gaylords completed their purchase of American General's entire entertainment division. They paid upwards of a quarter-billion dollars for it, with a guarantee to finance the modernization of the mansion and the hotel and the Nashville network. The entire package went for something in the neighborhood of a half-billion dollars. And at the heart of it all was that little donkey with the funny laugh!

In July 1983, the Gaylords held a press conference on the Opry stage to formally announce the acquisition. During his speech, Ed Gaylord stated that the reason the family had always been successful was because it always left business in the hands of the people best capable of running it.

I was seated in the front row, between Minnie Pearl and Roy Acuff, both of whom had worked behind the scenes to help convince American General to sell to the Gaylords. Among other things, Roy Acuff had let it be known he would no longer be a part of the Opry if it was sold to Budweiser Beer. It was in all of our interests to see this family, rather than a corporation, gain control of the Opry.

Once again, in spite of tumultuous happenings backstage, nothing had changed as far as our television audience could tell. However, perhaps inevitably, there were changes. Along with Frank and John, I was a partner in a postproduction center in Hollywood. Naturally, we used to edit *Hee Haw* there. When the Gaylords took over, we charged them our standard editing-facility fees. However, shortly after the acquisition, because the Opryland studios had fine editing facilities, I suggested we move our dubbing-and-editing operation to Nashville.

We built some new sets and added a few new faces. And, perhaps inevitably, we had to let some people go, including The Hagers, Lisa Todd, Don Harron, and a couple of the lesser known *Hee Haw* Honeys. Buck left, leaving Roy Clark as sole host.

We decided to stay with Roy Clark, as a single host, and each week team him with a different guest recording artist.

The concept worked for awhile. Roy enjoyed it, and so did the rest of the cast. Some of our cohosts included Roger Miller, June and Johnny Cash, Randy Travis, Patty Loveless, Minnie Pearl and Roy Acuff, Reba McEntire, and Barbara Mandrell. However, after a while we did away with guest cohosts. Not only did it wind up costing too much, it just didn't seem right to take the spotlight away from Roy, who had more than earned his solo moment. *Hee Haw* was his show, after all, and he was more than able to carry it on his shoulders.

Hosting by himself, knowing at last the show belonged to him, gave Roy a renewed energy.

Some of the old-timers were gone, too, such as Bob Boatman, a dear friend and former lighting director for the show in the early '70s, and who'd also worked with me on several major network specials. He had been *Hee Haw*'s director since 1973, helming nearly five hundred shows until he died suddenly and unexpectedly in the summer of 1989. It was a terrible loss for the show, cast, his family and all his friends, and of course my heart went out to his wife and children.

His replacement, Steve Schepman, became only the third director in *Hee Haw*'s twenty-five seasons. Steve was no stranger at least—he had been with the show since 1974. His first job with us was printing our cue cards. He then became stage manager and associate director before serving as director.

October 24, 1990, turned out to be my last day in the studio with the old *Hee Haw* gang. They didn't know it, but sales were down, and we were losing stations. I knew what was happening, though I didn't want to let go. But that day, when the director said, "It's a wrap," I felt it was the last time Roy Clark was going to be doing "Pickin' and Grinnin' " with the old gang, the last time they'd romp together in the Kornfield, the last time we'd see Minnie Pearl and her precious *Hee Haw* Jug Band.

At the wrap party that evening, I looked around at everybody and thought about saying, "Folks, this is the last time we'll all be together," but I didn't. I didn't want to say goodbye as long as there was any chance, no matter how remote, that we might somehow find a way to keep going.

Usually, at our wrap parties, I was the last to speak. It was obvious I wasn't the "old" Sam Lovullo, whooping it up, having a beer with friends, having a good time. I didn't even stay for the whole thing. I simply thanked everybody, said "See you next year," and left.

After editing the last batch of shows, I returned to my home in Los Angeles. In May of 1991 I received a call requesting I come to Nashville. I knew that discussions had taken place during the winter as to the future of the show—discussions which hadn't included me. When I got that call, I was sure that either the show was going to be canceled or I was going to be fired.

When I arrived at the show's corporate offices, the mood was grim. I was then told that additional cast changes had to be made—some fresh faces to "rejuvenate" the show.

If there was ever a time I felt I was going to die of a heart attack or develop an ulcer, it was when I had to call people like Misty Rowe, Gunilla Hutton, Marianne Rodgers, Cathy Baker, Roni Stoneman, Jeff Smith, the *Hee Haw* Band and Singers—all dear friends who had become so much a part of my life, responsible not only for the success of *Hee Haw*, but for my personal success as well—and tell them I was not exercising their options, that they were, in effect, gone.

It was hard to break up what had become a very real family to me. Besides, we'd already lost several key performers. Junior Samples, Archie Campbell and Kenny Price, the nerve center of our comedy, had all passed away.

The result was that everyone, with the exception of Roy Clark, Grandpa Jones, George Lindsey, Lulu Roman, Linda Thompson, Gailard Sartain, Gordie Tapp and Irlene Mandrell would go.

Early in 1991, we began auditions for new cast regulars. Some of the people we wound up hiring were the Norris Twins, Becky and Lindy from Branson, Missouri; Donna Stokes, a beautiful brunette from Nashville; Dawn McKinley, a model from Los Angeles; Alice Hathaway Ripley, a new Honey; and Pedro Tomas, a dancer from *The Louise Mandrell Touring Show*. These people were very talented, as good as many of the old-timers.

In the fall of 1991, the new cast was introduced to the American viewing public, wrapped in a "modern" format and a fancy new set with lots of hi-tech flashy lighting and sets. I tried to keep the show together as best I could. For twenty-five seasons, I had survived all the changes that had come in with country music, from traditional through modern traditional, to country pop, and even country rock. As these stylistic changes occurred, I tried to be very careful in my booking. I could never deny a Barbara Mandrell, or Reba

McEntire, and others who had drifted away from traditional country music.

But other things changed. When I was editing the old shows, I tried to see to it that if Barbara was singing a non-traditional country song, I didn't follow with the Kornfield or a traditional country spot. On the other hand, if I had a Roy Acuff in the next spot singing a traditional song, I could easily follow him with a Kornfield, or "Gloom, Despair and Agony."

However, with the new *Hee Haw*, it didn't bother me who sang what, or how they sang it. I just tried to give the show some balance. One thing I never lost sight of was that for every nontraditional, i.e., modern country performer, I tried to have a very traditional act on the same show.

In the fall of 1991, we shot twenty-two "new" *Hee Haw*s in twenty-eight days. In the past we had always done thirteen in the fall and thirteen in the spring. But by eliminating four shows, we could tape enough material for an entire season in one production period, and this amounted to a substantial savings. Among other things, doing all the shows at once prevented us from staying as musically current as we would have liked. Also, it didn't allow for any "fixing": inevitably, problems would crop up in editing which we could always fix in the following production period. Like it or not, though, the twenty-two "new" shows began airing in the winter of 1992. After sampling the first two "new format" shows, the audience dwindled.

We received twice as much mail as usual, nearly all of it negative. Our audience felt betrayed. I can remember sitting in my office on a Saturday night after one of the new shows aired, picking up my phone and hearing a fan on the other side literally crying into the receiver, pleading for me to bring back the old *Hee Haw*. I didn't know what to say. To avoid the humiliation, I told the caller, "I'm sorry, I'm just the janitor here, cleaning up the office."

In spite of my best effort to retain some of the traditional *Hee Haw* flavor, I knew in my heart that what Bernie Brillstein had said so many years ago had finally come true. The "Jackass" was dead.

After our last "new" *Hee Haw* show aired, on May 30th, 1992, we went into our rerun period. By this time, the ratings had dropped drastically, and the decision was made to cease production of new shows. Instead, we would come back in the fall with a series of best-of reruns called *Hee Haw Silver*.

I went back to our archives and selected twenty-six of our best "classic" shows. We did a total of fifty-two *Silver Hee Haw*s, with Roy as the host, who, by the way, did fifty-two in-tros and bumpers in a day and a half! Talk about a pro! We also brought back Cathy Baker, our sign-off signature person ("That's All!"), to entice the audience "to tune in the following week for another *Silver Hee Haw*."

Because the *Hee Haw* reruns were some of our better shows, filled with traditional humor and lots of silly anima-tion, we finally began to get back some of our faithful old view-ers, and we got some new young ones as well. Sure enough, before, long our ratings slowly began to rise.

I was tickled by this turn of events, but still downhearted. I knew that we could never go back to what we had been. Meanwhile, as the popularity of *Silver Hee Haw* increased, management realized that the *Hee Haw* audience consisted of the same people who regularly watched TNN (The Nashville Network). Why struggle in syndication when they had a per-fect outlet within the company? A decision was made to re-run all the old *Hee Haws* in their original form on The Nashville Network. The premier of the first *Hee Haw* rerun on TNN took place on October 2, 1993. It rated the network's sec-ond-highest-rated show.

Hee Haw was the longest running weekly first-run syndicated show in the history of television, a record likely never to be broken. The show spanned over four decades, from the late '60s to the early '90s, airing almost the same time, every Saturday night at 7:00. Roy Clark once remarked that *Hee Haw* was more than a TV show, it was an American institu-tion. I'd have to agree with him about that.

Not bad, for a bunch of shitkickers.

PART TWO

THE CAST

"Hee Haw *may have set me back, but it sure set me up.*"

—Roy Clark

*T*HE PILLARS that held the show together for season after season, during even the most chaotic of times, were its two cohosts, Roy Clark and Buck Owens—two of the most wonderful, talented fellows I have ever met. Every week, their faces as familiar as mom and dad, they came smiling into the homes of America, singing, laughing, cutting up, and spreading the good will of Kornfield Kounty. To anyone who tuned us in, they seemed great pals, with the remarkable ability to warm the heart and soothe the soul.

Backstage, however, it was a slightly different story. Negotiations to sign Buck and Roy proved quite difficult.

Frank and John approached Buck first, and, before his deal was finalized, they opened negotiations with Roy. Buck was crucial to *Hee Haw*'s original chemistry, so much so that we even brought aboard his personal manager, Jack McFadden, as talent coordinator, because when the show first went on the air, neither Frank, John nor I knew very much about country music.

In truth, I don't believe Buck, who was from Bakersfield, California, ever had any real use for Nashville. He had stopped playing the Grand Ole Opry ten years before he signed on with *Hee Haw*. He recorded for Capitol, which was located in Los Angeles, and as a result never felt a part of the Nashville music scene.

Still, it was decided that Buck would lead the way musically, since his greatest strength was that, not comedy. Responsibility for that would fall primarily on Roy's shoulders. Jim Halsey, Roy's manager, insisted that since the two were going to be cohosts, they should have equal terms, meaning equal salary and equal billing.

I became concerned when our starting date approached and contract negotiations with Roy were still not completed. The major stumbling block was the matter of billing—whose name would come first, Roy's or Buck's. I thought I'd settle it by announcing them in alphabetical order. However, that presented a new problem—first names (Buck Owens and Roy Clark!) or last (Roy Clark and Buck Owens!)?

While managers and agents jockeyed for position, I too got involved. I was able to convince both Buck and Roy not to continue their Abbott and Costello routine. To solve the situation, I suggested that for the first season I'd go with Buck, since the initial sound you hear is a "B," and "Starring Buck Owens and Roy Clark" sounded good. I asked them to at least try it this way, and promised Roy that in future seasons, we'd rotate the opening billing. One show we'd open with "Buck Owens and Roy Clark," the next with "Roy Clark and Buck Owens." It was costly, and a technical pain in the ass, because we had to shoot two openings and alternate them in postproduction, but a promise was a promise.

We did it that way until one day Roy came to me and said, "You know, Sam, I think it actually sounds better if you say Buck Owens and Roy Clark." Which was the way we left it.

When I thought we finally had the billing issue settled during those early negotiations, along came the money part. Again, both Jack McFadden and Jim Halsey wanted assurances that his artist was getting the same fee as the other. Dick Howard, at the time an agent at ICM who happened to be an associate of Jim Halsey, was a great help in convincing them all that I would give them the right deal. This proved a turning point in negotiations, as well as the beginning of my close friendship with both Roy and Buck.

Our production formula for Buck and Roy was unique. Buck would come in during the first part of the production cycle and do enough songs for thirteen shows. Later on in the schedule, Roy would join Buck for "Pickin' and Grinnin' " and the closing sing-alongs. To reflect their close cohost relationship we'd have them both do some comedy, usually in the Kornfield. We'd have Buck set up the joke and Roy deliver the punch line. Buck didn't really appreciate not being "the funny one," and more than once said to me, "Hey, Sam, if I can't be part of the joke, why don't you use somebody else?"

The remainder of the production schedule would be all Roy, *his* music, vocals and instrumentals, and hosting the comedy sketches. I managed to keep my two stars as far from each other as possible to keep them out of each other's hair. At times some friction did develop, but never anything serious. The gossip magazines that closely monitored us always found it difficult to believe we all got along as if we were one great big happy family, but the truth of the matter is, that's exactly how it felt. At least most of the time.

But definitely not all of the time. For instance, although there was nothing in either Roy or Buck's contract about equal time on the show, this was a never-ending problem with Buck. He and his manager, Jack McFadden, would watch the shows with a stopwatch, and I'd hear from his people if Roy got more airtime. I couldn't help that. While Buck was funny in his own way, Roy was and is a terrific comedian on and off the show. He's got those great facial expressions, and if you give him a line of dialogue that's not working, he can always make it work. All he has to do is smile, wiggle his nose or touch his ear, and it becomes funny.

All I really wanted to do in all this was keep the winning nucleus of the show together. As long as we were a success and everybody was making money, I figured, what the hell, an adjustment here and there wasn't needed.

Eventually, everyone found his and her own rhythm and place in the show, and we meshed together beautifully. I remember everyone with great fondness. Each contributed in his or her own way to making *Hee Haw* the unique program that it was.

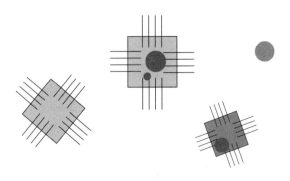

How-deee!

MINNIE PEARL

Minnie was on the very first *Hee Haw*, and became a regular on the thirteenth show. I've often said that one of the keys to *Hee Haw*'s success was her authentic, legendary Nashville presence.

I'd worked with Minnie on *The Jonathan Winters Show* and had gotten to know her quite well. In real life, Minnie, unlike the character she played, was a cultured, sophisticated woman. At first, we were a bit hesitant to oversimplify her "hat lady" character for *Hee Haw*, but she didn't seem to mind. She was a firm believer that country comedy energized the heart and soul, and was happy to be a part of the show. As a comedienne, her timing was the greatest.

Minnie's most famous *Hee Haw* sketch was, of course, "Minnie Pearl's Schoolhouse." She played the role of the schoolteacher and her "students" were members of the cast—

Roy, Junior Samples and others, dressed in cute little outfits as kids, complete with big suckers and balloons. Along with the show's animation, that sketch made us very popular with children.

Minnie was also a honky-tonk piano player. We often featured her at the upright. She enjoyed being the Jug Band bandmaster, which featured The *Hee Haw* Honeys—a lovely musical sight for young and old alike.

The death of Sarah Ophellia Cannon (Minnie Pearl) on Monday, March 4, 1996 in Nashville has left an emptiness in our lives. I'm so proud to have been around during her lifetime. We lost an ambassador of goodwill to the world.

Bored of education. Minnie Pearl's Schoolhouse

ARCHIE CAMPBELL

One of the first writers Peppiatt, Aylesworth and I hired was Archie Campbell. Archie was a member of the Grand Ole Opry and a natural country comedian. He was also responsible for helping to recruit some of the show's greatest talent.

He was no youngster when he signed on, and at first it was rough going for him because, though I didn't know it, he was also working Friday, Saturday and Sunday at Gatlinburg, up near Dollywood, Tennessee, where he owned and starred in his own comedy theater.

Gatlinburg's a three and a half hour drive from Nashville. Early each week Archie would slip into my office to examine my daily shooting schedule, which I kept on three-by-five-inch index cards on a board. If he saw he was scheduled for a Friday afternoon, he would just take that day's card (without telling me) and move it elsewhere, so he could be free to make the drive to Gatlinburg. If he found he was scheduled the following Monday, he'd switch that card too, so he wouldn't have to be back in Nashville until late Monday afternoon.

This caused me tremendous problems. Because we only had twenty days to do thirteen shows, I always worked out my schedule of set changes and talent availability in a very tightly coordinated rotation. At first I couldn't understand how I kept messing up so badly. Finally, one day I caught on to what Archie was doing and confronted him about it.

"Listen," I said, "you just can't arbitrarily come in and move the schedule around to suit yourself." He then explained his situation, and I agreed to work around him. But, as I told him, I didn't understand why he hadn't just come and talked to me about the situation. He said he was afraid he'd be fired because of a conflict of interest. I assured him that would never happen. Although I thought highly of Archie and valued his contribution to the show, I realized then and there he was not the most secure person in the world.

One day during our very first production schedule, Archie came into my office and made a suggestion about adding some country jingles on the show. One of them was something he called, "Pffft! You Were Gone." I liked it and agreed to use it on the very first *Hee Haw*.

With "Pffft," I wanted my performers to physically emulate the look of the famous painting "American Gothic": the gist of the jingle is how a boy feels when he discovers the girl of his dreams is no longer his.

Where oh where are you tonight
Why did you leave me here all alone?
I searched the world over
and thought I found true love
You met another and Pffft! You were gone . . .

It worked so well, I decided to make "Pffft" a part of our regular weekly format. We put the music on a track so that Archie could sing it not only with other regulars, but with guests as well. "Pffft" became one of the most successful sketches we ever did. We got a ton of mail on it, and the jingle became something of a national sensation. All over the country kids were singing "Pffft" all day in school.

In the music business you must be sure you know who the correct writer, composer and publishers of a song are, because writers get paid performance rights, and composers get publishing rights. Because the CBS network was very

Dr. Archie Campbell examines his nurse

particular about proper accreditation, I made it a point to be extra careful about the credits on "Pffft." But not careful enough, as I was soon to learn.

The first thing I needed to make sure of was that Archie was the actual composer. He assured me he was. In fact, he said the song was published by his own company, Archie Campbell Music. I said fine, listed it as such and sent it through the system.

Early on, during our next production schedule, I was sitting in my office when I noticed this frail, little old man who looked like he weighed 120 pounds, standing soaking wet in the hallway trying to get in to see me.

I was always extremely busy during production. My office had a constant stream of visitors, managers, agents, performers, musicians, and guests. I barely had time to take a deep breath when this little fellow tried to come in. I brushed him off, thinking he was probably someone wanting to try out for the show.

Finally, I had Marcia Minor, my associate producer, talk with him. After, she came to me and said, "Look, Sam, this gentleman is demanding to see you and I don't think it has anything to do with casting. He says he has a music copyright problem." When I heard that, I agreed to see the little fellow.

Marcia brought him in. He stood back, in the doorway arch, and said, "Are you Mr. Sam Lovullo?"

"Yes, I am."

"My name is Bix Reichner."

"Yes?"

Just about this time Archie Campbell came running in. "Chief! Chief! I want you to meet Bix Reichner! He's a friend of mine and a great songwriter! A great man! He's written for so many great people. By the way, *he's* the one who wrote "Pffft, You Were Gone!"

I looked at Archie. "What did you say?"

"Yes, Chief," he said. "This is the man who wrote 'Pffft, You Were Gone.' "

"But Archie," I said, "you told me you wrote it."

"That was just a temporary thing because I was unable to

find Bix. But now that he's here, we have to change the records!"

It was then I learned that Bix Reichner was an ASCAP composer who'd penned quite a number of songs, including many for Frank Sinatra and the Tommy Dorsey Orchestra during the big band era. He'd also written several novelty tunes, including "Papa Loves Mambo," a very big hit in the '50s, recorded as a duet by Minnie Pearl and Grandpa Jones.

Of course, I apologized to Bix and made all the necessary changes, so he would receive all his rightful royalties. Over the years, this proved quite a lucrative financial windfall for him and his family.

If you were a regular viewer of the show, I'm sure you noticed how Archie never aged. The reason was, he wore a hairpiece that was never out of place. I was told early on by his associates he was very sensitive about his "hair," and that I was never to question or talk to him about it. That was fine with me. As far as I was concerned, his toupee didn't exist.

One day, we were taping a new spot called "The Unknown Comedy Story." Someone would get up and tell a story that in his or her opinion no one had ever heard before, augmented by a bit of animation, while off-camera we'd hear the sounds of hound dogs. Video technology allowed us to run dogs on camera chasing the joke teller off-camera. It was our way of putting down the terrible joke teller.

Well, one day, Archie was telling a joke during the sketch and when he finished, in his haste to get out of the way of the "oncoming dogs," he fell flat on his rear end. The "dogs" went completely over him, and when he finally picked himself up, his hairpiece was gone!

A short while later, he came to the control room, very upset. "Now, Chief," he said, "I want to tell you something. I know how you like to edit the show, keeping all the mistakes and break-ups in. I just want to tell you, if you use that last take I'm going to sue you!"

And he meant it! I told him not to worry, that I wouldn't put it on the air. That still wasn't enough for Archie. "Chief, I would appreciate it if you would destroy that tape. I don't want anybody to see me without my hairpiece. Not even my wife knows that I wear one!"

That I found a little hard to believe!

In June 1987, Archie died of heart failure in a hospital in Knoxville, Tennessee. All during the last week of his life, I was in constant touch with his family, who kept telling me that all Archie talked about were the good things *Hee Haw* and "the Chief" had done for him. Not only had the show given his performing career a major boost, but it had allowed him to join the Writers Guild of America and utilize their excellent benefits.

Three days before Archie passed away, Chet Atkins went to see him. I wanted to go along, but he said not to bother making the trip. Later on, Chet told me Archie hadn't wanted me to see him without his hairpiece.

JUNIOR SAMPLES

Junior was from Cumming, Georgia. He had a third-grade education, and worked a variety of jobs, including what became his speciality, the manufacture of moonshine whiskey. By the age of eleven, he owned his own still.

He was constantly being arrested, until finally the judge told him the next time he saw Junior's face, he'd send him to the penitentiary. It was that warning which put an end to Junior's first career.

A year or so later, Junior's brother went down to the Gulf and caught a sea bass that weighed upwards of sixty pounds. He brought the head back to Georgia, where Junior mounted it and carried it around in the back of his pickup. Whenever anyone asked about the fish, Junior would say he caught it in a local pond.

The story spread through Georgia that Junior had caught the biggest fish in the history of the state! He was eventually invited onto a local radio show to tell the story. By then, the story had become somewhat embellished,

Junior Samples and friend. Would you buy a used car from this man?

in that special Junior Samples style. He told the DJ he wasn't sure how much the fish actually weighed, but as there were seven in his family, he figured he could feed them on it for a week.

The phone lines at the studio lit up, with people laughing their heads off. It also caught the attention of the state game commission. They pulled Junior in for questioning, he got scared he was going to go to the pen, and confessed the truth. They let him go, and Junior thought that was the end of it.

By this time, however, the tape of Junior's radio appearance was being passed around, other stations began playing it, and eventually it reached Nashville, where Archie Campbell and Chet Atkins heard it. Shortly after, Archie came into my office one day and said, "We need to hire this guy. He's perfect for the show."

The first time Junior came into my office, I remember sitting at my desk thinking, this guy actually *looks* funny. Here was this big, heavyset man in bib overalls with, as I couldn't help noticing, one green sock and one red. I said,

"Tell me, Junior, why do you have on two different-colored socks?"

"Well," he said, "The red is my right and the green is my left. That's how I tell one from the other."

The greatest line that's ever been told on *Hee Haw* was by Junior Samples on our very first show. "To get into show business," he said out of nowhere, "you just put a bunch of marbles in your mouth and start talkin'. The first thing you know, a marble'll come out, and by the time you lose all your marbles you're a star!"

Among his many contributions to the show, Junior was also our "used car salesman." You called "BR 549" if you wanted to buy a used car from him. We picked the number at random—only later did we discover there was a widow, living in Indiana, whose telephone number was BR-549.

One day I received a call from her attorney. He said if we didn't cease using the number his client was going to sue. She was an invalid, he said, unable to get to her phone every time it rang, and one time in her haste to get there, she had fallen and broken her hip! *The caller had wanted to buy a car!*

We solved that situation by adding another letter to Junior's phone number so no one could actually call.

During *Hee Haw*'s second season, Junior started to feel a little embarrassed by his appearances on the show. Part of his charm was his inability to deliver material as it was written, mainly because he could barely read. His "screwups" were hilarious, and endlessly endearing. However, he began to worry that he was coming off as a stupid person. He had street smarts galore, but, remember, no formal education. The more people laughed at him, the more uncomfortable he became.

One day he showed up for a taping with his wife, Grace Samples, a very charming, nice-looking, slightly frail woman. I liked her very much, but couldn't understand what she was doing there. Junior usually did his thing alone, had a couple of drinks, and made a good time out of his work day. He couldn't do that when his wife, who was as much a mother to him as a mate, was along for the ride. The reason, I soon discovered, was that he had asked her to help him "improve" his material.

I never gave scripts in advance to my performers. The first time they saw what they were to do and how we wanted them to do it was on the set. We always had cue cards ready, and as long as they got the general idea, that was fine.

This day, Junior kept demanding that he get his script in advance, and, very foolishly, somebody in the office gave it to him. He then took it back to his hotel, and he tried to memorize it while his wife read it aloud to him. When he came in the next day, he did his thing without any of the usual hilarious "Juniorisms." We taped a whole set of shows that way.

It wasn't until Junior saw those shows on television that he realized he was no longer being "Junior Samples." The following year, he returned as the "old" Junior, drinking, having a good time, breaking up, all of it. Much to his, and our, great relief.

GRANDPA JONES

We got Grandpa Jones, a sweet, caring, family man, from the Grand Ole Opry, on Gordie Tapp and Archie Campbell's strong recommendation. He was already a country legend long before he joined us on our very first show.

He's been playing the role of Grandpa, by the way, since he was twenty-six years old. He maintains that the boots he wears today are the same he wore when he first started.

In real life, 'Pa is a very educated, cosmopolitan man. He reads a great deal, and is well versed on many topics. However, when he's "Grandpa Jones," he's everybody's grandpa. There

Grandpa Jones in search of higher learning

isn't a soul in the country music world who doesn't just love him.

Of course, being the perfectionist that he is, he also has something of a temper. On the very first show, he actually gave me the idea for doing the "bloopers" when he was doing his act, strumming his banjo up over as he pulled it down. This time, he happened to break a string and he became furious! "Just a minute," he said, "I'll be right back." We kept the camera rolling, and it followed him as he tried to fix his banjo, all the while cussing out loud, saying, "This is my first chance to get national TV exposure and you're causing me to waste a lot of film!" He was talking to his banjo!

GORDIE TAPP

Before becoming part of the Nashville scene, Gordie Tapp had developed a successful country act in Canada, built on the character of "Uncle Clem," a country-style Frank Fontaine, the benevolent-drunk type. Gordie, who like Archie was a writer as well as performer, had starred in a number of Canadian TV shows, which is how Peppiatt and Aylesworth knew of him.

Gordie became our Kornfield Kounty general-store keeper. He was great at doing stand-up comedy, and could also sing quite well.

When it came to country humor, Gordie and Archie knew where to find the bodies. They were instrumental in introducing us to Stringbean, Junior Samples, and Don Harron. Thanks to Gordie and Archie they all became regulars.

Occasionally I'd let Gordie do his Clem act, but I didn't use it very often, because I felt it had an essentially Canadian identity and didn't really belong on a show so indigenous to the American South. Also, we were very big in the Bible Belt, where the people found little humor in drunkenness.

Don Harron with Hee Haw Honey Gunilla Hutton

DON HARRON

Still another person we brought down from Canada was Don Harron, who was Charlie Fargonson, our reporter in the KORN newsroom sketch each week. Incidentally, there was a real KORN, located in the Dakotas. When they found out about us, they were kind enough to grant us permission to use their name.

Don was a trained classical actor who'd played Shakespearean roles on Broadway. He wrote his own material for the KORN sketches (as Archie did for the barbershop and Gordie for the general store). Don's specialty was a satirical look at daily events. At times he would get way out there. To keep the *Hee Haw* identity, he played Charlie in an old sweater and cap, and "broadcast" out of a chicken coop. In many ways Don was the show's resident politician. He could bend the truth and always seem to get away with it.

STRINGBEAN

String was a six-foot-five-inch sweetheart of a man. He was a dear friend of Minnie Pearl and Grandpa Jones, and a favorite of the Grand Ole Opry. He and 'pa used to love to go fishing together, and were inseparable on the set. Anyplace you'd see Grandpa, you'd see String.

They played banjo duets on the show, and whenever String was scheduled to be on, he'd come into my office with a pipe sticking out of his mouth and say, "Hey boss, I got a letter from home, letter from home . . ." He'd pull the zipper down on his big overalls, sit there in my office, sometimes stand, and read these letters out loud, which I always found hilarious.

One day I said, "String, tell you what. You don't need any makeup, just be in the studio at three, I'll put the gang there, you read one of those letters and we'll see how it works." That's how he became a regular on *Hee Haw*.

String was very grateful for the success he enjoyed on *Hee Haw*. He always said that *Hee Haw* didn't make him wealthy, but it did make him a very comfortable man.

Now, String was not a believer in banking his money. He preferred cashing his check, taking his green money, hiding some under his mattress and carrying the rest around—sometimes huge sums—in his overalls. Often, in front of his friends, he'd pull out a big fat roll of bills, show them off and tell the world how good *Hee Haw* was to him. I suspect that one time some unsavory characters saw him do this, and this may have led to his death.

In any case, in 1974—and after all this time it's still hard for me to believe—String and his wife were brutally murdered.

THE BUCKAROOS

Our first regular house band was The Buckaroos, which accompanied all our musical guests. They were led by Don Rich, the group's lead guitarist, a terrific fiddle player and Buck's indispensable singing partner until he died in 1971 from injuries he sustained in a motorcycle accident on his way to Pizmo Beach. It was late at night, he hit the center divider and was killed instantly.

Don Rich's trademark was singing the high-part harmony behind Buck. Together they had a very special, irreplaceable sound that died along with Don in that accident. I believe his passing signaled the start of the gradual decline of Buck's career. Hit records stopped coming, because he could never duplicate that sound. Also, Don was like a son to Buck, and I don't believe he ever fully recovered emotionally from the shock of his singing partner's untimely death.

OUR NASHVILLE EDITION

Our Nashville Edition was *Hee Haw*'s regular back-up singers. The leader of this dedicated, versatile group was Joe Babcock, who sang lead and tenor, with Herschel Wiginton on bass, and Dolores Edgin and Wendy Suits on the upper parts. When they first came on the show, they were known as The Town and Country Singers. However, we had to change their name when another group claimed they'd used it first.

Backup singers are always crucial in giving a song its body. On television, this is especially true, because they add a visual presence as well.

Lulu Roman

LULU ROMAN

It was Buck who first introduced me to Lulu Roman. For many years, she had been a go–go dancer in and around the Dallas-Fort Worth area. She was a very happy, funny lady with a really pretty face, who used her considerable heft to great comedic advantage.

She first came to California to be in some of the early background videos we used on the show. She was quite funny on them, informally teamed with Pat McCormick, doing things like fighting to get the most space in front of the camera. From that point on, she became a regular on the show.

She was great fun in the studio, always laughing and bringing a great energy to the set. One day she was in the ladies' dressing room, and there was some confusion as to what she was supposed to wear. She threw a smock on and came to the control room to find out what I wanted her to put on. She asked me what she should do, and I didn't react, because I was concentrating on something else. "Just a minute, Lulu, I'll be right with you," I said. With that, she came right up behind me, took her smock, lifted the front, put it over my head and started shaking all around. I thought I'd been hit by a couple of waves in the ocean!

Unfortunately, Lulu was having some personal problems at the time. She was adopted as a child and was searching for her real parents. Along the way, she fell offtrack a bit, and became involved with drugs. She got caught up with the wrong crowd, was arrested in Texas, and in 1973 was put on probation.

I worked very hard to get her back on the show. I flew to Dallas to speak with the authorities, and was able to convince them that we would rehire her for the show, which was what they wanted to hear. All the time she was on probation, I made sure she remained on the payroll. Fortunately, I was soon able to secure her release and bring her back to Nashville with me.

I'm happy to say that she straightened her life out during this time and became a born-again Christian. Most of the people on the show were happy to see her, but there were a few who didn't want to work with her anymore, who felt that she was a bad influence, and that because she was on probation, she would have the authorities breathing down *their* necks. Also, there was some concern that our sponsors wouldn't want her to appear. I decided to keep Lulu out of group scenes, so that if the sponsors did raise a fuss, I could remove her bits without having to reshoot everyone else. If you look closely at any *Hee Haw* shows from the mid-'70s, you'll see that there was a period during which Lulu received no billing, wasn't highlighted at the top of the show, and was missing from "Pickin' and Grinnin'," as well as a lot of other group sketches.

Eventually, her probation ended, we put her back in the group sketches, and even gave her a chance to sing. Today she's part of the Christian circuit, traveling around the country trying to help others to avoid making some of the same mistakes she made.

THE HEE HAW HONEYS (AND SOME OF THEIR FRIENDS)

I always felt that a great deal of the success of *Hee Haw* had to do with all the pretty girls we featured. Although they weren't called "Honeys" back then, the original "sexy gals" on the show were Jennifer Bishop and Jeanine Riley. When we resumed production in November 1969, they were joined by Mary Taylor and Gunilla Hutton.

Gunilla had been on "Petticoat Junction," which had since been cancelled. When she became available, we signed her on. She's a very talented, intelligent actress who was always intensely into physical fitness. One of our writers, George Yanok, came up with the idea of making her our sexy "Nurse Goodbody" in Archie's doctor's office for Kornfield Kounty, which became one of our most popular recurring sketches.

T.G. Sheppard and the Hee Haw *Honeys. From left to right: Irlene Mandrell, Misty Rowe, Gunilla Hutton, and T.G. Sheppard*

Cathy Baker always practiced good dental hygiene

To this day, when she goes on tour, she'll put on her "Nurse Goodbody" uniform, to the great enjoyment of her fans.

Cathy Baker became our girl-next-door character and also our signature closer with her now-famous—"That's all!" Cathy had originally come to Nashville to be a writer, and took a job working as one of our set-design assistants. She always wore bib overalls and kept her hair combed straight down. One day I happened to walk by as she was painting sets. I loved her wholesome look and that's how she got the job as the show's sign-off girl. She eventually married the show's assistant art director, Bill Camden, responsible for so much of the show's early stylized "look."

Susan Raye was another of our original female cast members, but, although Buck had a thing for her and wanted us to put her in a Daisy Mae outfit and turn her into a Honey, she never really quite fit that image. She was more the girl next door, which is the role she came to play on the show.

By the way, we used to get quite a lot of fan mail from viewers in the Bible Belt, complaining about the Honeys, saying their blouses were too low-cut and their miniskirts a little too mini. There were, of course, an equal number of letters coming in from folks who loved the Honeys. Still, I decided that for one production period, thirteen shows, in June, 1974, I'd dress them up a bit and see what reaction that got. I called in my wardrobe designer, Ed Sunley, and told him what I wanted him to do.

He looked at me real funny and asked what the problem was. I showed him some of the letters and he said, "Sam, the beauty of *Hee Haw* is these gorgeous girls."

I said, "Ed, I like to follow what our audience tells me to do. I just want to try it, and if it doesn't work, we'll go right back to the way we were."

"Well," he said, "I'm not going to design any new clothes for the girls. I'll just go out and buy some stock products."

"Fair enough."

He stormed out of my office, and a few days later the Honeys were practically wearing turtleneck sweaters! He'd gone overboard on purpose, to make a statement.

Well, the first day the Honeys were in their new outfits, we taped a "Pickin' and Grinnin'" sketch. When the girls came out, everybody in the studio was shocked, but no one dared say anything. We shot the sketch, and as I remember, this was the first time we'd ever gotten through it without any mistakes, mainly because there was no pinching of the Honeys!

Immediately after, Stringbean came into my office. "Boss," he said, "I need to talk to you."

I looked up from my desk. "What's the matter, String?"

"Holy Moses, boss, but the only thing I had left in life was that there 'Pickin' and Grinnin'.' I'm always standing in the back 'cause I'm so tall, which gives me an opportunity to look down into them beautiful girls' bras whiles I'm doin' my lines. Now you've gone and taken this last pleasure away from me!"

As it turned out, String wasn't the only disappointed viewer. No sooner did that set of shows air than countless letters started coming in complaining about what I'd done. One I remember most vividly was a lady who said she'd been a fan from the first show, loved the comedy and the music, but felt we had made one horrible mistake. "Why did you dress up the girls?" she wrote. "You should never have done that. It was the one thing I could depend upon every week to turn my husband on!"

Buck Owens is sweet on the Hee Haw *Honeys. Bottom, from left: Victoria Hallman, Linda Thompson. Top, from left: Misty Rowe, Irlene Mandrell*

Sometimes just trying out for the Honeys or even saying you had was validation of sorts. Marla Maples claims to this day that she auditioned to be a Honey. I don't remember her doing so and haven't been able to find any record of it, but maybe she did send in a photo at one time or another. Anything's possible, I suppose.

One day, I was in the control room, and this model came in wearing a fur coat. While Marcia got a photographer, this gorgeous girl said to me, "Are you Sam Lovullo?"

I said yes, and was wondering what she was doing wearing a fur in hot weather.

"Well," she said, "I have a message for you." I thought she wanted to audition. All of a sudden, her coat opens up, she's standing there in nothing but a G-string, and written in lipstick on the front of her body is "Dear Sam, what is it going to take for me to get on your show?" That was followed by an arrow pointing to her crotch. I was stunned, and blushed all the way back to my office. We took some publicity pictures, but she never made it onto the show.

By 1973, *Hee Haw* was doing so well we decided to create a spin-off sitcom and call it *The Hee Haw Honeys Family.* Kenny Price played the "daddy" of the family that ran the Honeys' restaurant, where the show took place. Lulu Roman was his wife, the big lady behind the cash register. Gailard Sartain was their son the cook, Kathie Lee Johnson and Misty Rowe were sisters.

The show had a loose story line about people who passed through town and stopped by for something to eat. We were on the air for one year, before being canceled. We did well in the ratings but had made a poor business arrangement with our distributor, and because of that decided to let it go. Other shows since then have copied our original format and done very well, including the network sitcom *Alice* and *I-40 Paradise* on TNN.

Speaking of Kathie Lee, I found her in one of my periodic searches for new Honeys. I knew who she was because she'd gotten a lot of publicity when Anita Bryant was fired as the Sunkist Orange Juice spokesperson for something she'd said about homosexuals. Kathie Lee, who was then appearing on the *Name That Tune* show, became her much heralded replacement.

Roy Clark was familiar with her for another reason. Kathie Lee was a devout Christian and a graduate of Oral Roberts University in Tulsa, Oklahoma. Roy, who was a dear friend of Oral's, had seen Kathie Lee at the famous Crystal Palace. I had used her on the show once and was thinking of hiring her as a regular *Hee Haw* Honey when we hit upon the idea of putting her directly into the spin-off.

I must say that although Kathie isn't naturally country— she's more Broadway-belt-'em than anything else—she came through for us. It wasn't long before Kathie emerged as the "big find" of the *Hee Haw* Honeys sitcom.

After the show was canceled, Kathie got divorced from her first husband, moved to New York and landed a job on *Good Morning America.* One evening, a couple of years later, it must have been around seven or eight in the evening, I was in my office in Beverly Hills when the phone rang.

One of *Good Morning America*'s segment producers, Denise Schreiner (who happens to be an old friend as well as a coworker of mine in Nashville) and Kathie Lee were having a drink somewhere in New York City when my name came up. Denise mentioned that she used to have dinner with me every once in a while whenever both of us were in Nashville at the same time.

"No," Kathie said, "That's not possible. Nobody ever went out to dinner with Sam. He's a happily married man."

"Well, it's true," Denise said. To settle it, Kathie decided to call me. The first question she asked was if I'd ever gone to dinner with Denise. I said I did. And I added, "That's all I did."

"Well, are you still married to Grace?"

"Yes I am."

"Ah, honey, I wish I could find a man as trustworthy as Sam Lovullo. I'd marry him instantly."

"But Kathie," I said, "I'm an old man. You don't want an old man."

She laughed and said, "That doesn't matter." Sure enough, a few years later she married Frank Gifford, who is exactly the same age as I am!

Gunilla Hutton, one of the stars of the *Green Acres* sitcom, became a *Hee Haw* Honey when her show was canceled. She joined us at the start of our second full production cycle.

Lisa Todd, tall, dark, beautiful and sexy, was friends with one of our writers, Jack Burns, who was responsible for introducing her to me. She began on *Hee Haw* in June 1970 and stayed with us for fifteen years. She was from Hollywood, where she hoped to make it as an actress. She had worked as an extra on *The Jonathan Winters Show*, which was where she first met Jack. Lisa clarified the image of the gals on the show as "Honeys" for us. When she joined the show, we decided to make the girls our *Hee Haw* Honeys. Lisa, in particular, had quite a following. We paired her with Junior, and they made a great comic couple. Junior was the slow, gullible type, and Lisa the femme fatale. That setup gave us endless comedy possibilities.

Barbi Benton became a Honey in June 1972. We found her through the regular auditions we held from time to time in our Beverly Hills, California, offices.

I could tell immediately there was something really special about Barbi. Men just adored her, and she knew how to use that to her best advantage. After she was on the show for about a year, she came to me in March of 1974 and asked if I'd have Hugh Hefner on as a guest. She was living with him at the time in the famous Playboy mansion.

I said sure, I'd love to have him. The only problem was the obvious one. What would Hugh Hefner do on *Hee Haw*? After all, I thought to myself, his only real talent was publishing pictures of naked ladies! I finally decided to put him in a sing-along, surrounded by the entire cast in the Kornfield, a spot I reserved for just such unusual occasions. Actually, it was Archie Campbell who came up with a terrific idea. He suggested that the wardrobe people make a bunny outfit for Hef to wear in the kornfield. Archie fed him carrots and Hef managed to garble his lines beautifully!

Actor Will Geer with the Hee Haw *Honeys. Things never got this good on Walton's Mountain.*

One of the prettiest girls we ever had on the show was our own Miss Southern Belle from Georgia—Marianne Gordon. She became a Honey in 1972. One afternoon about a year later, while she was taping a bit, Kenny Rogers happened to walk into the studio. Kenny was in Nashville, having just left his rock-and-roll group, The First Edition. He was looking to get more heavily into country music.

Like every young fellow who came by the show, Kenny was very eager to check out the Honeys. It wasn't long before he made Marianne's acquaintance. A romance developed and shortly after, she came to me and asked if I would consider putting Kenny on the show. At the time, he was struggling with his career, and Marianne, to her credit, was very supportive of him.

I said I would, even though I wasn't sure he was country. I asked him what he wanted to sing. "When I was a youngster," Kenny said, "I lived in Texas, and used to do a song called 'There's an Old Man in Our Town,' accompanying myself on acoustic guitar." He did some of it for me, I liked what I heard, and put him on the show.

He worked out so well I decided to bring him back. George Ritchie brought Kenny a song he thought was right for him. The first time Kenny sang it anywhere was on his second *Hee Haw* appearance. The date was February 11, 1978.

Kenny Rogers met wife Marianne Gordon during a guest visit.

The song was "Lucille." Its exposure on *Hee Haw* changed Kenny's life.

Hee Haw not only helped make Kenny Rogers a country star, it also provided him with a wife, as he and Marianne were married shortly after. However, after "Lucille," I couldn't get Kenny to come back and do *Hee Haw*. I never really knew why, although I suspect it was a managerial decision. Suddenly, overnight, his people decided he was not the *Hee Haw* image.

In 1989, we did the *Twentieth Anniversary Hee Haw Special*. I wanted Kenny on it, and once again he turned me down, until I agreed to send a private plane to Atlanta to pick him up, and then a helicopter from the Oklahoma airport to the Lazy E Arena in Tulsa, where we were shooting the show. Kenny was the only one who ever demanded that kind of treatment.

Anyway, I thought the appropriate song for Kenny to sing on the show was "Twenty Years Ago." I got together with the fellow who'd written it and asked him to change some of the lyrics to make the song seem it was about *Hee Haw*. However, when I showed it to Kenny, he refused to sing it. He changed his mind the last minute, after we had already rehearsed another song, and he did sing "Twenty Years Ago," but without the special lyrics.

The women of Hee Haw *making music*

I like Kenny and it's unfortunate that these things happen. But they do.

THE HAGER TWINS

The Hager Twins were discovered by Buck Owens. They were orphans who'd been adopted by a Chicago couple. We knew very little about them when we hired them, other than that they were working at the time as maintenance men for a Chicago-based airline.

They joined us in midseason, 1969–1970. They were young, good-looking, and energetic, and they sang in the harmonic style of the Everly Brothers. There's no question that Buck helped make their career by bringing them to *Hee Haw*. The fact that they were identical twins became part of their "hook." Jim Hager played the guitar and sang lead. John did the harmonies and occasionally banged a tambourine.

They were a big hit on *Hee Haw*, and should have gone on to bigger and better things. We tried to develop a spin-off series for The Hagers. We shot a pilot called "The Hager Twins," a youth-oriented country music show. Unfortunately, it wasn't picked up.

Eventually, like so many young performers, they were tempted by the good life—and overindulged. As a result they kind of drifted out of sight.

Although they left the show in the big shake-up of 1986, they remained good friends to all the cast members, staff, and crew of the show.

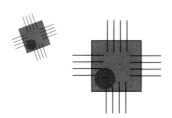

GEORGE "GOOBER" LINDSEY

George and I had first become friends in 1968, when he was a guest on *The Jonathan Winters Show.* He's a song-and-dance man and a very funny comedian. He was also on *The Andy Griffith Show,* and its spin-off, *Mayberry, RFD.*

In October 1971, he happened to be in Nashville and decided to come by and say hello to me and some of his friends on *Hee Haw.* He was great friends with Grandpa Jones, Archie Campbell, Roy Clark, and Minnie Pearl. When I heard he was in the studio, I went looking for him, found him, and we chatted for a bit. I asked him how long he was going to be in town. He said he'd be in Nashville for a few days and I asked him to stay put, figuring I might be able to get him involved with the show.

The next day I asked if he wanted to do a song for us, and so he did a traditional country song, "Just a Bowl of Butterbeans." It was a perfect vehicle to show off his country comedic "character." When he finished taping, I asked him when he could come back, and he said anytime I wanted him. From that moment on he was a regular.

George played the role of the simple country fellow on the

show, occasionally using his "Goober" character at the local gas station. Jack Burns, one of our writers who had also become a performer on the show, would be the city slicker. The sketch was always the same—the slicker knows it all but the country guy always wins.

In real life, George is a very sensitive person, and a perfectionist. Because he was essentially a West Coast performer, some of the born-and-bred Southerners on the show didn't completely accept him as "family" at first. They felt he was trying to move in on their turf, maybe even move them out. Ironically, these days George has a little trouble getting work in Hollywood, because of his long association with Nashville and *Hee Haw*. He currently lives in Nashville and travels the southern circuit. As a polished Broadway performer, he still hopes to someday be recognized as a "legitimate" actor. However, for now, "Goober" still prevails.

SHEB WOOLEY

Sheb Wooley was a successful film actor (playing, among many roles, a villain in *High Noon*) when we hired him as a regular cast member. Sheb was also a pretty good musician and comedian, and he did a "drunken-man" character by the name of Ben Colder. It was that character that Frank and John wanted when they decided to hire Sheb. It was a touchy decision since we didn't want to offend that segment of our audience that didn't appreciate drinking and "drunk" jokes.

Sheb, who was a pretty good songwriter, heard we were looking for a theme for the show. He took a group of musicians into his garage, recorded a riff loosely derived from "Mule Skinner Blues" which he called "Hee Haw," and copyrighted it through his own publishing company. He then asked us to listen to the tape. We liked it, and decided to use it for our theme. This turned into a very lucrative deal for Sheb.

Unfortunately, not long after the first *Hee Haw* aired, Sheb made a logistical error that would result in a far greater loss for him than whatever he'd gained through his ownership of the *Hee Haw* theme. After every critic in the country panned our first show, Sheb began to bad-mouth us around town, and it got back to Frank, John, and me. As a result we didn't renew his contract after the twelfth show. To this day, Sheb admits that if he'd kept his big mouth shut he could have been a regular for the whole twenty-five years. And he's absolutely right!

JIMMY RIDDLE AND JACKIE PHELPS

Jimmy Riddle and Jackie Phelps were the "Eefen and Hambone" team—hand-slapping palms to thighs and throat, and clacking spoons. Jimmy, the "eefen" half, was actually the harmonica player in Roy Acuff's band, and Jackie Phelps played guitar for Bill Monroe. They used to get together and fool around backstage at the Grand Ole Opry, which is where they developed their classic Eefen and Hambone routine.

One day in June 1970, Grandpa Jones and Archie came to me and said, hey, you ought to take a look at a nutty, hilarious act. I said sure, invited Jimmy and Jackie down and taped a bunch of their bits, which I then cut into the show for commercial bumpers.

The Eefen and Hambone skit was on the show for thirteen years, until 1981, when Jimmy died of cancer. At the time Jackie's health wasn't all that great either. He had developed a heart condition. It had become a tradition on Hee Haw that when people retired or died, we no longer did their sketches. When Junior passed away, for instance, we discontinued the used-car salesman, and when Archie died, so did his barbershop.

However, with Jackie, although I was no longer using the Eefen and Hambone, I didn't want to fire him because I was afraid he'd lose his AFTRA (American Federation of Television and Radio Artists) insurance. I decided to keep him on the payroll.

Sadly, Jackie passed away only a few years later. Not long after, I ran into his wife at a Nashville function. She came up to me and said, "Do you know who I am?"

"Yes," I said. "You're Jackie Phelps' wife."

A beautiful smile crossed her face. "I just wanted to come and thank you," she said, "for all the good things you did for him."

It was nice to know she felt that way. After Jimmy passed away, Jackie began to feel unappreciated. He kept after me to give him a bigger role on the show. I would have loved to, but there was nothing for him to do! He could play a little guitar, but we already had the best musicians in the business. I was glad to know that his wife didn't feel we had somehow misused or ignored her husband's talents; she knew that we genuinely cared for him, and watched out for his welfare.

ROY ACUFF

By 1972, I had begun to develop a feel for good country music but still had a lot to learn. For instance, I knew nothing at that time about Roy Acuff other than that he was the spokesperson for the Grand Ole Opry. I hadn't met him and really didn't understand his impact on country performers.

I rarely had time to socialize, which happens to be one of the best ways to get to know who's who in Nashville. Roy Clark, on the other hand, was and still is a happy-go-lucky type who loves life, loves to

Roy Acuff was a country music legend when he joined the cast of Hee Haw entertain, play the guitar, sing, hang out with his buddies, and get to know everybody.

One night after a taping, Roy said to me, "I think I'm going to head down to Broadway. Want to come along?"

Because I still had a lot of things to do, I declined, and thought he ought to as well. "Roy," I said, "we have a big day tomorrow."

"Go ahead and get your paperwork done. I'll call you. Maybe if you finish early you'll change your mind."

Later that evening, around nine, the phone in my office rang. I picked it up and heard Roy's voice on the other end. "Hoss, you still in the office?"

"Yeah."

"I want you down here *immediately!*" I knew he was out with his banjo player, Buck Trent, and that they were both roaring. "Come over to Roy Acuff's music shop, on Broadway. The place is closed so you won't be able to come through the front entrance. Drive to the back alley, park your car and you'll see two hurricane doors at ground level. That's the rear entrance."

I decided I had to check things out. When I arrived, I found the hurricane doors, but no bell. I started to pound on them until I heard a voice say, "We're coming, we're coming." All of a sudden, I heard a high, nasal voice say, "Young man, you step back now." The doors flew open and I was greeted by this elderly fellow whom I followed down the steps. As I did so, I said, "Hey, is Roy Clark here? I'm looking for Roy Clark."

Just then I saw Roy, who had a funny expression on his face. He put one hand on his lips and with the other pointed furiously at the old man. When I finally got inside, Roy quickly took me aside and said, "Don't you know who that is?"

"No."

"Lovullo, say hello to Roy Acuff!"

And that's how I first met the great man. Shortly after, I booked him on *Hee Haw*. His first show aired October 27, 1973, and soon after he became a regular.

When we moved *Hee Haw* to the Opryland complex, Roy Acuff would often sit and rest in his own dressing room between tapings, and Roy Clark and I would visit him there. Both Roys, Clark and Acuff, loved to play the fiddle. We'd sit around and all have a little cranberry juice and Jack Daniels, Roy Acuff's favorite drink.

More than once Roy Acuff turned to me and said, "My eventual replacement as host of the Opry should be Roy Clark. He's the only one who can properly carry on the tradition."

And I think in due time that's exactly what will happen.

In the late '80s, Roy Acuff had begun to show signs of physical deterioration. One day he came to me and said, "Sam, I just can't meet these early calls anymore." At his request, I cut his appearances back to maybe a song or two over several shows. I knew then the end was in sight, that his health wasn't good. In 1993, not long after we stopped production, he passed away.

Whenever I was in trouble and needed advice, I'd always go to Roy Acuff. He seemed to have the right answer to any question. Looking back, I'd have to say that Roy Acuff was the crucial link in a very long and beautiful chain.

PAT BUTTRAM

Already known to America's TV viewers, Pat was added to our staff of writers in 1969. Although he was a terrific and talented comedian, when he came on board we were still on the network and didn't have the room or budget for any more performers. Pat wrote for the last seventeen shows we did for CBS. He then became an occasional guest when we went into syndication. He could always be counted on to come up with the great one-liner, either on paper or in front of the camera.

Not many people know this, but Pat was also an outstanding speechwriter. He wrote dozens for Gene Autry, who used to love to take Pat along to the press box to watch California Angels baseball games. If the Angels could only play as well as Pat could write, they'd have a championship team!

BUDDY AND BUCK OWENS

Buddy Owens, Buck's son, was a semiregular singing partner of Buck's in 1969, when the show first started. He also participated in several comedy routines.

Nepotism was always a problem. It's sad, because sometimes talented people get hurt by it. There was a lot of resentment on the part of other cast members who felt that Buddy was only on the show because he was Buck's son. It became an uphill battle, and both of us knew it. He had a terrific voice, but he was forever singing in the shadow of his dad. He lasted three seasons, until he realized he didn't want to make a career out of country music. Today, Buddy runs Buck's radio station in Phoenix, Arizona.

Bonnie Owens, Buddy's mother, was an excellent backup singer, already in the process of getting divorced from Buck when he signed on to do the show. Along with Don Rich, Bonnie was crucial to the classic Buck Owens sound. After they divorced, she married Merle Haggard, and although they divorced as well, she's still singing with Merle in his live performances.

Gailard Sartain, a very funny man

GAILARD SARTAIN

Gailard, a graduate of the University of Tulsa, joined our show in 1974. We discovered him working at a local television station in Tulsa. He was a man of many characters, with a brilliant clown mind, not unlike Jonathan Winters.

Gailard was part of the infusion of talent we got from the Oklahoma-based Jim Halsey agency. Jim sent Frank, John and me a video of Gailard's TV show, where his job was to fill in comedy bits during commercial breaks of feature films. We all liked what we saw and decided he should be a regular on *Hee Haw*.

Gailard liked to clown around in the studio. Every time the station manager counted down—"Five, four, three, two"—when he got to "one," Gailard would make a loud, farting sound with his mouth. It was quite funny, but also a major distraction. When he was working with one or two others it was okay, but in a group sketch, such as "Pickin' and Grinnin'," or the Kornfield, it was a real problem.

One day in 1975, during "Pickin' and Grinnin'," he was in the background, and every time Buck said, "I'm a pickin,'" and Roy said, "And I'm a grinnin,'" Gailard made that noise. Roy became so furious, he walked off the set and shut the door behind him in the dressing room. When he cooled off, he came back, and sure enough, just as he was about to say his line, Gailard made that noise!

This time, I went right onto the set and pulled Gailard out of the sketch. We finished the taping without him. I was about ready to fire him!

He was a charmer, though, and I kept him on because he was such a key asset to the show. Among his many regular roles was the cook in the truck stop, which he also played on the *Honeys* spin-off series. He was also our sleazy ambulance-chasing attorney. He has since carved out a successful screen career, appearing in such movies as *Fried Green Tomatoes* and *Getting Even With Dad*.

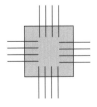

Roni Stoneman, between Victoria Hallman and Minnie Pearl

RONI STONEMAN

Roni was a great comedienne, a terrific singer and a banjo player. And a lovable scatterbrain. There's a country expression that fits her well—she's *squirrely*! She became a regular in 1973, when Gordie Tapp tagged her to play his wife in one of our most popular sketches, "The Naggers," which he developed. Gordie played the drunken, lazy husband, and she was the homemaker trying to get him to get off his rear end and provide for the family. She was always hitting him on the head with a rolling pin.

Roni is from a family of nine children steeped in country tradition. They traveled throughout the South, doing a lot of radio and television. Her father was a composer/song-writer/musician, and made sure that every family member played an instrument. Roni learned to play the banjo and was terrific at it.

We discovered her playing banjo in Printer's Alley one night, after the family act had been retired and she was trying to make it as a solo performer. Playing in Printer's Alley is as good a way as any to get discovered in Nashville. In Roni's case, it got her a regular role on *Hee Haw*. Later on, after Stringbean died, she replaced him in the Banjo Quartet.

KENNY PRICE

Kenny began his career as a winner on the old *Arthur Godfrey Talent Scouts* show, after which he became a regular on the *Louisiana Hayride* TV show, doing comedy bits and singing when we found him. He had a hit record, "The Sheriff of Boom County," which was why we wanted him to be a regular on *Hee Haw*.

Kenny was a lovable man, a good-time guy, big and fat, one of those robust Joes you want to put your arm around and hug and squeeze. We used to refer to him as "The Round Tones of Kenny Price."

Kenny was such a good comedian that people some-times had trouble taking him seriously, which im-peded the progress of his career. I believe he could have gone on to bigger and

He ain't heavy, he's my producer. Kenny Price and yours truly

better things, but he passed away prematurely. He loved to eat and drink, and one day his body just gave out. In 1987 he had a stroke and died shortly after. Grandpa Jones and I were honored to be lead pallbearers at his funeral. I miss him to this day.

JIMMY HENLEY

Back in 1976, Roy Clark was a very hot attraction on the road. One afternoon, he called me from Phoenix, Arizona, where he was making one of his sold-out appearances. Now, Roy is not one to pick up a phone and call anyone unless he's in a partying mood. So I was surprised when I picked up the receiver and heard Roy's voice on the other end. "Hey Sam," he said, "I've got a surprise for you. Listen to this."

For the next five minutes I heard the most beautiful banjo playing imaginable. When it finished, Roy said, "How did you like that?"

"Fantastic," I said. "You've been practicing!"

He let me go on and on, until, when I finished raving, he said, "That wasn't me, Sam, it was Jimmy Henley. *And he's only thirteen years old*!"

"Well then," I said, without missing a beat, "You have to bring him aboard!"

Jimmy came to Nashville, appeared on the show and was an immediate phenomenon. Bobby Thompson, one of our regular band members, marveled over Jimmy and considered him to be the greatest banjo player in the world. They established a great relationship, and often played together. Jimmy was a terrific addition to the *Hee Haw* family. Because we were on the air for so many years, America had the pleasure of watching him grow up every week right before its eyes.

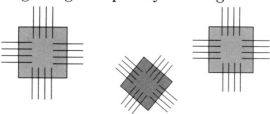

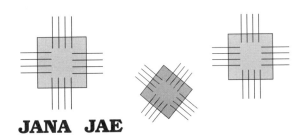

JANA JAE

Toward the end of 1976, a young lady by the name of Jana Jae was hired by Buck Owens as a regular member of The Buckaroos. She was a real beauty and a talented violinist. Today, Jana is known throughout the South as the spokesperson on Wal-Mart TV commercials.

I believe Buck first hired Jana as a possible replacement for Don Rich, but quickly took more than a casual liking to her. Either way, Jana, proved a great addition to the show. Buck then tried to push her into becoming a *Hee Haw* Honey, which was a problem for me, as she wasn't, in my opinion, Honey material. Her appeal was more on the maternal side.

When I refused to make her a Honey, Buck started pressuring me to feature her in some of the show's comedy routines. I did let her do one-liners while playing her fiddle like a female Henny Youngman, and occasionally I used her for lead-ins.

Somewhere along the line her personal relationship with Buck blossomed, and one day they announced they had gotten married. They took a short honeymoon, then returned to Bakersfield. Quite naturally, Jana was expecting to join Buck at his big ranch. However, he decided they ought to spend a couple of days in a hotel, to give him time to properly welcome her.

There were rumors that Buck was not yet over another woman, and it didn't take Jana long to figure it out. About a week later, we heard that Buck and Jana had split.

It got to the point where the two of them couldn't be in the same studio, and when it came right down to it, Jana was more expendable than Buck. Although she was an extremely talented woman—she was a great fiddle player—she just wasn't that important to the show. I needed another fiddler like I needed another guitar player, but there was only one Buck Owens!

At first, I tried to schedule her appearances when I knew Buck wouldn't be at the studio. One day, when we were in preproduction, someone told me Jana had arrived without being scheduled—this on a day Buck was going to tape—and I didn't know what to do. I figured the best thing was to avoid her, and she'd leave.

The moment I heard the front door to my outer office open, I ran into a small closet to hide! She kept waiting around, saying, "Well, his car is out there, I know he's here, he must be coming back . . ." Meanwhile, my assistant kept making excuses for me. It was a hot summer day, and I was forced to stay in that closet for two hours, until she finally gave up and left!

When I finally let her go, she hired Marvin Michelson, the famed divorce lawyer, and threatened to sue us, claiming I had been pressured by Buck to fire her, which of course wasn't true. Although there were a lot of threats that went back and forth, no lawsuit ever materialized.

JOHN HENRY FAULK

John was a a great southern storyteller, part Arthur Godfrey, part Will Rogers. He was a very successful radio broadcaster until he was accused by some in the '50s of being a Communist and was subsequently blacklisted.

One day in 1978, I was in my office and got a call from John Aylesworth. We'd been on the air about ten years, and Frank and John were looking to add a fresh spark to the show. "Sam," John said, "you ought to talk to John Henry Faulk and see if you can't make him a regular."

Which is exactly what I did. As soon as John joined the show we started getting quite a bit of attention, if not exactly the type we wanted. Here, after all, was a man who had just won a major libel suit against CBS for their having branded him a Communist. Our hiring him caused a bit of an unwanted stir.

My biggest problem with John Henry turned out to be how difficult he was to write for. Naturally, he wanted to continue where he'd left off, or been cut off, doing commentaries about the democratic system—what he thought was right about it and what he thought was wrong, often singling out members of Congress along the way. All of this was, quite obviously, very "un-*Hee Haw*."

Almost from the beginning we received a lot of negative feedback from our audience about his spots. I finally sat down with John to ask him if he would consider doing more traditional, patriotic material with an historical slant. "In 1779, the constitution . . . ," or, "Did you know that George Washington did not really chop down the cherry tree? Here's what really happened." That kind of thing.

John agreed, and I appreciated it.

In the early '80s, when we made our move from the WLAC studio to the Grand Ole Opry he came along with us, but it was apparent his health was beginning to fade. He taped his last spot in October 1981. After, he gave me a great big bear hug and said, "Thank you Sam, you put me back on the map!" He told me he'd come back to TV not for the money, which he didn't need, but because he'd had a tough time, being punished for doing nothing wrong or subversive, since he was and had always been a true American. He retired, and passed away not long after.

SLIM PICKENS

George Lindsey was friendly with character actor Slim Pickens, who expressed a desire to do *Hee Haw*. When George conveyed that message to me, I invited Slim to "Come on down!"

Slim was a very funny man and exuded great warmth. He made his first *Hee Haw* appearance on March 21, 1981, and proved so popular we brought him back several times. One of his best bits was "The Invisible Guy" character. People were always trying to guess who that voice belonged to. The following year I made him a regular.

I liked Slim so much, I invited him to appear on a new show that Frank Peppiatt, John Aylesworth and I were putting together for NBC, called *The Nashville Palace. The Palace* ran for a year, Saturday nights at 8:00, the lead-in to Barbara Mandrell's hit show.

In 1982, a noticeable change came over Slim. He became a little testier than usual, and began suffering violent headaches. He went to several doctors, and it was discovered he had an inoperable brain tumor. Not too long after, he passed on. He was a great addition to our show, and when he left us, was sorely missed.

THE QUARTETS—Gospel, Harmonica, Banjo, Fiddle

The show's greatest audience support always came from the Bible Belt. That's one of the reasons we chose the Gospel Quartet to close the show.

It began in the early '70s when Grandpa Jones, Roy Clark, Merle Travis, Buck Owens, Archie Campbell, Kenny Price, and that week's guest, Tennessee Ernie Ford were in the dressing room, trading country stories between set-ups for Tennessee's musical number. Gradually, they drifted into song, and began doing a gospel number. The harmony was simply outstanding.

Passing by in the hallway, I happened to overhear them and demanded more! I then asked them if they'd mind moving into the studio—and doing it quickly so they wouldn't lose their spontaneity. We taped their songs, and when we broadcast it, found we had a huge hit segment on our hands.

However, along with its success came problems. A quartet means four people. How was I supposed to get seven superstars to fit into a quartet? Ernie Ford was a great bass and fit the group perfectly. Once he finished his guest spot, though,

Archie Campbell wanted to take over his role. The only problem was, Archie sang tenor. Eventually, with Roy's help, Kenny Price filled the bill. The original Gospel Quartet that appeared regularly was Buck Owens, Roy Clark, Grandpa Jones, and Kenny Price. It's sad but true that when Kenny and Buck left, the group lost its unique sound.

When we discovered that musical "groupings" gave the show more family appeal, we developed the harmonica, banjo and fiddle quartets. Thereafter, we rotated each group in a regular sequence, so that every week one quartet would appear on the show.

The Harmonica Quartet featured Roy, Grandpa Jones, Gordie Tapp, and Charlie McCoy, and an occasional guest who could play harmonica. So sometimes we let it go to five. Who was counting?

In 1985, the great Stan Musial appeared on the show and sat in with the group. Stan, by the way, like Ernie, liked to fuel up with a little vodka-and-something before going on stage. Ernie liked his with tomato juice, Stan preferred Bloody Marys. I, of course, was the perfect bartender.

The Banjo Quartet consisted of Roy, Grandpa, Roni Stoneman (who replaced Stringbean after he died), and the great Bobby Thompson. Occasionally, Buck Trent and Tom T. Hall would sit in. This grouping was more visual than musical. The problem was, they could never settle on a song and then sit and rehearse it. These fellows (and gal) desperately needed a conductor!

The Fiddle Quartet was Roy Acuff, Roy Clark, Tommy Williams (a member of the show's regular band) and a lovely lady by the name of Ramona Jones—Grandpa's wife. Occasionally John Hartford would sit in with the group. All fiddles sound the same, so all the songs tended to sound alike. But thanks to Hartford, who was an amazingly fast player and clogger, we could break up the number with some of his dancing. I wanted to use Jana Jae in the spot, but she played a violin, and that word simply does not appear in any country dictionary.

The one and only Million Dollar Band

THE MILLION DOLLAR BAND

I think the biggest single accomplishment I made to the show was creating The Million Dollar Band. All odds were against my bringing these most talented individual musicians together. I was told—I can't tell you how many times—to just forget it, that I could never pull it off, but I did. The band featured the talented fingers of Floyd Kramer on piano, "Yakky" Boots Randolph on sax, "Breathless" Danny Davis on trumpet, "Wheelies" Roy Clark on guitar, "Slippery" Charlie McCoy on harmonica, "Smiling" Johnny Gimble on fiddle, Jethro Burns on mandolin, and "Cool" Chet Atkins on guitar. These outstanding musicians gave the show a million dollar's worth of ratings.

Word soon spread throughout Nashville whenever they were scheduled to tape a set for the show. Every musician in town was willing to hang from the rafters just to watch.

KINGFISH THE WONDER DOG

There were actually four dogs over the life span of the show. Kingfish, our first bloodhound, joined the show in 1969. His owner was the local prison warden. Kingfish had a contract, with a decent show fee and residuals. He was on the show for a year. We were unable to exercise our renewal option because he choked to death on a bone. It was a great loss, although no one missed his terrible smell.

Kingfish was replaced by Beauregard, who was with us from 1970 through 1975. His owners were our technical director, Joe Hostettler, and his wife, Anita, who worked in makeup. Joe agreed to let us have the dog as long as we fed him. Unfortunately, Beauregard also had an awful odor, and smelled his way out of a job.

He was replaced by Beauregard, Jr. (no relation), who was with us from 1976 through 1980. He left the studio one day and no one ever saw him again.

In 1980, a young law student who needed tuition money made a deal with us to use his dog, Buford. Buford was a very nervous dog. He was always passing gas on stage. I would have let him go sooner, but his owner was majoring in contract law and I was stuck with old Buford for five full years.

PART THREE

THE
GUESTS

"I thought they were crazy having little pigs dance across the screen. But after getting to know producer Sam Lovullo, I would have put up with anything to work with him."

—HANK WILLIAMS, JR.

FOR NEARLY twenty-five seasons and 585 shows, *Hee Haw* presented more than a thousand guests from every walk of show-business life. Certainly we had the cream of the country crop, and were responsible for breaking a number of unknown acts who went on to become today's country legends.

But we also had a fair number of performers who weren't country, who wanted to be on the show not because they were selling a record or promoting an upcoming tour, but strictly for the fun of it. That's really what was the heart of *Hee Haw*. We were like one big open-house party, where all our friendly neighbors were invited to come on down and have a good time.

On the following pages are highlights of some of the moments I shared with my *Hee Haw* family and our guests. I hope you'll remember their visits as I do, with warmth, affection, and great fun.

CHARLEY PRIDE—JUNE 15, 1969.

Charley received his first national television exposure on the premier episode of *Hee Haw*. He walked into my office during a break in the taping and said, "Mr. Sam"—everybody in the South calls everybody else by his first name with a Mr. in front of it—"thank you for giving me the opportunity to show the world I'm black. It's sad and unfortunate that in the pictures they use of me on my record albums, they're always making

NOTE: *The dates listed refer to the airdate of the guest artist/group's first appearance. For a complete listing of all guests and appearances, see Appendix B.*

me look lighter than I am." The truth was, he was proud to be black and wanted the public to know.

Charley appeared on *Hee Haw* several times, as well as on our twentieth anniversary special.

MERLE HAGGARD—JUNE 22, 1969.

Merle was on our second show. He was a part of Buck's Bakersfield "camp," which was how we got him. Merle was writing songs for Buck's publishing company, recording them for the same label Buck was on.

Merle didn't return to *Hee Haw* for nearly eleven years, until June 1980. That's when I found out he'd boycotted the show because of a falling out he'd had with Buck over some publishing problem. It was definitely our loss. *Hee Haw* was a perfect venue for Merle.

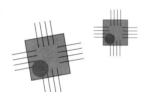

TAMMY WYNETTE—JUNE 29, 1969.

George Richey, a talented record producer, musician and songwriter, is married now to Tammy Wynette. They first met when Tammy was a guest on our show.

For our first twelve shows, Buck Owens and his manager, Jack McFadden, booked most of the talent on our show. They also acquired the services of Kelso Herston, a producer and studio musician, to help with the arrangements for guests. Kelso was also, at the time, Buck's producer at Capital Records. Then, one day Kelso was gone. Off the show. Buck brought George Richey on to replace Kelso.

I was in the audio room the day Tammy was rehearsing her first guest appearance. Now, Tammy is a gorgeous-looking lady. I'm not usually preoccupied with women's looks and all that, especially when I'm working. Still, this one time, I happen to be watching at the monitor, along with George and our audio-console operator, Larry Sullivan. Without thinking, I said out loud, "God, she's so gorgeous, I'd love to spend a night with her!"

Now the scene shifts, it's two years later, George and Tammy are married, George has left *Hee Haw* for what he believed were bigger and greener pastures. After much hesitation, possibly due to George's having left the show under less than perfect conditions, Tammy finally agreed to come back for another appearance on *Hee Haw*. She was scheduled for a Monday morning, and was exhausted, having toured all weekend and traveled all night on her bus to get to the studio.

Now, having worked on the show, George knew that I was an early riser.

At about eight-fifteen, he walked in to my office. George was a flashy zoot-suiter type, complete with gold chains. He said, "Come on, Chief, let's go, you wanted to give us an early call, we're ready, but you're not ready for us . . ."

I looked at him. "George," I said, "I thought being married to Tammy might have at least improved your taste in clothes. By the way, where is she?"

"Still on the bus. She says she's not coming out 'til you go in and get her."

I thought he was putting me on to stall for time. I decided to call his bluff. "All right then, come on, let's go get her." Although busses are usually locked, this one was opened, and I walked right in on Tammy just as she was getting out of bed. I was taken by surprise, and said, "Tammy! How are you, honey? I haven't seen you in a while. How's married life treating you?"

I went to hug her and George Richey came between us and said, "Don't you dare do that to my wife!" He then turned to Tammy and said, "Honey, I've got to tell you something. You all think he's an angel, but about two years ago, he wanted to make love to you!

"Yeah, he was in the audio room and said, 'Boy I'd like to spend a night with her!' "

I was absolutely stunned and humiliated! I could not believe what I was hearing!

Now it's ten years later, we've moved the show to Opryland, and I'm backstage the night of the CMA awards, broadcast from the stage of the Grand Ole Opry. (Because my *Hee Haw* office was in a trailer directly behind the stage, I had easy access to the Opry's backstage.)

This night, I happened to run into Tammy and, sure enough, jewelry-laden, zoot-suited George. I went up and said to Tammy, "So good to see you. What are you up to?" We chatted for a bit and then I headed back to my office.

Tammy got tired of waiting for her turn to perform, and decided to come to my trailer and continue our visit. The first thing I knew about it was, the door opened, I heard these footsteps, and then someone said, "I think he's in there."

The other person said, "Let me get ahead of you."

I didn't know who it was. Suddenly, Tammy was peeking in my door. "Hi, Sam."

"Hi, Tammy . . ."

"Shhh," she said. "Are you still after my body? I hope so, because I just have time for a quickie!"

In the background I could hear George trying hard as he could to stifle a great big hee-hawing laugh!

We all still kid about our "love affair." Keep dreaming, Tammy!

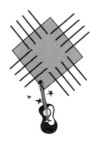

Jerry Lee Lewis banging the ivories

JERRY LEE LEWIS—JULY 13, 1969.

"The Killer" was always a little crazy. You never quite knew what was going to happen when he was around.

During the taping, because we wanted to show off his special style of singing and piano playing, Bill Davis, our director, suggested putting Jerry's sister, a regular singer in his nightclub act, on top of the upright piano to show off her beautiful legs. For some unknown reason, Jerry didn't like the idea, and he and Bill actually had hard words about it. After an embarrassing hassle, Jerry finally agreed to tape the number. He then walked off the set and never came back. I honestly think he was embarrassed by the fact that he'd created a scene, and thought because of it we didn't like him.

He did do the show one more time, years later, in the mid-'80s, and not a word was spoken about that unfortunate misunderstanding. Jerry is a great singer and piano player. I wish we could have had him on the show more often.

HANK WILLIAMS, JR.—DECEMBER 31, 1969.

Hank is one of my favorite guys. He's a real person and tells it like it is. For a long time, Hank lived in the very large shadow of his dad. Maybe that's why he was such a country music rebel/outlaw in the Willie Nelson/Waylon Jennings/Merle Haggard tradition. One of the reasons he loved doing *Hee Haw* was that no one seemed to care whose son he was. Quite honestly, at the time I didn't even know who Hank Williams, Sr., was, other than one of the pioneers of modern country music.

Shortly after Hank junior's appearance on our show, he had a terrible hunting accident which nearly killed him.

I felt especially privileged that when Hank returned to the music scene after his long convalescence, he chose *Hee Haw* as the venue for his reentry.

Hank junior always amazed me with how quickly he gets his job done. It's as if he's in some kind of great big hurry. Maybe it's due to his manager, Merle Kilgore. Merle, by the way, is also a very good singer. Both he and Hank performed together on a 1987 *Hee Haw.*

WANDA JACKSON—JANUARY 7, 1970.

At the time she made her appearance, I had no idea who Wanda Jackson was, other than that she was very hot in downtown Vegas casino clubs. I did know that she had given Roy Clark one of his big breaks early in his career, and that was good enough for me.

It's been said that during his unmarried days Roy had a crush on Wanda. I didn't see much eye contact between them when she did the show. Roy was, of course, by this time married to his lovely wife, Barbara.

Wanda went on to have a great career in gospel music. Unfortunately for us, that tended to limit her availability. Otherwise, she would have appeared far more often than she did.

HANK THOMPSON—JANUARY 14, 1970.

Hank Thompson is a genuine country legend. He plays guitar and sings traditional country songs that tell a story. People say that over the years, country music has changed. I don't agree. What *has* changed are the arrangements and instrumentation. The basic tune still hangs on story, love, marriage, divorce, broken hearts—the prime themes of country music. Hank Thompson's music carries that tradition on in a truly classic fashion.

GEORGE JONES—MARCH 11, 1970.

After George and Tammy Wynette's marriage began to fall apart and they separated, I booked each separately. For awhile, there was a feeling they might get back together again, but it didn't work out. George had a drinking problem, and Tammy couldn't put up with it. Worse, when Tammy divorced him, he fell apart.

With George Jones and his lovely wife, Nancy

Not long after, I attempted to book George. I called and said, "You know, George, you haven't done *Hee Haw* in a long time, no one has seen you, you've been tagged 'no-show George.' I think it's time you did the show, got some visibility and let people know you're alive."

He agreed and came down to our studios at Channel 5. I must say, it was quite an emotional visit. He was sober, but it was obvious he still had problems. He did a couple of his old standards, and when he finished, thanked me, put his arms around my shoulders and gave me a big hug. "You're the most understanding guy in the world," he whispered in my ear, before hastily leaving the studio.

A couple of weeks later, my phone rang, I picked up the receiver, and it was George. "Sam," he said, "I've been thinking about that taping. I don't believe I sang as well as I can. If you feel it was a bad performance, tell me and I'll be happy to redo my spot. Or if you just don't want to air it, that's okay too."

I said, "George, I know you weren't at your peak, but don't worry about it. With today's technology we can make you sound as good as you want to." I assured him I wouldn't air anything to embarrass him as a person, or hurt his career.

I worked very closely with my technicians to sweeten that track. When we aired the show, people saw he could still sing. As a result of that appearance on *Hee Haw*, George began what was to be his incredibly successful comeback.

After their divorce I actually did manage to bring George Jones and Tammy Wynette together one time. Nobody believed it was possible, but I convinced George and Tammy to cohost one edition of *Nashville Palace*.

Even after I'd made the booking, nobody believed George would actually show up. He and Tammy had just gotten divorced and George was still carrying the big torch. To make sure that he would, in fact, go through with his promise, I personally escorted him to the side entrance of the studio, and, standing there, gave him his show fee, $7,500 in cash.

Also, during this time when George was having personal

problems, he no longer trusted the people who surrounded him. He only agreed to do the show provided I give him adequate security.

This was his and Tammy's first joint appearance after the big breakup. They performed together, and it was a thrill to see them act so professionally toward one another. On the show that night George introduced (for the first time anywhere) "He Stopped Loving Her Today," which went on to become one of the biggest hits of his career.

Today, George is happily married to his lovely bride, Nancy. I believe she's responsible for his good health and his return to the top ranks of country music.

DOLLY PARTON—MARCH 18, 1970.

In those days, Dolly was doing a television show with Porter Wagoner. Early one morning, I was in my office when one of the show's secretaries called to say that Porter Wagoner was in the lobby and wanted to say hello.

We'd been on the air only about six months, and while I knew of Porter, I had never met him. I went upstairs and sure enough there he was, sitting with this gorgeous blonde I wasn't able to take my eyes off. "Sam," he said, "I'm Porter Wagoner, and this is . . ."

"You don't have to introduce her. I know who she is. It's a pleasure to meet you, Dolly Parton!"

"Dolly's going to be the next big country star."

Still looking at her, I said, "She already is, Porter."

There's no question Porter's a great talker and a natural salesman. I could tell he was really interested in promoting Dolly's career. There were rumors at the time of a romance between them, but I think that actually their relationship was strictly business. He had a genuine interest in her abilities as a songwriter. Later on, they opened up a very successful music publishing company.

On Porter's recommendation, I put Dolly on the show and she was excellent, of course.

At the time, incidentally, Porter said he wasn't interested in coming on the show with Dolly. He wanted her to have a solo shot. Later on, Porter came back and asked if I'd like to have Dolly back.

I said, "Absolutely."

"This time you have to have me too," he said, which was, of course, no problem.

Although we remained good friends, after those two performances, Dolly never again appeared on the show. I never "pressured" people to appear on *Hee Haw*. No matter who they were, if they declined, I went no further. That was one of the unbreakable rules of *Hee Haw*.

TOM T. HALL—NOVEMBER 10, 1970.

In my opinion, Tom T. Hall was the greatest singer-storyteller to ever appear on *Hee Haw*. Tom is funny, knowledgeable, personable, easygoing, and a not bad banjo player.

He's also quite wealthy, the result of owning his own music publishing company. The fact he was so well off became something of a running gag between us. I'll never forget one time he said to me, "Sam, I just bought a big farm ranch out here in Franklin, Tennessee, and my wife is just scared to death we're not going to be able to afford it, but I told her as long as there's Sam Lovullo I'll always be able to do *Hee Haw* and make enough money from it to pay it off!"

RAY CHARLES—DECEMBER 1, 1970.

When Ray agreed to do *Hee Haw*, the entire city of Nashville went crazy. Every musician in town wanted to come by and see the taping. There's no other way to put it except to say that Ray was a god to them. We made it a point not to book any other guests that day.

When late afternoon rolled in, I couldn't get him off the stage. He wanted to continue playing and singing, and he in-

When Ray Charles guested in 1970, everyone in Nashville wanted to see the taping

sisted on doing several comedy sketches, especially "The Kornfield," with the Honeys. Ray's appearance on *Hee Haw* marked the beginning of his longstanding love affair with Nashville.

Shortly after, he cut a country album, which was a huge success. From then on, whenever he'd come to Nashville, he'd call and ask if he could come on the show. We always had room for Ray.

His initial appearance, by the way, marked the first time we booked a singer who wasn't primarily country. Ray was very helpful to *Hee Haw* in convincing others from the West Coast, including Sammy Davis, Jr., to do the show. In a way, he helped "legitimatize" us to the show business mainstream. His appearance also marked the show as not merely creditable, but actually in danger of becoming "hip"!

ROY ROGERS AND DALE EVANS— DECEMBER 29, 1970.

Roy Rogers and Dale Evans were on two of the last ten shows that we did for CBS. We all knew each other from their days as guest stars on *The Jonathan Winters Show*. They used to do his show for one of the holidays—Christmas, Easter, or Thanksgiving.

When Roy first came to tape *Hee Haw*, I discovered he was a great bowler, with a very low handicap. It just so happened I was pretty good as well. After he finished taping, we decided to go bowling. Word spread throughout the alley that he was there, and people began coming up to him in a steady stream asking for his autograph. When he ran out of paper he took our score sheet and tore it into little pieces, signing each one "Trigger" and handing them out.

Oh yes, he beat me.

Roy and Dale are beautiful, talented, dedicated people, and it was a privilege to have them on *Hee Haw*.

ROGER MILLER—JANUARY 12, 1971.

I'm proud to say I had the privilege of working with the great Roger Miller, everybody's favorite, a great songwriter and a very funny man. We were able to get him on the show because of Roy Clark and George Lindsey, both of whom were friends of Roger and had worked with him many times.

We always had a great time with Roger, but whenever he was on he caused major scheduling problems for me. We were forever falling behind. I'd try to get him going and he'd say, "Hey, this isn't a show, this is a place to come over and have a good old time! Let's roll up the carpet, have a few drinks and have some fun!" He'd have such a good time it was always difficult to get him to leave!

He was quite impressed with our operation, and after his first appearance, he went to his agent and told him he'd like to do his own television show. And he wanted Sam Lovullo to produce it! Shortly after this, Roger's people did approach Frank and John at Yongestreet, and we all got very excited about the possibilities of doing a pilot. With Roger's brand of humor, his many friends and his music, we figured it had to be a hit.

We started thinking about sets, music, and guests. I wanted to sign Danny Davis—a country version of Doc Severinsen—and his Nashville Brass as Roger's TV band. Danny and I even had several meetings to discuss themes, play-ons, play-offs, all the things you need for a talk show. We had gotten almost to the point of contract negotiations when I suddenly got a call from Frank Peppiatt telling me the deal was off. To this day I don't know what happened.

It took a long time to get Roger to come back on *Hee Haw*. In fact we didn't see him again for nearly twelve years. When he finally did return, I tried to talk to him about it. Instead of "dwelling on the past," as he put it, he simply suggested we try again. I immediately began making plans, when, unfortunately, Roger became ill. Not long after, he passed away. His death was a terrible loss to country music.

That last *Hee Haw* that Roger Miller did was as a cohost, in December 1987. He came in flighty, funny and spry as ever, one joke after another, nonstop. I'll never forget that show. His wife, Mary, who had been a backup singer in Kenny Rogers's former band, The First Edition, was on the set that day. They had recently moved to New Mexico and adopted a child. Mary was a great stabilizing influence on Roger. I'm not sure if she knew about Roger's illness at the time.

He did a medley of his hits, and as Mary and I watched him perform, I'm not sure how it happened, but there was eye contact between them. She suddenly took off her shoes, walked on stage, stood next to one of our backup singers and joined in. It was a great, culminating moment for all of us, filled with warmth, a sense of family, tradition, and togetherness: everything *Hee Haw* had come to represent.

I never saw Roger again after that.

MICKEY MANTLE AND BOBBY MURCER (MANTLE)—JANUARY 5, 1971; (MURCER)— JANUARY 12, 1971.

We were looking to expand the appeal of the show in the big northern cities, where we never really did as well as in the South. One day we hit upon the idea of booking major-league legends, like Bobby Murcer and Mickey Mantle.

What was important about Mickey's and Bobby's appearances was that it proved early on that we could attract talent beyond the boundaries of country music, which in turn helped us enlarge our viewing audience. Neither Mickey nor Bobby could sing, but it didn't matter. It was their physical presence alone that gave the show a real boost. I seem to recall thinking they came to Nashville to see the Honeys, but left having fallen in love with Junior Samples.

AMANDA BLAKE—OCTOBER 2, 1971.

Amanda Blake—"Kitty" on *Gunsmoke*—was the first non-country music performer to appear on *Hee Haw*. *Gunsmoke* had just been cancelled. To maintain our network image and for all those CBS stations who were with us in syndication, Amanda was an ideal marketing opportunity. Viewers wrote in to tell us how nice it was to see another side of her. She did some comedy vignettes, including a *Gunsmoke* takeoff, sang with the whole *Hee Haw* gang, and was a pleasure to work with. After her taping, she and her husband invited the entire cast out to dinner.

When her *Hee Haw* show aired, we had a surge in our ratings, which made us all feel extra good, seeing as how we all understood what it meant to be canceled by CBS and then experience a surge of audience interest. Once again we had managed to outfox the big boys.

JOHNNY BENCH/STANLEY SIEGEL/TOMMY LASORDA/VIC DAMONE—(BENCH)—FEBRUARY 5, 1972; (SIEGAL)—MARCH 16, 1974; 1978 (LASORDA/DAMONE)—MARCH 10, 1984.

Not many people know it, but Johnny Bench is a pretty good singer. Every so often we'd bring him on to do some comedy routine and sing a country tune. He was always willing, mostly I think because he loved hanging out with the *Hee Haw* Honeys, particularly Cathy Baker.

One time we had him scheduled to tape the same day as Stanley Siegel, the talk-show host and a real crazy guy. At the time, Stanley had a morning talk show out of New York that was all the rage. He used to do wild things, like bring his psychiatrist on the show for a televised session, or eat dog food out of a can.

After his New York show completed its run, he began a local talk show in Nashville, and that's when I decided to book him on *Hee Haw*. He could always be counted on to do crazy, unscripted things, with my blessing. "Stanley," I told him, "just go out and do your thing and whatever we can use we'll cut into the show." Which he did and we did.

This particular time, Johnny Bench was in the control room watching Stanley carrying on. Somebody then suggested the perfect way to tag off the segment would be to hit Stanley in the face with a pie. I set it up so that Buck Owens would do it.

By this time, Buck had had more than enough of Stanley and welcomed the opportunity. Sure enough, at just the right time, he hit Stanley square in the face with a big whipped-cream pie. Stanley, bless his heart, loved every minute of it. Johnny, however, couldn't believe what he saw. "No son of a bitch is ever going to hit me in the face with a pie," he announced.

Of course, that was all I had to hear.

Johnny was scheduled to tape that afternoon. He was

supposed to sing "Johnnie B. Goode," then go to the front of the famous *Hee Haw* board fence and do a quick gag. As he rehearsed, I stayed back in the control room trying to figure out how to get him with the pie. "Ah, there's no way," one of the crew said.

I said, "Keep him going, I'll find a way." I knew that Johnny had gone out the night before with Cathy and a couple of other cast members, so I called her over. "Listen," I said to her, "I need you to do something." When I told her what I wanted her to do, she said, "Oh no, I can't!"

"Yes you can."

"He'll kill me."

"That's okay," I said. "Whatever happens, we'll have it on tape."

Reluctantly, Cathy went to Johnny and sure enough his eyes lit up. I then pretended we had a screwup in the control room and went down to the set to personally apologize to Johnny for having to give us one more take. When I finished, I said, "Cathy, get out of the way, you're getting him all excited!"

That was the prearranged cue. She stepped to the side and we handed her a pie. He never saw it coming. He started singing and BANG, she hit him right in the kisser! Johnny looked straight into the camera and said, "Damn you, Sam . . . Getting hit with that pie was worse than losing to the Los Angeles Dodgers!"

After our production season ended, I made a copy of that bit, and when I got back to Los Angeles, showed it to Tommy Lasorda. He couldn't believe it. "Tommy," I said, "I'd like to take you into a local studio, record your response and cut it into Johnny's show when it airs."

Tommy came with me to the Goldwyn Studios that afternoon. All he said on camera was, "Only a hell of a catcher would know that!" I had that bit edited into Johnny's show.

A couple of months later, on a Sunday afternoon, he was playing golf in the Bing Crosby tournament in northern California, near Monterey, and it so happened the local station was running *Hee Haw*. While Johnny was on the golf course someone came to tell him he was on TV. He raced into the clubhouse, arrived just in time to see himself get hit with the pie in the face, and, for the first time, heard Lasorda's reply.

He was furious! He reached for the nearest phone, dialed my number and screamed into the receiver, "You son of a bitch, Lovullo! How could you do this to me?"

It was all in good fun, of course, and Johnny knew it. In fact, he really loved the idea of Tommy's going to all that trouble to tape a response. So did Tommy. Best of all, so did our viewers.

From that point on, Tommy was forever after me to have him come to Nashville and appear on the show as a guest. I finally invited him on. When Vic Damone, who's a very good friend of Tom's, heard that Lasorda was going to do the show he invited himself to come along. It was a real wild show, one of the craziest *Hee Haw*s I ever put together. I found myself doing an Italian version of *Hee Haw*! Even Lasorda sang a song!

Tommy fell in love with Nashville and developed quite a local following. A group of nuns from the Sister of Mercy Convent, who lived in an old, dilapidated convent, were trying to put together a fund-raiser to help build a new one. John Hobbs, a good Catholic and a local real-estate developer with several businesses near Opryland, called upon Tommy, who was staying at John's Ramada Inn, and asked him to be a principal in the project. I was then asked to produce.

It turned into a great three-hour extravaganza, held on the Grand Ole Opry stage, with Vic Damone, Kathy Mattea, Loretta Lynn, George "Goober" Lindsey, Irlene Mandrell, Robert Wagner, Vin Scully, ESPN's Roy Firestone, and many, many more who donated their time and talent.

We raised $50,000 from the sale of tickets, and Tommy surprised everyone by having Orel Hersheiser and Kirk Gibson make an appearance and donate an additional $50,000— money they'd made from a bet with Tommy that he couldn't lose a certain amount of weight by the night of the show. He lost the bet and the nuns got the money. I haven't been able to keep Tommy away from Nashville since.

BRENDA LEE—FEBRUARY 19, 1972.

Brenda Lee began her career in country, crossed over to rock and roll in her teens, then faded from the charts, and from sight, until *Hee Haw* brought her back. Her appearance on our show was the key to reestablishing her career. Hers is one of the great comeback stories of country music.

WAYLON JENNINGS AND JESSI COLTER— FEBRUARY 26, 1972.

I booked Waylon Jennings and his beautiful wife, Jessi Colter, even though, in those days, Waylon was still a bit wild and unpredictable. I have nothing but praise for Jessi for having stood by him all these years. She also happens to be a great singer and piano player.

I had the pleasure of introducing "I'm Not Lisa," by Jessi Colter, on *Hee Haw*. I believe the only reason Waylon agreed to do the show was to help Jessi promote that song. She sang it accompanying herself on the piano in the living-room set. Everyone in the studio, from the staff in the control room to the cameramen on the floor, was riveted by both the song and her performance.

However, two days later I got a call from Waylon, who was adamant about not using Jessi's song on the show. He'd decided he wanted to go back into the recording studio and re-arrange it, and he didn't want the current version aired. A day or two later, he showed up at the studio in a wild mood, ready for a real serious discussion with me about that song.

I finally calmed him down and said, "Tell you what, Waylon, I think I'm going to go with it." It was such a great song. Frankly, I believe one of the reasons it took off and became a hit was because we presented it on *Hee Haw*.

Still, because of that it was a long time before Waylon came back on *Hee Haw*. I think he felt that some of us in Nashville didn't care about him. I truly believe he was overly sensitive for a while, stemming from his personal problems. And of course there was that outlaw-image thing.

When he finally did return, in 1989, he cohosted with Roy. By then, he had completely cleaned himself up and was just wonderful to be around. We were in the makeup room the day of the taping and got around to talking about the time he wanted me to pull Jessi's song. Waylon looked at me funny and said, "Goddamn it, Sam, I don't remember that at all."

Today, Waylon carries on in his unique way.

RAY STEVENS—SEPTEMBER 16, 1972.

Ray Stevens was one of my favorite *Hee Haw* guests. He is a talented writer and performer, and perhaps one of the smartest businessmen in the industry. However, because he is a perfectionist, he could be difficult at times. Things had to be exactly right with him, creatively as well as technically.

Ray introduced several of his most popular tunes on *Hee Haw*, including "The Shriner's Song." Whenever he taped the show he'd say, "Sam, when you edit this one let me know." I'd call, and he'd then check to see where his song was on the *Billboard* Country charts. If it was moving up, he'd say, "Sam, air it." His appearance would always shoot it to the top of the charts.

I must confess I always enjoyed that kind of interest and input from our artists. If they knew the airdate of their show, they would tell their live audiences to make sure and tune in to watch *Hee Haw*. It was a very friendly two-way street. We'd help artists promote their songs, and they'd help boost our ratings.

DIZZY DEAN—September 16, 1972.

I had heard that Dizzy wanted to be on the show. I figured he'd be perfect, as his "character" and *Hee Haw* seemed to fit together so well. I called him at his home in Mississippi. He told me *Hee Haw* was his favorite show and that he really wanted to do it, but was concerned his regular television sponsor, Falstaff Beer, to whom he was under exclusive contract, wouldn't allow it. At the time, he was doing color on the weekly NBC Saturday-afternoon *Baseball Game of the Week*.

I was finally able to convince him to at least come to Nashville, and we'd worry about his sponsors later. I assured him he could come early in the day and we'd get him back home by a chartered plane the same evening.

I decided to put Dizzy in the barbershop with Archie Campbell. At one point, Dizzy looked at Archie Campbell and said, "Well, fellow, aren't you going to try to get me to sing 'Wabash Cannonball'?" Diz used to occasionally sing it on radio, sometimes during slow spots in the ball game. Now, he'd decided to sing it right from the barber's chair! Roy Clark grabbed a guitar and backed him up. It was an outstanding segment, made special by Dizzy so obviously struck by being with the whole *Hee Haw* gang.

After the taping, he autographed baseballs for everyone. Just before he left the studio for his flight home, he came into my office. As was our custom, I had his contract ready, and a check. All he had to do was sign for it, but instead he waved me off. "Sam," he said, "I had such a great time, you don't need to pay me. I really don't need the money."

"Diz," I said, "This is business, you have to be paid. Plus, it's our way of saying thanks for coming out to do the show."

"Son," he said, "If I get paid I'm going to have a problem with Falstaff. Can't we treat this as some kind of cameo appearance?"

"You need to get paid," I insisted.

At that point, he picked up my phone and called the Falstaff people. Someone on the other end gave him static, saying he should have asked permission first, that kind of thing. I remember Dizzy saying into the receiver, "Look, fellow, I've already done the show, I got a chance to sing 'Wabash Cannonball,' and besides, I'm sitting right here holding a check 'cause I just got paid! These folks are the greatest people in the world to work with. They pay off like a slot machine in Las Vegas!"

RAY PRICE—OCTOBER 7, 1972.

Ray Price introduced "Lay Your Head on My Pillow," on *Hee Haw*. However, he didn't return to the show until February 10, 1979. It was a real struggle to try to book him. I guess he had a bad experience with another producer on a different TV show and was a bit camera shy.

When he did return, he insisted on a full orchestra complete with strings. I told him we couldn't afford that, and even if we could, it wasn't the *Hee Haw* image. He finally reluctantly agreed to come on and do his song with our regular house band.

When he arrived at the studio, I asked him if he'd consider doing some comedy. He refused. "I'm only here to sing, Sam. No Kornfield, no Moonshiners, no 'PFFFT,' no straw hat." He laid down the law and that was it.

After finishing his song he went off to visit with Grandpa Jones. I decided to say hello to Ray's wife, who told me, "He's having such a good time, he really won't mind getting into a pair of overalls and a straw hat." I asked Ray again, and he said okay, he'd do a few bits for us.

It wasn't until later that I found out why he'd been so against doing any comedy. Years earlier, the producers of *The Dean Martin Show* were doing a country music special and booked Ray as a guest. They insisted he wear a straw hat, which he felt took his dignity away. The difference was, on our show we celebrated, instead of making fun of, traditional country values.

PATTI PAGE—DECEMBER 2, 1972.

What do you do with Patti Page? Have her sing "Tennessee Waltz," of course. We invited her to come on to do her most famous country song.

She arrived in Nashville by plane the night before from somewhere in the Midwest. I arranged for John Gallagher, the show's runner, to pick her up at the airport and take her to the hotel. I called a bit later and told her I needed her at the studio early the next day so we could track her song in the right key and add a vocal background. I planned to tape her in our gorgeous living-room set. By prerecording the track, we could shoot her "live" by the fireplace.

"Fine," she said. "What time do you want me?"

"Eight o'clock in the morning."

"Oh," she said, "I can't sing at that hour!"

"You don't have to," I said. "All you have to do is help us select a key to record the track."

The next morning, she arrived at the studio in a pair of slacks, and I could see it was quite early for her. Our musical director, Charlie McCoy, then informed me that our bass backup singer, Herschel Wiginton, who loved to stay out late and party, hadn't as yet arrived. I got on the phone, called his home and was told he was on his way. When eight-thirty rolled around and he still hadn't showed up, Patti came to me and said, "Uh, Sam, you got me out of bed early to come in and do the track and you're not ready."

"Oh," I said, "We're ready."

"Really?"

"You bet."

I called everyone together, and then moved in the backup singers and *sang the bass part myself!* It was the first time that anybody on my staff had ever heard me sing, and I think it blew their minds! When I was finished, my associate producer, good old Marcia Minor, came up to me with her clipboard and a release form, and she asked for my union card!

A little while later, our director, Bill Davis, arrived. He came in, checked the track, took me aside and asked, "How did you get that sound without Hershel?"

Somebody then told him I had sung the part, but he didn't believe it. He played the track back again, and then, with a note of quiet disbelief in his voice, said, "Pretty damn good, Lovullo."

BARBARA MANDRELL—December 16, 1972.

Barbara started out very young as a singer and steel-guitar player, and quickly picked up on virtually every instrument there was. She was always full of energy, hardworking and very nervous, constantly smoking cigarettes and drinking Coca-Cola.

She made her national television debut on *Hee Haw*, an appearance that gave her the opportunity to demonstrate her versatility. On one show she sang a song while at the same time playing the steel guitar, horns, and saxaphone. At the end of her number, she pretended to be exhausted, and "collapsed" out of camera shot.

I don't think there's any question that Barbara's rise to fame began on *Hee Haw*. Not long after her first appearance on *Hee Haw*, she got her own network show, on NBC. *The Nashville Palace* series that I produced with John and Frank was her lead-in. Because of the success of *Hee Haw*, NBC was, at the time, trying to make Saturday an evening of country music. Ironically, we wound up competing with "ourselves" in several markets, as both *Hee Haw* and *The Nashville Palace* often aired at the same time!

Grant Tinker, at that time the head of NBC programming, was concerned that both Barbara's show and *The Nashville Palace* were competing for the same guest stars. Because of this, we only lasted one season.

Barbara and her family became personal friends of mine. Her parents, Mary and Irby, raised very talented ladies. Barbara's sister, Louise, appeared on *Hee Haw* several times, and we were fortunate to have Irlene as a regular. She may have come off as a dumb blonde, but she was one smart cookie.

My only regret was that I never got the chance to produce a show for the Mandrell sisters.

ORAL ROBERTS—FEBRUARY 10, 1973.

Oral Roberts made a personal request to appear on *Hee Haw*. Although gospel music was a regular feature on *Hee Haw*, everyone was nervous and uptight about Oral Roberts's appearance. As it happened, he was a big fan of *Hee Haw*, and a lot of the performers were personal favorites of his, especially Roy Clark, who'd done a lot charity work for Oral Roberts University.

Still, it was an unusual booking for us, to say the least. Not that we had to clean up our act or anything. We were, after all, one of the most family-oriented shows in the history of television. But we didn't know what to do with him. We certainly didn't want him to come on and preach, he didn't sing, and we weren't about to put him in the Kornfield with the *Hee Haw* Honeys! I finally decided that because he was such a great storyteller, the best place to use him was in the barbershop.

When he arrived at the studio, I personally escorted him into makeup and introduced him to everybody on the show. By the time we were ready to tape, everyone felt quite comfortable with his presence.

The barbershop sketch always began the same way: some background music and someone coming in for a haircut. As usual, Archie kicked it off. "Well, if it isn't Oral Roberts," he said. As a gesture of friendship, everyone waiting for a haircut gave up his place in line to allow Oral to get his hair cut first.

He got into the chair, and Archie Campbell, the Kornfield

Kounty barber (he was the only man who never got a haircut, because of his toupee), put an apron around Oral's neck. "How's it goin', Oral?" he said, and casually hit him on the right arm.

"Okay," Oral said, "but quit hittin' me there. That's the arm that heals!"

DONNA FARGO—FEBRUARY 24, 1973.

Donna Fargo introduced her big hit, "Funny Girl," on *Hee Haw*. She was originally a schoolteacher in West Covina, California, but had always wanted to be a country singer/songwriter. Her life changed when she met her husband, Stan, a stocky, bushy-bearded music arranger/conductor who took over the management of her career.

From that point on, every time she did our show she had to be cleared through him. If she was in the studio, he insisted on being in the audio room, supervising the engineer. Donna could never relax around him.

One time we were ready to roll tape and all signals were go, except that Stan was tied up on a long-distance phone call, which meant we all had to wait. I was in the control room talking to my director, Bill Davis, who was anxious to get through this session. So I finally suggested we start to roll tape without Stan.

Just at that moment, Stan slipped back into the control room. I happened to look back and see him, but didn't react or respond or make any mention that he was there. It was then Bill Davis said, not knowing Stan was there, "By God, she's a gorgeous girl! I'd love to spend an evening with her!"

CHARLIE RICH—FEBRUARY 24, 1973.

Charlie is a very good-looking man, with a striking head of white hair that really stands out when he sits at a black piano and wears a white tuxedo. They don't call him "The Silver Fox" for nothing!

I first came across him when he was playing Roger Miller's King of the Road club.

Charlie's public-relations person had called me to come by and catch Charlie's act. She said that although he was currently singing rock and roll, he was about to go into the studio and cut some country songs.

Whenever I go to see artists, I don't like them to know I'm there, or they'll pick up my tab. I don't want to feel committed in any way, or place any added pressure on them by my presence. Therefore, I didn't introduce myself to Charlie that night until after his first set. Before I left, I told him and his manager that I was impressed, but didn't think his songs were right for *Hee Haw*.

One evening not long after, Bill Davis, *Hee Haw*'s director at the time, went out with the cast and partied a little. They ended up at Charlie Rich's show. He must have had a great time, because when I arrived at the studio the next morning, Bill was late and nowhere to be found.

Charlie Rich, however, was there in the lobby, bright eyed and bushy tailed, along with his PR person, Audrey Winters. I took one look at them and realized that neither had as yet been to bed. I went over, said hello, and asked Charlie how his show was going. His associate then said to me, "You know we're doing *Hee Haw* today."

"What?"

"Yessir. We were with Bill Davis last night, your director . . . and he asked us to come in this morning and tape a couple of songs."

I said, "Well, gee, that's fine, but we're not prepared. It's not on my schedule." However, inasmuch as Bill had invited them, I agreed to work Charlie in. We always kept our living-room-for-musical-performances set ready for just such "drop-ins."

Around eight-thirty Bill Davis showed up and started mumbling about having run into Charlie Rich the night before. "It was too late to call you . . . you know, I had a great idea. Why don't we put him in the living room set and let him do a few tunes?"

I told him I hoped that for all his trouble he'd at least had a great time last night! I then went to Charlie and asked him what he wanted to sing. He suggested "Behind Closed Doors," and "Take It on Home." I told him we might have a problem, since the band wasn't on call and I didn't have a prerecorded reference track.

"Don't worry, my man," he said. "I have one." With that, he produced a quarter-inch prerecorded tape. I put him into makeup, moved him to the stage, taped the two songs (the fastest anyone ever taped for *Hee Haw*), paid him, and that was it.

A couple of weeks later, I was in Los Angeles doing postproduction editing, and as I watched the tape I began to feel that Charlie Rich was going to break in a big way. I went to the video editor and asked him to remove "Behind Closed Doors" from the show and dub off a separate copy of it for me. I then hand-carried it to my office in Beverly Hills and threw it in a desk drawer.

Sure enough, six months later Charlie Rich was huge, and no one could buy him for a TV appearance. But I had that song, the only live performance of "Behind Closed Doors." I edited it into the September 29 show, sent Charlie a check for its use and ran it just as it topped the charts! To this day Charlie has never figured out how I got him on *Hee Haw* that second time!

Tennessee Ernie Ford helps out Buck and Roy

TENNESSEE ERNIE FORD—MARCH 10, 1973.

Ernie was a little hesitant about doing *Hee Haw*. At the time, he was a very big draw in Las Vegas and although he was pure country and loved Grandpa Jones, he wasn't sure it was a good idea to be seen on network television in straw hats and overalls.

We were finally able to book him when we went into syndication. As I mentioned earlier, he was part of the formation of the Gospel Quartet, which for seven years, from 1976 through 1982, won the Music City Award as the favorite gospel singing group in the nation.

TANYA TUCKER—October 13, 1973.

In my opinion, Tanya continues to get better and more beautiful every day. I honestly think if I were a film producer today, I would try to make her a movie star.

Her dad manages her career. They're a close-knit family who believe in and support one another. I sometimes wondered if she didn't ever want to make an amicable separation from her dad and branch out on her own.

Tanya first did *Hee Haw* in 1973, when she was fourteen years old, right after "Delta Dawn" had established her as a star. She was a little brat all right, but really cute, and she followed instructions well.

I booked her again a year or two later and I could see immediately how much she'd matured, both as a singer and a person. She had developed a truly wonderful voice, and it was apparent she was going to be a superstar. Over the years she became a *Hee Haw* favorite. There wasn't a season that went by when we didn't have her on the show. Everyone connected with the show adored her, and she became part of our family.

Tanya was very bright and knew how to act, which allowed us to develop great sketches for her. One of the last shows we did with her, she played a fortune-teller. All we did was to give her the lead lines, and she carried on using her own words quite beautifully. As a result, I was forever fighting off our fifty-two "regulars," who were constantly after me to work with Tanya.

When we did our twentieth anniversary special, I called Tanya's daddy about arranging to have her on, and he told me I needed to talk to her brother, who was also her road manager.

Unfortunately, there was always some kind of communications barrier between her brother and me. Sure enough, I didn't get a good vibe from him about Tanya doing the show. I kept stressing how important I felt it was, since she was so much a part of the *Hee Haw* family, and finally he said he'd try to get her to do it. At the time, I wasn't smart enough to understand there had to be a reason I was talking to her brother and not directly to her.

Right up until the day I arrived in Guthrie, Oklahoma, to tape the special, I wasn't sure if she was going to show. That evening I went over the list of the stars scheduled to perform, and next to Tanya's name I put a question mark, which I knew was going to cause a small problem. Unlike *Hee Haw*, which we did in bits and pieces, the special was shot live before an audience of five thousand people. Everything had to be planned down to the last detail.

I was walking about the arena the next day, watching all the artists and guests arriving (including Kenny Rogers in his helicopter), when suddenly in the distance I saw this pretty but drawn-looking young lady, with no makeup or lipstick, coming toward me. It took me awhile to realize it was Tanya. She came up and said, "Sam, I want so much to be a part of this." I hugged her and told her how much I appreciated her coming.

It wasn't until a couple of days later that I found out that Tanya had been in rehabilitation at the Betty Ford Clinic, and that they'd decided only at the last minute to let her out for the show, provided she came right back afterward. I'd like to think that *Hee Haw* proved to be good therapy for Tanya.

RONNIE MILSAP—DECEMBER 15, 1973.

I discovered Ronnie Milsap while he was performing at Roger Miller's King of the Road Lounge. I've always thought he was a very talented performer, a genius really, blessed with a great voice and terrific style at the piano. He is meticulous in his arrangements, uses the best musicians, and has a great ear.

All of which became part of the problem booking him. Although he was blind, Ronnie always wanted to take part in all the technical aspects of his segments. Because the quality of his sound was so important to him, he liked to spend most of the day taping one song. All well and good, except the

Hee Haw style was to tape a week's worth of performances in a day.

He also loved getting into the Kornfield and visiting the barbershop. He'd always ask for a script and turn it over to one of his associates who would read it aloud to him. Ronnie would then transfer his parts to a braille machine.

There was one period of time, almost eight years, when Ronnie didn't do *Hee Haw*. I was never sure, but I suspect it might have stemmed from an incident that occurred during the twenty-fifth anniversary Country Music Association (CMA) Award show, for an audience that included President Reagan, Vice President George Bush and several members of Congress.

I produced that show with Gary Smith and Dwight Hemion, from Washington, D.C.'s Constitution Hall, an old armory with no dressing rooms and no backstage; it was not particularly suitable as a television studio, but we used it because of its historical atmosphere.

For one segment of the show, I wanted Mickey Gilley, Ray Charles and Ronnie Milsap to do a song together, followed by our finale—a solo rendition of "America the Beautiful" performed by Ray Charles, as the show's entire cast came out and stood around his huge grand piano. I believe this offended Ronnie Milsap who felt he and Ray should have been playing back-to-back pianos in the finale. As a result, he may have decided to boycott *Hee Haw*.

He finally returned in February 1992 and it was great to have him back.

RALPH EMERY—FEBRUARY 2, 1974.

Ralph's a very knowledgeable TV and radio personality. He was on *Hee Haw* back when he still was a radio disk jockey at WSM. In the early '70s we had a sketch on the show called "The Disk Jockey Spot." Each week we'd feature a different DJ to talk about the hit songs of the week, what was up-and-coming as tabulated by their local station. The main complaint about the spot from the guest DJs was that it was too short. It never really worked the way we wanted it to, and was dropped from the show.

Still, Ralph always loved doing the show for one very simple reason. Whenever he'd do *Hee Haw* we'd hand him his check and he'd beam. "A thousand dollars for two and a half minutes work! Unheard of!"

JOHNNY CASH—FEBRUARY 16, 1974.

One of the toughest bookings I ever had was Johnny Cash, because when we started, he was our "country competition" on ABC. After he was canceled in 1971 and we became friends, he told me he felt some lingering bitterness toward ABC for pressuring him to "modernize" his approach to country. He believed if he'd stayed traditional, he would have been on the air a lot longer. I have to say that later on the networks made the same mistake with Dolly Parton.

I think Johnny was embarrassed when his show was canceled. He became something of a recluse, and didn't do any TV for awhile. Three years later, in 1974, Yongestreet and I produced a John Wayne special for NBC called "Swing Out Sweet Land." It was a very patriotic show, and one of the segments showed the introduction of the train and how important it was in helping to unify the states.

Johnny Cash was my natural choice to host that segment, because of his many train songs. It took a lot of convincing, but he finally agreed to do it.

We shot the segment at Knotts Berry Farm, in Anaheim, California. I'll never forget that day. I was a little nervous because it was shortly after Johnny's wife, June Carter, had given birth to baby John-John. That morning, I called my wife, Grace, and asked her if she could come out and help June with the new baby while we shot the segment.

Grace spent most of the day with June. When the time came to change the baby's diaper, we were outside and there was no place to lay a blanket, so Grace and June used Johnny's guitar case!

A few months later, Johnny was shooting a Pennzoil commercial at the Channel 5 studios in Nashville. I asked him if he'd appear on *Hee Haw*, and this time he said he'd be delighted to tape a couple of shows.

I was so happy to get him, the day of his taping I threw a special barbecue luncheon for him and his group and our staff. Johnny wound up giving us enough material for several shows. I wasn't expecting him to do any comedy, but he insisted, saying he especially wanted to appear in "Pffft! You Were Gone."

The one thing he was able to accomplish on the show that no one else would have done was hitting Archie Campbell in the face with a pie. To this day, whenever I see John he always says, "I got to hit Archie Campbell in the pusser with a cream pie!"

In 1988, after Buck left the show, I invited John to cohost one show. He agreed, as long as his wife, June Carter, could come along. I was told to watch out for June, that she liked to control whatever she was involved in.

Well, I soon found out that she may be tough, but she's also good. And she certainly knew how to control the studio. She was terrific in the comedy sketches. This was the first time I'd gotten a good look at what June Carter could do. If I hadn't been under pressure to bring more youth onto the show, I would have made her a regular. Of course, she has a royal lineage, her mother being the legendary Mabel Carter. That put her right up there in the category of such country authentics as Minnie Pearl and Grandpa Jones. June would have made a terrific addition to the cast of *Hee Haw*.

PAT BOONE—FEBRUARY 23, 1974.

The first time Pat did the show, he was in an awful hurry to catch a plane. Unfortunately, we ran late and didn't finish taping his segment until ten minutes before it was scheduled to take off. It was nobody's fault. He was meticulous about his sound, and there had been a lot of interruptions because his family was from Nashville and everybody wanted to come by and say hello.

When he finally finished, I assured him he'd get to the airport on time. "Don't worry, Pat," I told him, "I'll take you there myself." It's about a five-minute ride from the studio to the airport. We arrived just in time, thanks to Pat, who prayed all the way!

ERNEST BORGNINE—SEPTEMBER 14, 1974.

Ernie's arrival created quite a scene at the Nashville airport. Back then, not many Hollywood stars came to Nashville, so this was a big deal. The press and hundreds of fans came out to greet him.

I was there as well, along with George "Goober" Lindsey. When I first met Ernest I gave him a pair of oversize *Hee Haw* overalls, which served as his introduction to country music.

JIMMY DEAN—OCTOBER 9, 1976.

Jimmy's a good friend. I think if he weren't filthy rich from all his sausage money he'd do a lot more television. He's a good singer and terrifically funny storyteller, and plays a number of instruments besides his famous accordion.

In January 1983, when Roger Miller finally returned to *Hee Haw* after his long self-imposed exile, I had heard that Jimmy was in town, and I decided to invite him down. Of course when Jimmy came on, as always, he took charge of everything.

Now, no two performers were ever more different than Roger and Jimmy, yet so similar. Roger was always crazy, into drinking, pills, on every wagon there was. Fortunately for him (and us), he'd recently sobered up and was learning what a kick it is to be clearheaded. Jimmy, on the other hand, is the consummate professional. He approached every appearance as a "job." Roger loved Jimmy, and at one point during the show turned to him and said, "You know, we're so straight it's driving me crazy!"

One of the things I picked up on during Jimmy's first guest appearance was a bit of distance between him and Roy. Before, whenever I'd brought up the possibility of bringing Jimmy on the show, I'd get a strange look from Roy. I never understood why, until I learned that back in the '50s, Roy had been in Jimmy's band, and had been fired by him for always being late. Today we're all good friends. Jimmy sometimes comes on strong, but he truly has a heart of gold.

LARRY GATLIN—December 11, 1976.

In June 1976, a young kid by the name of Larry Gatlin was our prop person. Larry had come to Nashville from Texas, looking to break into the music business. On the same day Archie got hit with the pie, Larry Gatlin approached Johnny Cash, said he was a songwriter and wanted to give him some songs.

About a year later I got an invitation from John to come to his place and watch a "guitar pulling session," an informal living room setting where musicians get together in a three-quarters circle, play songs and talk about their music. Johnny had also invited George "Goober" Lindsey to inject some humor into the evening. And there was Larry Gatlin!

John had chosen the occasion to showcase several young performers, including Larry and up-and-coming Canadian singer, Gordon Lightfoot. It was clear to me that Johnny had invited me so I would see what Larry and Gordon could do. Shortly after, I booked Larry on the show.

He went on to great things, of course, and was a featured guest on the *Hee Haw* tenth anniversary special that we did for CBS television.

ERNEST TUBB—February 26, 1977.

In the hierarchy of Nashville country legends, Ernest was second only to Roy Acuff. His biggest hit was "Walking the Floor Over You." He was the ultimate father figure to many female country stars, including Loretta Lynn, Patsy Cline, Barbara Mandrell, and Kitty Wells.

Ernest was only on the show a couple of times. It wasn't that he didn't want to be on more often. It was just that, of all the country artists I've known, Ernest was the busiest. He was always on the road, and therefore almost impossible to book. It was said that if a young up-and-coming musician had the privilege of recording and playing with Ernest Tubb, it was a sure ticket to the big time. One of our band members, Leon Rhodes, had such an opportunity, and it was one of the big breaks of his career.

Roy Clark once pointed out to me that the best way to tell a real country music fan from a pretender was that a real fan would never call the great Ernest Tubb "Ernie Tubbs."

THE "DUKE OF PADUCAH" (BENJAMIN FORD)—September 17, 1977.

"The Duke of Paducah" was one of the most talented comedians in country humor. He wore big boots, with a long, loud, green jacket, a scarf and a funny hat. We first auditioned him to be a potential "regular" in 1969, but he didn't come off very well. It wasn't until much later that I found out he'd been very nervous during the tryout.

Years later, in June 1977, I heard that I'd offended the Duke because in all the time we'd been on the air I had never booked him. To correct this oversight, I booked him, used him in the Kornfield, and, sure enough, he proved much funnier than I thought he could be. I booked him a few times after that.

Not long after, I discovered that the Duke had a very deep inventory of valuable comedy material. Partly to help him out, and partly to increase our own inventory, *Hee Haw* bought out his joke library for $7,500. He kept his jokes on index cards filed in shoe boxes. The shoe boxes were alphabetized and broken down into subcategories—"love joke," "sex joke," etc.

From what my writers told me, it was apparent that the Duke had "compiled" his jokes from some very interesting sources. On more than one occasion we'd use a joke from the shoe boxes that had originated with us, back in the early years of the show! We eventually realized he was selling us our own jokes!

DENNIS WEAVER—NOVEMBER 11, 1977.

One day, singer Hoyt Axton's mother, Mae Axton, a sweet woman who was Dennis Weaver's manager and knew everybody in Nashville, called to tell me Dennis Weaver was coming to town. In addition to his acting, he sang, wrote music, was a lyricist and a musician, and he really wanted to do *Hee Haw*. I asked her to extend my personal invitation.

I scheduled him thinking I'd let him sing a song and then do several of our comedy bits. He agreed to do a little comedy, but he insisted he really wanted to sing some songs he had written. I reluctantly agreed.

Dennis "McCloud" Weaver donned overalls for his visit

Because he's a vegetarian, we had to put a special refrigerator in his hotel room filled with nonfat foods and a lot of fruit and vegetables. I considered him a special person who deserved the red-carpet treatment.

As it turned out, it was far more difficult to deal with his music than with him. His songs were okay, but not necessarily country, and his performance wasn't all that spectacular. This was his national TV debut as a singer, and I remember thinking that if he was hoping to use it as a springboard to a career in country music, it wasn't going to bounce him very high.

However, Dennis felt he'd done a great job, and his last remarks to me were, "Hey, Sam, when you edit the show please send me a copy." I made a "diplomatic mistake" by having my backup singers overdub his track with lush vocals and my audio people sweeten his overall performance.

When we finished, I sent Dennis the tape. He was quite pleased, not knowing the extent to which I'd worked on it—he thought he sounded sensational. From that point on, every time he came on the show, I'd have to have my backup singers come in after and augment his vocals. Ironically, this routine brought Dennis the fame he sought as a singer.

VERNON PRESLEY—JANUARY 7, 1978.

Linda Thompson joined the show as a regular in June 1976, a few months before Elvis died. At the time, she was living with him in Memphis.

I met Elvis once, earlier that year, on a plane traveling from Memphis to Los Angeles, and all during the flight he kept telling me how crazy he was about the show. I invited him to come on, and he said, "I'd like to, Sam, but we'd have to do it in the middle of the night. And we couldn't tell the Colonel [Elvis' manager]. If he found out, you'd never get me. I'd do your show for nothing 'cause I want to have a good time and meet some of them girls!"

I didn't know then that he and Linda Thompson were living

together. I believe after that flight Elvis made a few phone calls to see what he could do about getting Linda on the show. Eventually, Ed Hoodstratten, a friend of Elvis, called and asked me if I'd consider having Linda. I put her on.

Two months later Elvis was dead. A month after his funeral, Linda, a warm, earthy woman, told me that Vernon, Elvis' dad, was coming into Nashville. He dropped by the studio. I could see he was very down, obviously still grieving quite hard. I asked him if he'd like to say something about Elvis to all his fans who watched *Hee Haw*.

He came on with no script and talked about how Elvis had been a big fan of the show. He also said that although he was gone, the world would always remember him with love. That minute and a half was *Hee Haw*'s farewell salute to Elvis.

BILLY CARTER—JANUARY 14, 1978.

While Jimmy Carter was president, his brother Billy was a favorite of the press. We, in the meantime, became a favorite of Billy's, and because of it used to get free cases of Billy Beer delivered to the show.

First Brother Billy Carter and the women of Hee Haw

I tried forever to get him to come on. After many calls, not to the White House but to the local gas station in Georgia, Billy agreed to make an appearance, and that's when I discovered that he didn't do anything unless he had a can of beer in his hand.

We held a big reception for him at a local country club, and invited the members of the Nashville Chamber of Commerce and all the local Democrats. Unfortunately, before most of the guests arrived, Billy was out of it. Because of his inclination to be plastered before noon, we had trouble taping all the segments we'd planned for him.

One had him playing himself sitting on a milk crate in front of his famous gasoline station, beer in hand. However, we had planned an afternoon shoot and he failed to show up. We didn't have enough room to build a set in the studio, so we decided to go on location.

We found a nearby gas station, and designed the sketch so that a car would pull up to the pump and Billy would walk over to see what the customer wanted. It would be one of the *Hee Haw* regulars who would invite him to come to the studio and get in the Kornfield. Billy would then get into the car and they'd drive off. We shot all the close-ups in the studio and just needed one wide shot of him walking up to the car.

But Billy didn't show up. So, because he and I were about the same size, I put on a wig and glasses, stood in for the wide shots, and played his part!

A year later, Grace and I were in Washington, D.C., invited to the White House because I was a member of the Country Music Association which President Carter was honoring. The night before, I said to Grace, "You know, we ought to bring a pair of overalls for the president's daughter, Amy."

The actual dinner was very informal. Not long after we ate, guitars came out and everyone sat around having a great time, though.

At one point Jimmy Carter told me he was a big fan of the show, and I said, without thinking, we'd just had Jimmy on as a guest. "No," he said smiling. "That was Billy. *I'm* Jimmy."

In spite of my gaffe, it turned out to be a real *Hee Haw* kind of day down at the president's place!

Interestingly, Billy hadn't been invited.

ALAN KING—JANUARY 28, 1978.

Everybody who comes to Nashville sooner or later stops at Printer's Alley. Alan King happened to be passing through Nashville and, like everyone else, wanted to go there. He ran into Skull, who, as always, was in his *Hee Haw* overalls. Alan King asked about them, and Skull said he wore them because he was close with the *Hee Haw* "brass." Sure enough, Skull called me the next morning to say that Alan King was going to drop by and pay us a visit.

He did, we chatted, and I asked him to appear on the show. No one on the show knew who he was, except the writers and Roy Clark. During rehearsal, he tried some of his own jokes and they didn't work. Okay, I figured, hey, the barn's up, we'll put him in "Pickin' and Grinnin'," get some jokes from the writers, and that'll do it. Alan fit himself in perfectly, had a great time doing the show, and provided us with yet another of those unique *Hee Haw* guest-star "non sequiturs."

RUTH BUZZI— FEBRUARY 25, 1978.

Often, my regular performers couldn't understand why I'd have someone non-country like a Ruth Buzzi on *Hee Haw*. In this instance, they were pleasantly surprised

Former Laugh-In *star Ruth Buzzi and Roy Clark*

when she proved to be an excellent guest. Ruth, a very funny lady, took over the whole studio. When I found out she could sing a bit, I came up with an old Jimmy Dickens novelty song for her to do, "May The Bird of Paradise Fly Up Your Nose." I played it for her, she fell in love with it, performed it on the show, and was hilarious.

JOHN RITTER—October 7, 1978.

John, the son of the legendary Tex Ritter, was very friendly with the Hager twins, who brought him to the studio one day. John always had a great, natural ability for comedy. He loved the opportunity to do "Pickin' and Grinnin'," "Pffft! You Were Gone," and of course to hang out with the Honeys.

John added a little something to everything he did. This was another instance of a West Coast-based talent passing through town and agreeing to appear on our show.

JIM STAFFORD—January 27, 1979.

Jim's a very funny, talented fellow. Whenever I'd book him, he'd say, "Hey chief, what do you want me to do?" We'd sit and talk, pick out a song from the stacks of music I had in my office, and he'd develop a little comedy sketch around the Honeys.

Most people consider Jim a singing comedian. On *Hee Haw*, he showed he could also play guitar and banjo; he was in fact a one-man band. There's no mystery as to why his is the most successful theater in Branson, Missouri.

JOE FRAZIER—October 13, 1979.

The folks in the South are not really into boxing. Their big sports are fishing and golf. When Joe first arrived at the studio, no one except Roy Clark, who'd been an amateur boxer in his younger days, knew who he was or what he did. Joe drew a complete blank from the rest of my people, including Minnie Pearl and Grandpa Jones. But he was a welcome addition to the show anyway, and once everyone realized who he was, the atmosphere became quite friendly.

Roy was particularly excited about having Joe on. During taping sessions, they'd huddle together at the back of the studio and talk about boxing for hours. We even got Roy and Buck together with Joe, who wanted to do a medley of country tunes. It wasn't the best singing I've ever heard, but the good feeling among them all was so infectious, the piece turned out incredibly well.

ED McMAHON—JANUARY 5, 1980.

Ed, TV's roaming ambassador of good will, was a natural for *Hee Haw*. I always thought he'd be perfect in a sitcom. He had several opportunities to do one during his career, but always remained faithful to Johnny Carson. Personally, I think a large measure of Johnny's success was due to Ed.

Ed's also a big country music fan and had wanted to do *Hee Haw* for the longest time. The only problem was, he could never fit us into his busy schedule. I worked with him in 1973, though, when I produced the John Wayne special. Ed played the bartender in our saloon scene. The show was sponsored by Budweiser, so Ed, who at the time was their spokesperson, became the natural choice to play the role.

When he finally did appear on *Hee Haw*, he was a big hit, and made several follow-up appearances. Ed liked to sing and had a pretty good voice, so I thought we'd let him do a tune or two. The first time he sang he did a very entertaining version of "The Hatfields and McCoys." After so many years of doing *The Tonight Show*, he fit quite easily into our comedy sketches.

When it came to Ed McMahon, I had an open-door policy. They don't come any classier.

LOUISE MANDRELL—February 9, 1980.

Louise got her start in country music on *Hee Haw*.

Like her sisters, she is extremely talented, and very conscientious about her work. She plans her routines and rehearses them down to the last note. She was a terrific asset to *Hee Haw*, both as a dancer and singer, and we always loved having her on the show.

BOXCAR WILLIE—February 16, 1980.

When Boxcar first arrived in Nashville in the late '70s, he didn't have a penny. One day, he stopped by our studio looking for a job. Archie Campbell and Grandpa Jones invited him to lunch, but Box hesitated because he didn't have enough money. Archie graciously insisted on picking up the tab.

It was during this time that George Jones had opened The Possum Parlor, a nightclub in Printer's Alley. He appeared there once in a while, and when he did, liked to invite locals to come in and play. With the help of *Hee Haw* cast member Roni Stoneman, Box managed to get a gig there one night. He came out in his trademark hobo garb, sang, played his guitar and brought the house down.

I happened to be there that night, and after the show invited him to come to the *Hee Haw* studio. He came by a day or two later, when we happened to be shooting comedy spots, including Kenny Price's routine at the railroad ticket booth at the station. The sketch was a very popular one, and the possibilities were endless—the wrong ticket, refunds, overcharging, that kind of humor.

Across the studio we had set up the Empty Arms Hotel, Roy's regular spot, where people who would come from out of town would stay when they came to visit.

Box arrived early and sat in the lobby for a good part of the morning. I finally got a chance to go out, say hello and visit a little. During our chat, I said, "Box, why don't you grab your guitar and come with me?" As he was dressed like a hobo, I thought he'd make a good porter for the train sketch. Box then said, "You know, I do a lot of train songs. I think I could do a medley for you."

"Just you and your guitar?"

"Yeah."

"Well," I said, "be my guest." And that's how he got his first television exposure. That appearance led to another, Roy Acuff took notice, invited him on to the Grand Ole Opry, and Boxcar Willie was on his way. He was eventually able to open his own theater in Branson, Missouri, where he remains one of the most popular acts in country music. To this day, whenever Box is on stage, he always cites that spur-of-the-moment medley he did on *Hee Haw* as the turning point of his career.

ETHEL MERMAN—SEPTEMBER 13, 1980.

One day, out of the blue, through a friend of a friend in New York I received a request from Ethel Merman to be on the show. At first I didn't think it was possible. What could she possibly do on *Hee Haw*? However, the more I thought about it, the more I realized we ought to give it a try. After all, she had done *Annie Get Your Gun* on Broadway, a country-style musical comedy not that far removed from what we did.

I decided to call her and talk it over. At one point in our conversation she said, "Honey, all I want to do is get in the Kornfield with Junior Samples, have some fun with your pretty girls and say hello to Roy and Buck and the whole gang."

I said, "Fine, Ethel, but what about singing?" "Well," she said, "call me again in a couple of days and we'll talk about it." I got the feeling she honestly didn't want to sing. She was a big fan of the show and just wanted to come down, meet everybody, do a little comedy and leave it at that.

I called her back and somehow convinced her to do a song.

"How about 'Buttons and Bows'?" she asked. "I can have

Buck, me, Ethel Merman, and Roy

my arranger and piano player call your guys and they can work it out."

I said, "Ethel, we don't read music down here."

"What?"

"Well," I said, "we usually work off a record, because most of the time a guest will do a song he or she's recorded. My boys can lift the arrangement by ear and make up their own charts. All you need, really, is Roy and Clark to provide the rhythm section."

"Then that's the way we'll go," she said. "When do we rehearse?"

"Why don't we do it right now?"

"My orchestra leader isn't here."

"I don't need him. I need you."

"What do you mean?"

"You sing and I'll write down the lyrics."

"I've never done it that way. This'll be the first time, but I'll give it a try."

With that, she started singing over the phone as I wrote down the lyrics. When she finished, I said, "Let's go back to the top. We'll have an intro and possibly a little vamp, and then Buck'll say, 'Ladies and gentlemen, here's Ethel Merman with the *Hee Haw* gang joining in to sing "Buttons and

Bows,"'" and everyone'll cheer. You sing the first four lines, Buck'll do the next, and so forth."

"How do you know what key I sing in?"

"Don't worry, Buck and Roy will figure it out. Kick it off and let's see how it works." She did the first four lines and then said, "Is that where Buck comes in?"

"Yeah," and then I sang Buck's part back to her! And Roy's as well! By the end of the song we were harmonizing beautifully! She kept on wanting to do it over and over again. When we finished she said to me, "You know, you're pretty damn good, Sam. Why don't you and I do the number together and forget Buck and Roy?" It was tempting, but I decided that Buck and Roy needed the work.

When she came down to the show, she got into the *Hee Haw* overalls and straw hat and had a really good time. Didn't question a thing. We were anxious to have her back, but she became ill and a short time later, passed away. She was one of the most fun guests we ever had on the show.

HENNY YOUNGMAN—November 11, 1980.

Henny Youngman lives in Florida, and used to watch us all the time on our Miami affiliate. One day he decided he wanted to be on the show. Being a one-liner comedian made him a natural for *Hee Haw*, since our style of comedy was based so much on that concept. For that reason, I thought he'd be especially perfect for the Kornfield.

When Henny arrived at our studio the day of his taping, I went to the dressing room to greet him. I held out my hand and said, "Good to meet you, Mr. Henny." He stared at me as if I were completely out of my mind. He's one of those comedians who never laughs. Instead, he shook his head and said, "Uh-huh, uh-huh, let's get on with it, boy."

Well, I don't know if he was ready for us, but one thing's for certain, we weren't ready for him. I had scripted a lot of material for the Kornfield, mostly setup lines. "Tell us about this, tell us about that," someone in the Kornfield would say, and he'd deliver the punch line. Simple, right?

You might think so, but not for my *Hee Haw* cast that day. They had a very rough time with Henny. To begin with, they didn't really know who he was, and weren't familiar with his type of humor. They were so uneasy, a lot of them didn't want to be in the same Kornfield with him! I think they felt his humor had a bit of the put-down about it, and they didn't like that.

I decided to make some changes in the script. I thought the best way to handle it was to put Henny in the Kornfield with Don Harron's "Charlie Fargonson." Don had a background in New York theater, had even done some Shakespeare! I figured that out of everyone in the cast, Don would feel most comfortable with Henny. I therefore rescripted everything for just the two of them, and asked Don to let Henny go wherever he wanted to and I'd edit the acceptable pieces throughout the show. I told Don not to worry if he broke up, I could cut away and come back ten minutes later with them still laughing, turning it into a running gag, which is exactly what happened, and it worked beautifully.

However, given his appearance, it almost didn't happen at all, because when it came time to dress Henny in his straw hat and overalls, he absolutely refused to wear anything but the suit he was wearing. He told Clara Franklin, our wardrobe person, there was no way he was going to put on overalls. "Besides," he said, "You haven't got a pair in the whole studio that would fit me."

I said, "Henny, you need to get into some overalls."

"No way, boy. That is not my image."

"But that's the fun part of it! Some of your friends in New York'll get to see you in overalls, and they'll love it!"

"No way, boy!"

I took Clara aside and told her to get me a pair of Junior's old overalls. Junior had since passed away, but we still had some of his size-55 overalls in the wardrobe department, all washed and cleaned. A few minutes later, she returned and I said to Henny, "How about getting into these?"

"Boy, I told you I'm not going to get into them!"

I then said, out of nowhere, "Say, Henny, do you remember Al Jolson?"

"What the hell has that got to do with me being on *Hee Haw*?"

"Remember when Al used to get down on one knee and sing 'Mammy?'" With that, I went down on my knee, and began to put the overalls on him, right over his clothes. Well, Henny cracked up! He couldn't believe what I was doing! Before long, he was giving me his other foot. He laughed and laughed and, like Sammy Davis, Jr., couldn't get over the things I was prepared to do for my guests. In Henny's case, he said it was the first time a producer of a television show had become his personal dresser!

ROGER MARIS—NOVEMBER 22, 1980.

In the summer of 1980, Roy Clark mentioned to me he'd met baseball-great Roger Maris at a golf tournament and it turned out he was a huge *Hee Haw* fan. Although Roger had no interest in being on the show, he did tell Roy he wouldn't mind stopping by the studio the next time he was in Nashville and watching a taping.

That's all Roy had to tell me. I immediately asked my associate producer, Marcia Minor, to track Roger down and invite him to come to Nashville as our guest.

The day he came to the studio, Roy was taping some comedy skits, including "The Empty Arms Hotel." When Roger showed up, everyone in the studio asked him for his autograph, which made him very happy. I then asked him if he would like to do a comedy segment with Roy. Very politely he said, "Hey, Sam, I'm a baseball player, not an actor."

However, he couldn't refuse Roy, and sure enough, made the appearance. He played an out-of-towner looking to check into the Empty Arms Hotel. Roy signed him in, and when he looked at the name said, "By any chance are you *the* Roger Maris?"

"Yes, I am."

They then chatted about the famous sixty-first home run.

Roger enjoyed being on the show, but afterwards, told everybody that hitting that last home run and breaking Babe Ruth's record, which many fans were not happy to see, was the hardest thing he'd ever had to do in his life.

JOE MAPHIS (AND MARTY STEWART)— DECEMBER 13, 1980.

Grandpa Jones and his wife, Ramona, were great friends with Rosie and Joe Maphis. Joe was a traditional country performer whose specialty was the double-neck guitar. He was never a national star, but well-known and respected in the industry. Among his many achievements was teaching Barbara Mandrell how to play steel guitar.

I decided to invite Joe and his wife on the show. Their appearance proved quite popular, and generated a great deal of audience response. Because of that, I invited Joe back and told him the next time he came, he would play with Roy Clark.

Roy was extremely impressed with Joe's fingering ability. So much so that Roy asked me to get him clips from the show of Joe playing guitar, for his personal collection. In all the years of the show, the only two clips Roy ever asked for were one of Joe Maphis and one of Merle Travis.

The next time Joe came on, he brought along an aspiring singer by the name of Marty Stewart. Marty was in Johnny Cash's band, and an excellent studio musician. During rehearsals, Roy and Joe played a number together and Joe suggested bringing Marty out to join them on mandolin. That was Marty's first national TV exposure.

REBA McENTIRE—JANUARY 24, 1981.

Reba was discovered singing at a rodeo in Oklahoma by Red Steagall. At the time she was married to an older rancher, and

Reba McEntire got her start on Hee Haw.

was a schoolteacher who happened to have this wonderful voice. Red, a great singer/songwriter himself, happens to be a personal friend of mine. In November 1980, he called and asked me if I would book Reba on the show. On the strength of his recommendation, I did.

She was, understandably, a little nervous during rehearsals. This was, after all, her first nationwide exposure. After, she came up to me and said, "Sam, I'm country and if I make it in this business, I'm going to stay country. I'll always sing traditional country music." That's always led me to wonder why she recorded the pop tune, "Sunday Kind of Love."

Of course, she went on to great fame and fortune. She's a mighty talented lady and astute businessperson who deserves everything she's gotten. She suffered a terrible tragedy in her life when she lost her band in an airplane crash; a tragedy that nearly destroyed her career. She's a brave lady, and continues to grow in every way.

Reba is a joy to work with, unselfish, and kind to everyone

on the set. I believe that she will go on to become a major motion-picture star. When I'm retired, I'll be proud to say I got the chance to work with her.

PAUL ANKA—JANUARY 31, 1981.

In November 1980, Paul Anka was in town and wanted to come to our studio during lunch hour to tape a promotional spot for his annual charity telethon with the whole *Hee Haw* gang.

Normally, during our lunch hour, I made everyone leave the building to breathe some fresh air and come back ready to work for the rest of the afternoon.

However, on this one occasion, to accommodate Paul, I asked everyone to return a little earlier than usual to get ready for him. We had worked it out so that he would "unexpectedly" drop by the studio while Buck was taping a song. Buck would stop playing and say, "Well, look who just walked in, if it isn't Paul Anka! Come on over and visit!" Paul would then segue into his promotional message.

Paul looked at me for a long time, thought it over and finally said, "Hey, I like that." It came off beautifully, without so much as a rehearsal. After, he said to me, "You know, Sam, I'm going to be in town two or three more days. Would you like me to make a guest appearance on the show?"

It was something I didn't expect, but certainly welcomed. "Absolutely," I said.

About twelve-thirty the day we were scheduled to tape his spot, I got a call from his manager, who said, "Hey, it's twelve-thirty, where's the limousine?"

"What limousine?"

"The one for Paul."

"I don't use limos on this show," I told him. "I use a runner who drives my black sedan to pick up guests. He'll be right by to pick up Paul."

"No way. Paul Anka only travels in limousines."

I repeated that we never used limousines.

"Well, I'm sorry, but Paul insists he must have a limousine."

Finally, and quite reluctantly, I said I would look into it. I went to Marcia and said, "I hate to tell you this but we need to get a limousine for Paul Anka."

She said, "No way. We're not going to do it. We've never done it before and we're not going to start now!"

"But, Marcia, we'll lose Paul."

She said, "If you want to order a limousine, fine, you do it, I'm not going to break precedent."

"Fine," I said, and called a local service. The only problem was, it never arrived at the studio. The driver picked Paul up at his hotel, went one block, stalled and wouldn't go another foot. When he called ahead to tell us what was going on, Marcia came running into my office, screaming, "We did it! We did it! Our Go-fer is picking up Anka!"

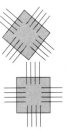

Paul finally arrived, and dutifully worked with us the rest of the day. Not only did he do his songs, but he also appeared in several comedy bits. The show turned out so well, I decided to put that episode up as our representative nomination for a 1981 Emmy award.

After Paul finished, he hung around to watch the others do their thing until it was time for him to go the airport. I personally carried all his luggage out to my car. As I was loading up the trunk, he thanked me for sending the limousine and apologized for all the problems it had created.

I then proceeded to tell him the whole story. "Damn it," he said, "That's managers for you. If I'd had known about your custom, I would have had no problem taking the car!"

ALABAMA—OCTOBER 10, 1981.

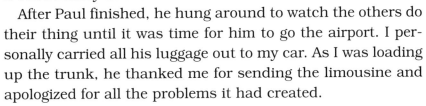

Like so many other country superstars, Alabama got their first national exposure on our show. When we first discovered them, they were a very good bar band. It was only after they appeared on *Hee Haw* that they shot into the stratosphere, and then it was the old story; their management was reluctant to let them come back as often as we would have liked.

They went from a situation of no visibility to a fear of overexposure!

Still, whenever they had a new country record to introduce, they'd do the show. The guys themselves loved coming on, not to sing, but to do some comedy in the Kornfield with the Honeys. We always loved having them on because of their humor. Some of the guys in the group are good enough comic actors to star in their own sitcoms.

BIG BIRD—OCTOBER 24, 1981.

The Jim Henson organization decided to let Big Bird sing, and they thought it would be nice to have him come on *Hee Haw* and do a country song. It would never have occurred to me in a million years to have anyone from Sesame Street on *Hee Haw*, but as soon as it was suggested I knew it would make a terrific booking.

I learned a lot about puppeteering from Big Bird's visit. For instance, the people "inside" have a very limited amount of time before it gets too hot and stuffy. I was forever being hounded by Jim Henson's people to start taping exactly on time and to only do "quick" shoots. As it happened, the fellow playing Big Bird was having such a good time working with Roy and Slim Pickens he either didn't realize or didn't care that he was slowly turning into Big Roasted Bird.

DOC SEVERINSON—NOVEMBER 7, 1981.

My buddy, Skull, called to tell me that Doc was coming to Nashville to make an appearance with the Nashville Symphony. I got ahold of him and asked if he'd like to be on *Hee Haw*. He very graciously agreed.

When I arrived at the studio the morning he was scheduled to tape, Doc was already there, earlier than most of the staff. He had come in to practice his scales on the horn.

He performed a solo trumpet number, and a duet with Roy

on guitar. He also sat in with the Million Dollar Band and increased its value by another million. Every musician in town wanted to be in the studio that day to watch Doc do his thing. Perhaps, because he was on *The Tonight Show* all those years, the public never got enough of Doc and his solo work. All the Nashville musicians had enormous respect for him and considered it a privilege to hear him play live. And so did I.

By the way, this one time I didn't suggest that our guest wear overalls.

LESLIE NIELSEN—JANUARY 9, 1982.

For many years, Leslie Nielsen had a career as a serious screen actor. As he got older, there was less demand for his services, and he made what can only be described as a spectacular shift into comedy.

I first met Leslie in 1980, at the George Lindsey Special Olympics golf tournament in Montgomery, Alabama. We used to help George out by putting on a *Hee Haw*-type show for the people who came to the tournament. I asked Leslie to be on the *Hee Haw* TV show, although I had no idea how I'd use him. It was one of those instances where it just felt right, and I knew I could work it out in the studio.

Leslie had this little green rubber contraption he carried around with him. Whenever he'd be talking to a group of people, he'd squeeze it, and everybody would think somebody farted. This kept everyone crazy the entire time he was on the set.

We didn't exactly "turn" Leslie into a country star, but we did help keep him in the public eye, until he successfully resurrected his film career.

SAMMY DAVIS, JR.—OCTOBER 16, 1982.

Early in 1982, after recording a country-music album, Sammy Davis, Jr. decided he wanted to do more concert

Sammy Davis, Jr. and Minnie Pearl

venues, especially country fair dates. He signed on with
Buddy Lee, a very well-known Nashville booking agent who
handles such country greats as Garth Brooks and Willie
Nelson.

When Buddy called to tell me Sammy was available, I
thought it would be an exciting booking and decided to go for
it, as long as Sammy would meet us halfway and forget about
his twenty-piece band. Even if we could afford it, which we
couldn't, that wasn't what *Hee Haw* was all about. Buddy
talked it over with Sammy, who said it was no problem, and
we set a date.

As always, when dealing with someone not used to the way
we did things, I tried not to lock Sammy into a specific schedule. I just told him to come down the morning we were taping. There were certain procedures on the show we always
followed. No matter how big or small our guest stars were, I
always made sure they were warmly greeted by someone,
usually a person from make-up or wardrobe, and taken di-

rectly to a dressing room. After they settled in, I'd make it a point to personally stop by and say hello, thank them for coming down, ask if they needed anything, give them a run-down of the show and tell them what I expected from them.

Shortly after he arrived, I met Sammy in his dressing room, we spoke a while, and I then asked him what he wanted to sing. He wasn't quite sure, something from his new country album, he said. No problem. Prior to his arrival, our band had listened to his album and were ready.

After my visit with Sammy, the parade of requests began. First, his orchestra leader wanted to talk things over. Then his piano player. Then his arranger. Then his backup singers. Then his wardrobe person. I told them all I was sorry, but we were only going to use our house band behind Sammy. "But you only have six or seven guys," his orchestra leader said.

"That's *Hee Haw*," I replied. "We also have four backup singers."

"Well, you're going to have to rehearse them, you'll need charts."

"I don't think you understand," I said. "Just tell us what song Sammy wants do and we'll be ready. In fact," I went on, "all we need for you to do is bring Sammy into the studio to block out his camera shots and give us a sound check."

The fellow just shook his head. Sammy's wardrobe person was trying to figure out what Sammy should wear. "Just let him go out the way he is," I told him. Sammy had come in dressed in black, and looked fine to me. A little makeup was all I thought he needed.

Just before he went on, Sammy turned to me and said, "I have to have a drink."

I told him I'd be right back. Sammy liked screwdrivers—vodka and orange juice. When I handed him his drink, he looked at me and said, "Hot damn, I've never seen a TV producer play waiter before!"

Sammy wound up doing four songs for us from his album. He had arrived at ten in the morning and was finished by noon. I was ready to say good-bye and wish him well, when he insisted on returning after lunch to do some comedy.

It so happened this was the day of the week we had one of our famous *Hee Haw* chili lunches. Charlie Barnhardt, a stagehand on the show, cooked it for everyone outside our studio, right there on the grounds of the Grand Ole Opry. He used giant oil barrels cut in half, rough edges and all, which he'd put on top of a gas burner and go to town. Sammy decided to join in and had such a great time he made an impromptu speech to everyone about how this was the only way to live!

That afternoon, back at the studio he donned a straw hat and overalls, decorated with his famous jewelry, and had a ball! He did "Pickin' and Grinnin'," went into the Kornfield, and fooled around with the *Hee Haw* Honeys. All the while, his people sat on folding chairs against the back wall staring in disbelief! They couldn't understand how we had managed to pull it all off without them!

At one point, Sammy turned to me and said, "Get Roy out here. I want to do a song with him." Even though we weren't set up to do music that afternoon, Roy came right out and together they performed an impromptu version of Hank Williams' "Oh, Lonesome Me," which wasn't even on Sammy's album. Roy sang and played a gorgeous guitar accompaniment that sounded as if it had to have been rehearsed for weeks.

Sammy and Roy hit it off so well, they wound up doing a half-dozen additional songs. Just before the last one, Sammy ad-libbed into the camera, saying how much he had enjoyed himself, and how terrific everyone was, and how he wanted to thank everyone who'd made his stay so enjoyable, especially Sam Lovullo!

I was floored! As much as I appreciated it, I didn't think a "thank you" to me made sense over the air, so we wiped the speech from the final mix. However, I could never erase Sammy's words from my heart.

PAUL WILLIAMS—November 6, 1982.

Paul is a great songwriter and performer, as well as a terrific piano player. I first met him six years before he did the show, in circumstances that were fairly embarrassing.

In the '70s, Wesley Rose, Jr., the son of the legendary Wesley Rose of the Acuff-Rose publishing company, was the president of NARAS, the organization that puts on the Grammies. One morning in Los Angeles I got a call from Wesley saying he was going to make a pitch to have the Grammies broadcast from Nashville, and would appreciate my assistance in approaching Pierre Cossette, the producer of the Grammy Award television show.

I took the next plane to Nashville, and during the flight happened to sit behind Paul Williams, who was also going to the NARAS meeting. He had had a couple of drinks, and soon began to talk so loudly that I couldn't help overhearing part of his conversation. He kept saying to his associate that he didn't quite understand why he had to go to Nashville, that he didn't really want to make the trip but was doing so only because Wesley Rose had insisted. Plus, he'd heard they'd brought in a consultant, someone named Lovullo, and who the hell was he? At the time I had no idea he was a performer. I thought he was a board member. I thought to myself, oh my God, this is really embarrassing! Wait until he meets me at the first meeting and realizes we sat near each other on the same plane!

Sure enough, the next morning I arrived at Wesley's office, walked in, and there was Paul Williams. When he saw me, his jaw dropped!

It wasn't until he did the show five or six years later, in June of '82, that I had a chance to say to him, "Paul, remember me?" He looked the other way, somewhat embarrassed and said, "Vaguely."

But he enjoyed being a part of *Hee Haw*. He was prepared to come on and simply do a song or two, but when he discovered what we were all about, he was more than eager to become a part of the overall fabric of the show.

PHIL HARRIS—NOVEMBER 13, 1982.

In the summer of 1982, Roy Clark played the Phil Harris Golf Tournament. Phil happened to mention to Roy that he'd like to come down to Nashville and check out the country scene for himself. Roy invited him to make an appearance on *Hee Haw.*

When Phil arrived at the studio, everyone was just all over him. One of his biggest fans was our own Grandpa Jones. Everyone wanted to ask about the old days, when he was cutting records, making movies and appearing with Jack Benny. Phil did his big hit, "Smoke Smoke Smoke That Cigarette," on the show. He was joined by Roy for a duet, and appeared in a "Pickin' and Grinnin'" skit. Everyone had a great time that day. Just before he left, he told me his wife, Alice Faye, had instructed him to come right back home when he was finished and to forget those Honeys!

WILLARD SCOTT—MARCH 12, 1983.

I'd heard that Willard loved the Grand Ole Opry and was a great fan of Grandpa Jones and Roy Acuff. I figured we could have some fun if we invited him on the show. I called his office in New York, and sure enough he called me back himself because he wanted to tell me how much he loved *Hee Haw.* All he wanted to do was talk about Minnie Pearl, Roy Acuff, and Grandpa Jones.

I told him I wanted him to be a guest and he said he'd love to but really didn't see how, as he worked five days a week on *The Today Show.* I asked him what time he got out of work in the morning and he said he was usually finished by ten.

I said, "I'll tell you what, Willard, let me check something." I always kept airline schedules on my desk, because if I really wanted people badly and they weren't in the Nashville area, I could pretty much figure how to fly them in with the least amount of hassle and loss of time. "Willard," I said, "there's a flight out of La Guardia at 11:40 A.M. to Nashville that arrives at 1:00. I'll have someone pick you up at the airport."

He agreed, and I had our runner waiting for Willard when he landed. We were ready to go as soon as he walked into the studio. When he arrived, everybody gave him a big cheer. I had the whole cast on stage for "Pickin' and Grinnin'," then brought him from the dressing room through the studio doors, and said, "Hey, gang, let's give a great big *Hee Haw* welcome to Willard Scott!"

That's all it took, and he was home! He had such a good time, he didn't think about eating or drinking, or making his return flight to New York, 5:00 that same afternoon.

We used him in several sketches, including the Kornfield with the Honeys. As we were finishing up, he took me by complete surprise, saying he wanted to sing a song! As this was a comedy-taping day, our house band wasn't even in the studio. But okay, I figured, I'd go with it. "What do you want to sing?"

"'Mountain Dew,' and I want Grandpa Jones to sing with me, and Roy Clark on the guitar." Years ago, "Mountain Dew" had been a big hit for Grandpa Jones, and he was thrilled that Willard knew that. Prior to rehearsal, Willard said, "Now when I get to this part, I want you all to cheer me on, and then join in the chorus."

He really set us up. We rehearsed the song and did it just as he wanted. However, when we got to this one part where everyone was supposed to cheer, he suddenly raised his hands and said, "Stop the music!" He then gave us a weather report! "Now, it's 70 degrees in New York, 85 degrees in Los Angeles, and mighty hot and happy here. Start the music!" When he finished his weather report, he went right back to the song! He had the entire cast and crew in stitches!

We got him to the airport in time, and I didn't hear from Willard again for about two months, until one day he called and said, "Sam, you ain't gonna believe this, but some folks saw me on your show and guess what? I'm going to do a *USA Today* newspaper commercial and they want me to sing!" To this day, Willard attributes his "singing" career to that appearance on *Hee Haw*.

GEORGE STRAIT—November 12, 1983.

By the mid-80s, country music had entered its "hat" era—not the Minnie Pearl type, with the price tag still dangling, but modern cowboy hats. The first to wear one on *Hee Haw* was George Strait.

George had been kicking around Texas for a long time before hitting it big with "All My Ex's are in Texas." Although he's a classically handsome man, by the time he made it he wasn't really all that young, and I think maybe he wore that hat to try and disguise his age.

George never came back after his first visit and to this day I can't tell you why. Maybe all his ex's were in Tennessee! I know he liked the idea of working with our cast, and of course those Honeys. Unbeknownst to George, there was a time when we considered making him a regular. We were looking for a "hunk" and George seemed the perfect choice.

GRANT TURNER—November 26, 1983.

Grant Turner was the legendary "voice" of the Grand Ole Opry. Anyone who was ever a fan of the Opry radio broadcasts would instantly recognize the sound of his voice. I put him on the show one time, in the Kornfield.

One Saturday night not long after, I ran into Grant in the greenroom of the Opry. His entire family was there and he insisted on introducing me to all of them—his wife, his daughter, the grandchildren. Grant turned to everyone and said, "This is the man who put me on television."

I was awakened the next morning and told that Grant, who

was in his eighties, had died in his sleep during the night. He was a wonderful man, and never stopped thanking me for finally giving a face to a voice that millions knew and loved.

LEE GREENWOOD—October 6, 1984.

In March 1984, I got a call from my old friend Skull, extolling the talents of a singer he'd "discovered." Skull used to take local groups on gambling junkets to Las Vegas. Among his own many and varied talents has always been his ability to spot new talent. He was forever calling to tell me about some new singer I ought to see, and that's what this call was about. On one of those Las Vegas junkets, Skull happened to see Lee Greenwood.

For many years, before he hit it big, Lee was a Las Vegas lounge performer, bouncing from hotel to hotel, never making it into the main rooms. To this day, he will tell you whatever success he's had in country music he owes to Skull Schulman and Sam Lovullo, Skull for bringing him to Nashville, me for putting him on *Hee Haw*.

Lee appeared on several shows, often playing instruments his fans didn't know he could handle, including the saxophone. Among the most enjoyable moments with Lee were his jamming duets with Roy.

THE JUDDS—October 6, 1984.

Naomi Judd was a nurse before she made her mark as a singer, and that was when she got acquainted with one of my production assistants, Betsy Haney. Naomi started coming around the old Channel 5 studios in the late '70s. No one at the time knew she was a singer. As far as anyone was concerned, she was just hanging out, visiting her friend. Occasionally she would help out around the office, do a little photocopying and typing while she waited for Betsy to get off work.

It was only after I got to know Naomi that she told me she was into Christian music and suggested I book The Stamps, one of Elvis' backup groups. I found out later that the reason she recommended them was because she was going with one of its members. I told her I thought we already had enough Christian music on the show, especially our own Gospel Quartet.

Now, I've been a little bald since I was a young man. One day, the nursing side of Naomi noticed I had a lump on my scalp. I knew it was there, and to tell you the truth was scared to deal with it. I feared it might be cancerous, and so kept putting off going to a doctor.

She started bringing me a salve to put on the lump. Eventually, she convinced me to go see a doctor. I did, discovered it was a noncancerous cyst and had it surgically removed.

Not long after, Naomi and her daughter Wynona cut a demo that was good enough to get them a record deal with RCA. One of their first singles, "Mama He's Crazy," was a huge hit. Because of it, I had the extreme pleasure of booking them on *Hee Haw*.

Years later, Naomi and I ran into each other at an awards show. Naomi came up, put her arms around me and asked, "How is that cyst you used to have on your head?"

I bent over and said, "Look, it's all gone." And then in came her entourage, several of whom moved in to break us up. They weren't comfortable with me dealing directly with her. That's part of the problem so many stars have today—they become overcontrolled by their "management," who are really doing little more than justifying their existence. I believe that the restrictive lifestyle, and perhaps a couple of bad management decisions—and of course her health—were responsible for Naomi's deciding to break up the duo and the business. It's a shame, because she's too good to be out of the business.

AMY GRANT—OCTOBER 27, 1984.

One day I got a phone call from Amy Grant's management saying she wanted to do the show. I was pleasantly surprised, as she was at the time still heavily into Christian music. She always struck me as having a great personality, nice looks, and an ability to get a message across to a youthful audience.

I decided to float her name around the studio to find out how everybody felt about having her on the show. It turned out everybody felt fine about it, but like me, had no idea what we could with her. Finally, I said, why don't we just let her come on and do her own thing?

I put her into our nightclub set and she did a contemporary, up-tempo song. Like every other guest, she fell in love with the *Hee Haw* cast, and decided she wanted to do some comedy bits.

After her appearance, I got a call from her management asking if I'd be interested in developing a network special for her. I took that as a real compliment, and while I wasn't able to free up the time, I had no doubt that she could easily cross over into the secular mainstream with a great deal of success, which is exactly what she did.

LORRIE MORGAN—NOVEMBER 3, 1984.

Lorrie is the daughter of the legendary George Morgan ("Candy Kisses"), who was a longtime favorite of the Grand Ole Opry right up until his untimely passing. George used to take little Lorrie with him whenever he played the Opry. She was everybody's favorite, and when she was old enough to sing, her daddy brought her on to the Opry. I personally think she's as good a songwriter as she is a singer.

When Lorrie first did our show, she was appearing as a regular on *Nashville Now*, Ralph Emery's nightly TNN show. I would see her at the eleven-thirty mass every Sunday at St. Joseph's church in Nashville, a stone's throw from Opryland.

I asked her to come on the show just as she was invited to be a member of the Grand Ole Opry.

Although she didn't as yet have a recording contract, it was obvious to me that Lorrie was going to be a big star. However, early on she had some personal problems. Her second marriage, to Keith Whitley, a recording artist with RCA, ended when Keith died of the long-term effects of alcoholism.

Lorrie did *Hee Haw* many times. She's a beautiful-looking woman, and with her gorgeous blonde hair and big eyes, quite telegenic. One of her most unforgettable appearances on the show was when she sang her daddy's big hit, "Candy Kisses," with Roy Clark.

Lorrie is a strong woman, and today, in spite of setbacks, she has become a top country star. The best years of her life are still ahead of her.

STAN FREESE—November 17, 1984.

Stan is the entertainment director for Disneyland in Anaheim, California. He is also a great tuba player and songwriter, which is how we first met. In 1983, a friend of mine I'd worked with at CBS recommended Stan for a guest shot on *Hee Haw*.

This was just about the time brass instruments were becoming an acceptable part of country music. I was curious to see how everyone on the show would react to a tuba player. I told Roy first. He laughed and said sure, sounds great. Of course, Roy was always ready, willing and able to try anything.

The spot proved terrific, and Stan became a semiregular. Although he lived in California, he was in Nashville quite often, and he would always come by and do the show. Most evenings he'd be jamming down in Printer's Alley or Music Row. Musicians used to call up during our production periods to find out if he was in town and where he was going to be that night.

The last several years, eight o'clock every Christmas morning the phone rings, I pick it up and all I hear is the sound of a tuba playing "We Wish You A Merry Christmas."

KATHY MATTEA—DECEMBER 15, 1984.

We introduced Kathy in 1985 as a "newcomer" to country music, although she'd actually been kicking around in Nashville for a few years. Like so many others, she got her first nationwide television exposure on *Hee Haw*. Before that, she'd worked as a waitress, at a music-publishing company and several other jobs, all the while looking for a chance to cut a record.

Kathy is a real sweetheart with a terrific voice. In the course of bouncing around she took a few wrong turns but managed to straighten herself out and find a nice man. Today she is once again on the verge of superstardom.

I consider her one of my special friends. First of all, I love brunettes. The people in my office used to tease me by asking, what is it with you and Kathy Mattea? That was an easy one to answer. She was an Italian girl from West Virginia!

WILLIE NELSON (WITH KRIS KRISTOFFERSON)—FEBRUARY 2, 1985.

Another person I consider important to me in Nashville is a fellow by the name of Billy Deaton. Billy was a country musician who spent a lot of years in Texas before moving to Nashville, where he liked to hang around with his pals Merle Haggard, Willie Nelson, Charley Pride and Ernest Tubb backstage on Music Row.

One day in October 1984, I happened to run into him there with Kris Kristofferson and Willie, neither of whom I'd ever been able to get to come on *Hee Haw*. Not because they didn't want to do it, it's just that they were basically "road" entertainers, never in one place long enough to do anything but set up, perform, break down, and move on.

This time, with Billy's help, I was able to convince Kris and Willie to come to our studio and be on *Hee Haw*. Because it happened on the spur of the moment, I thought I might have to juggle some guests. I asked Billy what time he and the boys would be coming down. "Sam, all I can tell you is, we can't give you a specific time. You'll just have to wait for them to show up."

I decided to keep to my original schedule, and as luck would have it, just after the last guest finished taping, Willie and Kris walked in. I went up to greet them. They were polite, but I could tell they didn't recognize who I was or that I was the producer of the show. Willie, who was a little uptight, sized me up and said, "Well, what would you like us to do?"

"Whatever you want will be fine. Consider this your studio."

Willie Nelson and Kris Kristofferson in the Kornfield

"Okay, then," he said, "I'll do some songs, but I really came here to get in the Kornfield with those Honeys!"

"Me too," Kris added in that deep drawl of his.

I wanted them both to do the Kornfield first, so I could get it out of the way and send everybody else home. However, Willie decided he wanted to sing alone first, so that's the way we went. He did some songs, and Kris did as well. When they finally finished singing what must have been a dozen songs, they wanted to get into the Kornfield again and have some fun! Unfortunately for them, most of the girls had gone home!

Both Willie and Kris had such a good time they tried for the longest time to come back and do the show again, but just couldn't coordinate their schedules. Willie, in particular, was very eager to come back and play with The Million Dollar Band. It's too bad he never came back. We would have loved to have him sit in.

MINNESOTA FATS—OCTOBER 26, 1985.

Minnesota had to be pushing eighty when he did the show. He was hanging around Nashville, playing pool, still very much into the game, if not as sharp as he once was. His steady gig was serving as the host for the Hermitage Hotel in Nashville, the way Joe Louis hosted for Caesar's Palace in Las Vegas.

Minnesota got word to me he wanted to make an appearance on *Hee Haw*, and I was happy to arrange it, although I wasn't quite sure what we'd do with him. Set up a pool table and let him make some fancy shots? Too obvious. I decided to put him in the barber shop and have him do a couple of routines with Archie. Much to my surprise, it turned out he was a natural comic. Unless he was hustling me, of course.

MARIE OSMOND—November 30, 1985.

I first met Marie when she was a guest on one of the many Perry Como specials that Frank, John, and Nick Vanoff produced. Also on that show, which aired in the mid-'70s, was Archie Campbell. Everyone knows that Perry Como had been a barber before he made it as a singer. So, in a sketch written by Frank and John, Perry went to Archie, "the barber," for a haircut, and he kept criticizing his technique.

I was at the taping and saw Marie sing her big hit, "Paper Roses." I was so impressed with her performance, I asked her to come on *Hee Haw* and do that song, which she did.

Marie was always a joy to work with, a total professional. She liked to bring her children along when she taped her spots for us, I think because it made her feel a little more relaxed and at home. I had her on *Hee Haw* many times, and was always impressed with her talent and generosity, especially her many appearances to help good Christian causes.

RANDY TRAVIS—October 11, 1986.

Like so many others who went on to become superstars, Randy received his first national TV exposure on *Hee Haw*. At the time, he was managed by Liz Hatcher, whom he later married.

Randy had a reputation as a "bad boy" when he was a youngster—he'd been in a little trouble with the law. He credits Liz, and I believe rightfully so, for helping to straighten him out.

When they first met, she was running her own business in California. She divorced, moved to Nashville, and took Randy with her. She went to work managing the Nashville Palace, owned by John Hobbs, within earshot of the Grand Ole Opry. In addition to being a waiter and helping out in the restaurant's kitchen, Randy was also the club's regular singer.

Randy Travis with Gunilla Hutton

One day he came to the attention of Roy Acuff, who liked to give struggling acts a shot, and Randy wound up getting a one-time invitation to sing at the Grand Ole Opry. He was an instant hit, and the machinery started to roll. Not long after, Liz landed Randy a record deal. It all happened so fast he didn't know what hit him. He made his network TV debut on *Hee Haw*, and six months later was a national sensation.

DWIGHT YOAKAM—November 1, 1986.

Although Dwight is originally from Kentucky, he is associated with the Bakersfield sound. He's a great fan of Buck Owens, and if you compare the two, you'll find their phrasing is quite similar. You can really hear it on their duet, "Streets of Bakersfield." I think Dwight was largely responsible for Buck coming out of semiretirement to record that song.

Dwight was also very fond of Grandpa Jones, and because of that and his association with Buck, was a big fan of *Hee Haw*. One time he was passing through Nashville, and called up to see if I could get him on. Although I was happy to book him, he hadn't as yet broken big and I must say he didn't impress me at the time as someone who was about to become a star. There was something about him I found a little strange. Whenever he spoke to me, he looked over my shoulder rather than in my eyes.

I guess Dwight doesn't particularly like Nashville, but he has enormous respect for Grandpa and Minnie Pearl.

LYLE LOVETT—March 28, 1987.

Lyle, who's quite an interesting fellow, is another one who got his first nationwide television exposure on *Hee Haw*. But I don't think that down deep in his heart he's a country singer. He's really more of a rocker. Offstage, he's very laid back, never talks out of turn, never speaks out about anything. He was never very willing to do much in the way of comedy, and like so many of the greats, was really fussy about his music. He always insisted on having the best musicians behind him. Because his sound was so special, I let him bring on his own musicians.

PATTY LOVELESS—October 17, 1987.

Patty caught my eye during an appearance at the Grand Ole Opry. She's sweet, very personable, and has a great voice. If she has any shortcoming, it's her shyness, which I believe is part of the reason she struggled for so long to get to the top.

Because my office was in a trailer right outside our studio and next to the back wall of the Grand Ole Opry, I'd occasionally wander over to watch the show from backstage. That's how I first heard Patty. I had my production coordinator, Jack Kirby, approach her as soon as she came off stage and asked if she'd have her manager call to arrange a booking on *Hee Haw*. She was still an unknown, and skeptical about my invitation, which I believe was a manifestation of her shyness. She finally consented to do the show, was a big hit, went on to have her first hit record, and was on her way.

Also, although she was married, she didn't reveal it right away, and I think her belated admission turned a lot of people off. Her career suffered because of it, although quite honestly I'm not sure why, unless it's because she's so beautiful and people had this fantasy about her that was shattered. She certainly should be at the top of the charts, and now that she's signed with a new label, I'm sure she will be.

K.T. OSLIN—JANUARY 16, 1988.

After K.T. made her first and only appearance on *Hee Haw*, I got a flood of phone calls from women all over the country, thanking us for having her on and saying what a great performance she'd given.

From the start, I wanted K.T., a northeasterner, to feel as if she were a welcome guest in Nashville, a member of the *Hee Haw* family. At the same time I wanted my people to see that she was not only a great singer, pianist and songwriter, but a talented comedienne as well.

Her appearance turned out wonderfully, and we received a very high rating that week. Naturally, I wanted to book her for a return visit, and was surprised when she turned me down. I couldn't understand why. Stan Moress, her personal manager, was a little embarrassed when he had to tell me she didn't want to do *Hee Haw* again.

Two years later, I was invited to the Talent Buyers Association seminar in Los Angeles to give a talk about my experiences booking talent for *Hee Haw*. As it happened, K.T. was also there, to give the performer's perspective. We wound up sitting next to each other on the dais. I turned to K.T., smiled and said, "Gee, how you been? I haven't seen you in awhile."

"I'm fine, Sam," she said, smiling back. "I see *Hee Haw*'s doing alright."

I decided to bring up the obvious. "K.T.," I said, "how come you haven't done the show again?"

She didn't hesitate for a second and came back straight ahead, which I appreciated. "Sam, I did not like the way the *Hee Haw* Honeys and some of the other female performers were dressed on the show. I don't think you were being respectful to them as women." She went to explain that she didn't like the low-cut blouses and felt we were sexually exploiting the Honeys for the sake of ratings.

I was absolutely stunned. "K.T., I'm sorry you feel that way."

"There's no need to be sorry, Sam. That's your show. There's nothing wrong with it, I just didn't appreciate it and don't want to be a part of it again. That's all."

It was an amicable discussion, but after, I got to thinking that maybe I had done something wrong by surrounding her with our Honeys in some of our comedy skits. After all, K.T. isn't exactly Honey material.

K.D. LANG—FEBRUARY 27, 1988.

I first discovered k.d. when she appeared as a guest on *The David Letterman Show*. She wore a weird skirt, black nylons ripped to shreds, and sang a modern pop/country tune. She later wore the same outfit on *Hee Haw* and told me the skirt had been fashioned by her grandmother out of old kitchen curtains.

I happened to be tuned in to Letterman that night and was impressed by her singing ability, as well as by her look. I was always searching for performers who could make a lasting impression—people whose unique talents and abilities might become one of the instantly visual definitions of *Hee Haw*. After seeing k.d., I thought she'd be perfect for us.

The next day, I had someone in my office call Letterman's production office to find out how to get in touch with her. I must say, his people were not very cooperative. We got bounced around from person to person. No one seemed to know anything about her, or care that we were interested. I began to wonder if perhaps Letterman hadn't been as impressed as I was with k.d.'s performance.

Tired of the runaround, I finally picked up the phone myself, called the show, and was put through to the head writer, who wanted to say hello to me. Through the years, David has continually poked fun at *Hee Haw*, especially George "Goober" Lindsey and Kenny Price. Both, in fact, have appeared several times on his famous "Top Ten" list, which I always took as a compliment: it meant someone on David's show was a regular viewer of *Hee Haw*.

I finally got a lead on k.d. and discovered that she was from Vancouver, Canada. I called and caught her manager completely by surprise. His initial reaction was, "Do you really think she's right for *Hee Haw*?"

I couldn't give him an answer because, quite frankly, I didn't know. So I said, "Bring her down to Nashville and we'll find out."

When I posted k.d.'s name on our shooting schedule, almost no one knew who she was. The few who did, thought she was not right for us. I told them all the same thing. "Wait until you see her perform."

When k.d. arrived, she insisted we do nothing to change her style, or the arrangements of her songs. To that end, we made an exception to one of our house policies, that performers had to play with the *Hee Haw* house band. I decided to let her sing and play with her own people.

I also gave her a separate dressing room, which, to my surprise, she rejected, insisting on staying with the boys in her band, her "guys" as she called them. I was surprised, although in truth she didn't have to do much dressing—just change into those nylons and that odd skirt. As we got closer to show time, k.d. announced she didn't want to wear any makeup. "Well," I told my staff, "we'll just have to let her go natural."

Which is exactly what we did.

I immediately fell in love with k.d.'s kookiness, and we developed a kind of father-daughter relationship. I have to admit, my staff couldn't understand why I liked her so much, or see what k.d. could possibly contribute to the show, and they were sure her appearance would land me flat on my face.

Finally, when it was time for her to sing her songs, I must say k.d. didn't let me down. Nobody in the studio could believe what they saw. We had a near riot! Everyone from the entire studio and adjoining complex had crammed into the studio to find out what all the commotion was. I finally had to call security to control the situation. There were so many people on the floor—stagehands, mechanics, even nearby Opryland workers—we literally couldn't move a muscle! Word spread like wildfire that there was a genuine kook on our stage, giving a performance that couldn't be missed!

She pulled out all the stops, slid around on the floor (which I realized was why her nylons were always so torn up), sang her heart out, and just about tore the place apart. Her appearance was a great success. I've never heard the kind of applause k.d. received that day. She was overwhelmed by it, got down on her knees, bowed down, thanked everybody, and left the stage.

Back in the dressing room, I said to her, "You must be pooped."

"No, not really," she said. "I could have done a lot more." She paused and added, "I really love the people in this town."

"You ought to," I said. "They love you."

She suddenly looked at me and said, "Do you think I could meet Minnie Pearl?"

I said, "Minnie isn't scheduled to be at the studio today. Where are you going to be tonight?"

"I'm not sure if we're leaving tonight or tomorrow."

I told her to stay in town until the next day, and I'd arrange a meeting. Minnie happened to be doing *Nashville Now* that night, Ralph Emery's TNN talk show. I told k.d. to meet me at seven fifteen by the stage entrance to Ralph's studio.

As it happened, k.d. was late and the show had already started. I was standing backstage, wondering where she was.

What I didn't know was, she was having trouble getting past the guards. Finally, she convinced them she was supposed to meet me, walked down the backstage hallway, and ran directly into Minnie!

Later on, Minnie told me she had no idea who this strange-looking person was, or what she wanted, but k.d. managed to ingratiate herself, and they became quite fond of each other.

Then k.d. went on to become a big hit in Nashville, and recorded a country album produced by the legendary Owen Bradley, Patsy Cline's producer. There's no question that *Hee Haw* was the catalyst for that, responsible for first bringing her, and her special brand of country music, to Nashville.

VINCE GILL—APRIL 30, 1988.

I was surprised when Vince made it in Nashville as a country singer. He's originally from Los Angeles, and before he turned to country he was a member of a pop group that played every night in a club in Long Beach. The word on him back then was not so much about his singing, as it was his guitar playing.

I'm happy he found his niche. Vince is a terrific musician. He's also easy to get along with, thoughtful, naturally modest, and a family-minded person. And, may I add, one hell of a golfer. Because of his winning personality and brilliant mind, I believe he would make a terrific talk-show host.

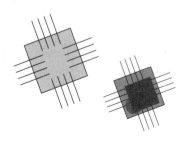

With John Denver and Grandpa Jones in 1989

JOHN DENVER—FEBRUARY 25, 1989.

When I found out John Denver was in town I decided to invite him on the show. He said he was quite busy but was a fan of ours and would at least come by to say hello to Grandpa Jones and Roy. He did, and he wound up doing a quick guest spot for us.

John wasn't really prepared to sing. However, once he arrived at the studio, he was so impressed with our operation, he said, "Well, I'm here, and I'd be delighted to do a medley of my hits." In spite of no rehearsal or advance warning, the taping came off perfectly, one of the advantages of having the caliber of musicians we were fortunate enough to have at our disposal.

KYLE AND RICHARD PETTY—APRIL 29, 1989.

In the late '80s, TNN began televising the NASCAR races. It was just about this time that Kyle Petty was making his move into country music. I must say, for an auto racer, he isn't a bad singer.

One day I got a call from Don Light, an agent who's been around as long as Prince Albert. Don wanted me to know he was now handling Kyle, who'd just recorded a Rodney Crowell song, "King Richard," and wanted to be on *Hee Haw*. I booked him, and added how great I thought it would be if his father, Richard, came along. Don said he'd try to arrange it. On the day of Kyle's scheduled appearance, Richard showed up and said he'd do the show—you guessed it—as long as he could get into the Kornfield with those Honeys.

ROBIN LEACH—OCTOBER 28, 1989.

Robin was a natural. His visit came about after I received a call from Barry Adelman, a former *Hee Haw* writer before joining Dick Clark. Dick wanted to use Robin Leach in an interview spot on one of his TV award shows. Unfortunately, Robin wasn't going to be available to do it live, so Dick arranged to pretape his bit. The only problem was, he couldn't find the right location. Barry, who'd been to my home in Los Angeles several times, suggested using it. Dick's people called and I agreed.

As it happened, the day of the shoot, the producer was also shooting a spot with Jackie Collins, and wound up taping them both in my home. While Dick's crew was setting up, Robin and I began to chat, and that's when he first found out I was the producer of *Hee Haw*.

I always keep a handful of *Hee Haw* merchandising items in my home. When Robin told me he was a fan of the show, I went into my closet and pulled out a pair of *Hee Haw* overalls for him. And, just so Jackie wouldn't feel left out, I gave her a *Hee Haw* carrying bag. I also told Robin I'd be calling him to do the show. That was good enough for him. As soon as he got back to his office in New York, he had *his* people call *me.*

I opened Robin's appearance with a sketch featuring him on the phone, talking to his agent, when suddenly he says in that thick, Cockney accent of his, "What? What's *Hee Haw*? A jackass? What's 'Pickin' and Grinnin'?" We also put him in our running skit, "The Naggers." He came down to Kornfield Kounty looking for The Naggers (which he referred to as "The Poor-and-Unknowns") to feature on his program.

For the "finale," I came up with a musical bit with The Instrumental Band: Roy on the banjo, Charlie McCoy on harmonica, guest David Holt on washboard, and Robin on paper bag—nothing more than a blown-up gold-painted grocery bag with one end tied with a piece of cord that you hit against your hand.

Robin had one hell of a time doing *Hee Haw*! His image may be champagne, but his heart is strictly moonshine!

CLINT BLACK—November 11, 1989.

Clint is a great singer-songwriter from Texas. Because of his dark features and prominent bone structure I've often been asked numerous times if he's got Italian roots. To the best of my knowledge he doesn't.

Clint's married to Lisa Hartman, whose sister, Marilyn Hartman, used to work as a production assistant on *Hee Haw*. Lisa and Marilyn's mother is a very reputable publicist, who, I believe, played a key role in resurrecting Clint's career.

Clint was as excited to be on *Hee Haw* as we were to have him. The day he taped his song, I couldn't find him. Eventually someone told me he was on the stage floor, watching the crew set up. He was talking to a friend, and didn't hear me approaching. He put his hand on his buddy's shoulder and said, "Doing this show has always been my dream. If only my family could see me now!"

Garth Brooks up to his neck in Hee Haw *Honeys*

GARTH BROOKS—JANUARY 13, 1990.

Garth is a naturally aggressive performer as well as a marketing whiz, which was his major in college.

After graduating from Oklahoma State, he kicked around Nashville for a long time before making it. He'd come to town, stay with friends, make demos and play the local clubs. He struggled mightily, and then suddenly, seemingly out of nowhere, shot to the top. Sometimes, when you go up that fast, you fall just as quickly, but happily, that hasn't been the case with Garth.

I booked him on *Hee Haw* after I saw him perform his first

big hit, "If Tomorrow Never Comes," on the Grand Ole Opry stage. I remember watching one of the Opry's production assistants, Debbie Logue, being absolutely mesmerized by the song and Garth's performance of it.

When he performed "If Tomorrow Never Comes" on *Hee Haw*, the reaction of our studio audience was exactly the same. Stunned silence. Shortly after that performance, things began to happen for Garth.

One Saturday night some time later, I happened to run into him backstage at the Opry. He was a big star now, but to me, still the same lovable good ol' boy. "Sam," he said, "I'll tell you what. Call the office. I'd love to do a couple of new songs for you."

Not long after, I called his office, and was told Garth couldn't do the show because he'd gone on vacation. "There must be some mistake," I said. "He gave me a specific date."

"Well, we're sorry, Sam, but he's on vacation. There's no way he'll be able to do it."

Garth and his wife had decided to fly to New England, rent a car, and drive the countryside to see the fall foliage. He made it a point, however, to shorten his vacation by one day and fly down to Nashville to make the taping. He had forgotten to tell his people, but I kept the date open, and he showed up exactly on time. *That's* Garth Brooks.

ALAN JACKSON—SEPTEMBER 22, 1990.

Alan began his musical career in 1983, right in my office, working as a mailroom boy for TNN. One day he dropped a demo tape off on my desk and ran out before I could say a word. I listened to it, liked what I heard, put it aside and forgot about it. A few years later he was discovered by Glen Campbell and became one of country's biggest stars.

He came on *Hee Haw*, and the day he taped I happened to run into him at the Opryhouse bathroom. "Alan," I said, "how are you?"

He looked at me. "Boy, I sure came a long way in a short time, didn't I?"

"You sure did. By the way, do you want the demo you gave me a few years ago?"

He said he did. "And I'm going to throw it away!"

No matter what Alan says, it wasn't that bad!

JIM DE PAIVA—November 3, 1990.

Jim, the star of the soap opera *One Life To Live*, is married to Misty Rowe, one of our *Hee Haw* Honeys. They were, in fact, married in my Los Angeles home.

Charlie called me one day and said he wanted to do something with the *Hee Haw* Honeys. (Charlie Chase, from *The Crook and Chase Show*, does occasional specials for The Nashville Network, called "Funny People," a *Candid Camera*-type production.) We had a regular segment on our show—the Jug Band—with Minnie Pearl at the piano, surrounded by the Honeys. The gals sang the same song each week, with different topical, sometimes risqué lyrics. I came up with the idea of having a "gorilla" come into the studio during the sketch; it would come after the girls, concentrating on Misty. There was, of course, a twist.

Charlie loved the idea. Unbeknownst to Misty, I asked Jim De Paiva to play the gorilla. He agreed, and flew down from New York to do it. And, of course, we kept it a secret from Misty.

During rehearsals, a regular *Hee Haw* cast member, Jim Smith, played the gorilla. To make sure Misty knew it was this Jim, we had him wear only the legs of the costume, supposedly because he claimed it was too hot to wear the whole outfit. What Misty didn't know was, we had flown Jim De Paiva in, picked him up at the airport and snuck him into the studio. Now, when the "gorilla" returned, De Paiva was inside. As part of the gag, we told him to start getting a little too familiar with Misty.

The director then announced we were ready to do a take. The "gorilla" appeared, and as the sketch progressed, Jim kept moving closer to Misty, and she kept moving farther back. At one point he actually grabbed her from behind and started pulling at her dress. She got so angry she finally turned, pulled his hood off, ready to smack Jim Smith—only to find it was her husband smiling back at her!

CONWAY TWITTY—NOVEMBER 3, 1990.

Conway was never that enthusiastic about doing *Hee Haw.* He was a shy person, very sophisticated, both on stage and off, and wasn't into straw hats, overalls and "Pickin' and Grinnin'." He was one of the few male guests we ever had on who didn't come to me and say, hey, put me in the Kornfield with the Honeys. He was the epitome of class, and his premature passing was a sad day in the history of country music.

TRAVIS TRITT—DECEMBER 1, 1990.

One thing I never lost sight of was that for every nontraditional, i.e., modern country performer, I made sure I had someone on the same show who was very traditional. Travis was one of our "modern" performers, and like a lot of the younger singers, refused to do any comedy. They saw it as a generational thing, better left to the old-timers. I never agreed with that philosophy, but always respected those who did.

ALLISON KRAUSS—FEBRUARY 16, 1991.

It was always difficult for Roy to sit in the studio and watch guests perform. He was aware that because of his legendary status, his very presence could be intimidating, and never wanted anyone to feel he or she was being scrutinized.

The only time I ever saw Roy actually go out and find himself a place in the studio to watch a guest perform was when

Allison Krauss did the show. He watched Allison sing and play her fiddle, and I have to say seemed totally in awe. After, when I asked him what he thought, he looked at me and said, "Sam, she's outstanding. What a pure voice for harmonizing."

Allison continues to get better all the time. I believe the mainstream will one day part its waters to welcome her.

TRICIA YEARWOOD—JANUARY 18, 1992.

Tricia is from Georgia, and like all those Georgia peaches, incredibly pretty. She is also a formally trained musician with a degree in music, and she sang all through her school years. She was discovered singing on the Nashville club circuit.

When Tricia came in to tape her segments, I went to her dressing room to greet her. I always wanted to make my guests feel at home. I said, "Hi, Tricia, I'm Sam Lovullo." I could tell she was extremely nervous about making her national television debut.

We talked for a bit about her songs, and then she said, "I used to watch the show when I was three years old. It was my parents' favorite show!"

Did you ever have one of those moments when you suddenly felt every second of your age?

Pickin' and Grinnin'—Hee Haw *style*

CLOSING CREDITS

Creators

Frank Peppiatt	1969–1990
John Aylesworth	1969–1990

Executive Producers

Frank Peppiatt	1969–1982
John Aylesworth	1969–1982
Elmer Alley	1989–1991

Producer

Sam Lovullo	1969–1991

Directors

Bill Davis	1969–1972
Bob Boatman	1973–1989
Steve Schepman	1989–1991

Writers

John Aylesworth	1969–1984
Jack Burns	1969–1970
Pat Buttram	1969
Archie Campbell	1969–1987
Frank Peppiatt	1969–1984
Gordie Tapp	1969–1989
Bud Wingard	1969–1989
George Yanok	1969–1971
Stan Ascough	1970
Tom Lutz	1970–1981
Don Harron	1972–1985

David Cox	1977–1979
Barry Adelman	1979–1989
Barry Silver	1979–1980
Tom Finnigan	1985
Sam Lovullo	1985–1989
Kent Wildman	1986–1989
Sharon Bell	1989
Steve Campbell	1989–1991
Mary Eta Cook	1989
Herbert Fox	1989–1991
J. R. Miller	1989–1991
Mike Price	1989
Robert Wynn	1989
Steve Arwood	1991

Associate Producers

Marcia Minor	1977–1988
Patricia Branan Wendell	1989–1991

Music Directors

Bob Alberti	1969
Kelso Herston	1969
Don Rich	1969–1970
George Richey	1970–1977
Charlie McCoy	1978–1991

Art Directors

Bill Camden	1969–1971, 1978
Gene McAvoy	1969–1970, 1980
Bill Gernert	1972–1977, 1979
Jim Stanley	1980–1991

Assistants to the Producer

Rita Scott	1969
Lily LaCava	1969–1970
Ellen Brown	1970–1973
Marcia Minor	1973–1976
Sandy Liles	1979–1991

Associate Directors

Dick Harwood	1969–1972
Peter Barth	1973
Bonnie Burns	1973
Bob Bowker	1974
Claude Lawrence	1975
Van Fox	1976

Ellen Brown	1977–1978
Steve Schepman	1979–1989
Connie Mansfield	1989–1991

Choreographer
Diane Lovullo	1983–1991

Talent Coordinator
Jack McFadden	1969

Stage Managers
Phil Dell'Isola	1969–1970
Jimmy Norton	1969–1972
Rick Zarro	1970
Ted Ray	1972–1973
John Sprague	1974–1977
Steve Schepman	1978
Gary Hood	1979–1986
Russ Nunnally	1987–1991

Unit Managers
Al Simon	1969
Bill Williams	1973–1976
Ann Rice	1977–1979
Danny Wendell	1980–1983
Patricia Branan Wendell	1983–1988

Scenic Designers
Bill Gernet	1970–1971
Chris Tibbott	1978–1991
Bill Briggs	1990–1991
Bill Camden	1991

Set Decorators
Bill Camden	1969
Lee Clayton	1969–1970
Kay Munson Nunnally	1971–1981
Russ Nunnally	1982–1986
Jeff Nunnally	1987–1991

Production Assistants
Ellen Brown	1969–1970
Brigit Jensen	1969
Doris Kentner	1969
Marcia Minor	1969–1972
Amy Kimmelman	1970–1971
William Robert	1972

Sandy Liles	1972–1978
Joe Doster	1973
Sandy Zajack	1973
Belva Cunningham	1979
Betsy Haney	1980–1983
Francesca Peppiatt	1982
Sandy Broadway	1983
Michelle Gabler	1984–1985
Mary Jo Talley	1984–1985
Katy Bach	1986–1988
Melissa Cross	1986–1987
Colleen O'Connell	1988–1989
Jan Ray	1988
Jill Jackson	1989–1990
Myra Godby	1990
Jackie Guidry	1991
Missy Whitchurch	1991

Production Coordinators

Bill Williams	1969–1972
Jennie Farrell	1974
Sandy Zajack	1974
Belva Cunningham	1975–1978
Michelle Gabler	1975–1978
Betsy Haney	1979
Francesca Peppiatt	1980–1981
Martin Clayton	1982–1984
John Gallagher	1985–1991
Donna York	1985–1991
Jackie Guidry	1990
Lela Long	1991

Production Staff

Joyce Thomas	1969–1983
J.M. Kuno	1973
Ellen Edmunson McNamara	1973
Gordie Steele	1973
Jack Kirby	1979–1981
Kathy Ingram	1980
Pat Johnson	1980
Susan Pitts	1980
Nedria Wence	1981
Ronnie Hassell	1982
Collen O'Connell	1982–1986
Patricia Bannon Wendell	1982

Beth Wendell	1982
Florian Schereck	1983
Brian Hughes	1984–1985
Betty Holleman	1986–1988
Glennise Perkins	1986
C. C. Cunningham	1988–1991
Lela Long	1989–1990
Jack Kirby	1991

Wardrobe Designers

Ed Sunley	1969–1976, 1983
Faye Sloane	1977–1982
Clara Franklin	1984–1991

Wardrobe Assistants

Lucille Taylor	1969–1975
Dewey Perrigo	1974
Faye Sloane	1976
Lurlyne Traughber	1977–1978
Betty Chapman	1979
Clara Franklin	1980–1983
Diane Lovullo	1983–1991

Makeup Artists

Jo Coulter	1969
Charles Nash	1969–1973
Elizabeth Linneman	1970–1989
Paul Sanchez	1973
Bill Knaggs	1974
Bob Ryan	1974
Caren Daay	1974
Anita Hostettler	1975–1989
Genie Freeman	1986–1989
Candy Smathers Johnson	1989–1991
Valerie Cole	1989–1991
Joyce Daniel	1989–1991

Hair Stylists

Donna Norton	1969
Yolie Stefanko	1969–1972
Caren Daay	1973–1975
Richard Cardenas	1974
Gwen Anken Bauer	1976–1989
Linda Demith	1983–1985
Cindy Rich	1989–1991

Lighting Designers

Art Roberts	1969
Bob Boatman	1969–1972
Mike Turner	1973–1974
Leard Davis	1974–1986
Ted Wells	1986–1987
Richard Kennedy	1987–1991

Lighting Directors

Mike Turner	1972
Richard Kennedy	1976–1979
Bobby Trull	1977–1979
Art Brown	1980–1991
Mike Gillen	1989–1991

Technical Directors

Joe Hostettler	1969–1989
Kent Green	1980
Bill Williams	1981–1991

Audio Mixers

Larry Sullivan	1969–1974
	1975–1979
Steve Abbott	1976
Dan Newman	1976–1977
Terry Farris	1980–1981
John Long	1982–1988
Ron Worrell	1988–1991

Audio Assistants

Paul Resch	1980–1981
Conrad Jones	1980–1983
John Long	1981
Kim Raymer	1982
Glen Trew	1982
Ron Worrell	1982–1984
Jerry Baker	1983–1984
P.C. Salter	1985–1991

Post Audio Production

Charlie Douglas	1969–1972
John Pratt	1973–1977
Carroll Pratt	1978–1980
J. L. Meyers	1981–1991

Craig Porter	1981–1986
Rick Hemot	1986–1991

Videotape Recordists

Reed Skinner	1969–1979
Robert Britton	1980
Jim Ferguson	1981–1983
Marti Vacek	1983–1985
Dennis Grandinetti	1986–1991

Videotape Editors

Fred Gayton	1969
Bill Kendall	1969–1970
Lewis W. Smith	1969
Marco Zappia	1970
Jack Calaway	1970–1971
Barney Robinson	1972–1973
Lynn Coulon	1973–1977
Terry Climer	1978
Jeff Bass	1979
Joe Bella	1981–1982
Rocco Zappia, Jr.	1983
Alex Gimenez	1984
Tom Edwards	1985–1987
Craig Garrett	1988–1991

Videotape Assistants

Joe Askin	1978
Kevin Muldoon	1980
Tim Wheeler	1981
Eric Yang	1981, 1984
Jacki Robison	1982
Marc Breaux	1983
Elliott Michell	1985–1986
Phil Jones	1986

Camera Video

Bob McKenny	1969
Bob Sowell	1969–1971
Truett Smith	1972–1974
	1980–1983
Cliff Boswell	1974–1979
Larry Bearden	1981, 1984
Mickey Caruthers	1985–1991

Cameras

Bob Derryberry	1969–1978
Alan Fuqua	1969–1979
Bobby Trull	1969–1978
	1983–1991
Gentry Hughes	1969–1979
Damon Freeman	1979, 1988
Bob Morrison	1980–1981
Dan Preston	1980
Rick Reale	1980–1981
Ronnie Smith	1980–1981
Pat Gleason	1981, 1991
Don Lewis	1981
Wayne Womack	1981
Larry Copeland	1982
Ron Smith	1982–1984
Rick Reddy	1985–1991
David Owens	1986–1991

Technical and Maintenance

Jody Karlovic	1980–1982
Mike Schofil	1980–1991
Andy York	1980–1986
Mike Gillen	1981–1989
Gaylon Holloway	1981
Dick Hargett	1981
Andy Jones	1981
Don Claggett	1982
Tommy Fisher	1983
Shipley Landiss	1983–1986
Barclay Randall	1989

Stagehands

Charlie Barnhardt	1969–1982
Mike Mason	1969–1986
Oot Sullivan	1969–1991
Jay Murphy	1981–1985
Frank Bess	1984
Jim Brown	1984–1991
James Reed	1985–1988
John Bryan	1986–1991
Tim Bess	1986
Terry Cox	1986
Paul Franklin	1986
George Lunn	1986–1991

Terry McDonald	1986–1991
Mike Smith	1987–1991
Tom Stokes	1987
Bill Wood	1987
Ray Perrin	1990
Jim Robertson	1990–1991
Danny Barber	1991
Ken Henley	1991

Construction Crew

Tom Merritt	1969–1978
	1980–1991
Reed Moyer	1969–1978
	1980–1991
Tony Pennington	1980–1991
David Wade	1983–1991

Cue Cards

Stan Ascough	1969–1970
Tom Lutz	1969–1970
Fred Porter	1970
John Sprage	1970–1973
Steve Schepman	1972–1977
Bob Vogeli	1974
Martin Clayton	1978–1980
Peter Alex	1980–1982
Susan Rettig	1980
Julie Watson	1980–1981
Chuck Shockley	1981–1982
Mike Alley	1982
Jimmy Corbitt	1983–1989
Brian Hughes	1983–1984
Suzanne Edems	1984–1988
Gary Hood	1984–1988
Rita Buck	1985–1991
Chris Hill	1987–1991
Stephanie Reeves	1989–1991

Photographers

Tony Esparza	1969–1970
Marv Newton	1972–1973
Greg Zajack	1974–1975
Marshall Paulk	1976–1977
Ralph Nelson	1978–1980
Jim Frey	1981–1984

Dean Dixon	1985–1991
Harold McBroyen	1991

Publicists

Bonnie Bucy	1969–1974
David Ward	1975–1980
Jerry Franken	1981–1983
Cliff Dektar	1984–1989
Bernie Illson	1990–1991

Puppeteer

Tom Tichenor	1980–1982

Titles and Animations

Format Films:

Hank Jordan	1969–1991
Herb Klynn	1969–1991
Joe Siracusa	1969–1991

Production Studios

WLAC and WTVF-TV—Nashville	1969–1980
Opryland, USA	1980–1991

Production Credits

Yongestreet Productions in Association with CBS	1969–1970
Yongestreet Productions in syndication	1971–1981
Gaylord Program Services in syndication	1982–1991

Buck Owens asking me for a raise. Not subtle, but effective

THE *HEE HAW* BROADCAST SCHEDULE

1969–1992
A COMPLETE LISTING
OF AIRDATES AND GUESTS

HEE HAW
CBS-NETWORK
BROADCAST SCHEDULE
1969 SUMMER SEASON

Show Number	Airdate	Guests
1)	6/15/69	Loretta Lynn Charley Pride The Hagers
2)	6/22/69	Merle Haggard The Hagers
3)	6/29/69	Tammy Wynette George Jones Faron Young
4)	7/6/69	Sonny James Waylon Jennings Connie Smith
5)	7/13/69	Ferlin Husky Jerry Lee Lewis The Hagers
6)	7/27/69	Charley Pride Tammy Wynette George Jones
7)	8/3/69	Merle Haggard Bonnie Owens Eddie Fukano
8)	8/10/69	Waylon Jennings Loretta Lynn
9)	8/17/69	Conway Twitty Jerry Lee Lewis
10)	8/24/69	Merle Haggard Bonnie Owens The Hagers
11)	8/31/69	Tammy Wynette Sonny James The Hagers
12)	9/7/69	Charley Pride Loretta Lynn Jerry Lee Lewis The Hagers

Loretta Lynn guested in 1973.

Show Number	Airdate	Guests
13)	12/17/69	Tammy Wynette Merle Haggard
14)	12/24/69	Loretta Lynn Dillard & Expedition
15)	12/31/69	Hank Williams, Jr. Dottie West
16)	1/7/70	Wanda Jackson Henson Cargill
17)	1/14/70	Hank Thompson Lynn Anderson Buddy Alan
18)	1/21/70	Sonny James Tammy Wynette
19)	1/28/70	Loretta Lynn Merle Haggard
20)	2/4/70	Ferlin Husky Dottie West
21)	2/11/70	Lynn Anderson George Jones
22)	2/18/70	Merle Haggard Henson Cargill Tammy Wynette
23)	2/25/70	Loretta Lynn Charley Pride
24)	3/4/70	Wanda Jackson Sonny James
25)	3/11/70	Dottie West George Jones

208   LIFE IN THE KORNFIELD

Show Number	Airdate	Guests
26)	3/18/70	Faron Young
		Dolly Parton
27)	3/25/70	Connie Smith
		Stan Hitchcock
28)	4/1/70	Merle Haggard
		Linda Ronstadt
29)	4/8/70	Tammy Wynette
		George Jones

HEE HAW
CBS-NETWORK
BROADCAST SCHEDULE
1970–71 SEASON

Show Number	Airdate	Guests
30)	9/15/70	Roy Rogers
		Dale Evans
		Bobby Bare
31)	9/22/70	Charley Pride
		Jeannie C. Riley

More Pickin' and Grinnin' with Buck and Roy

Show Number	Airdate	Guests
32)	9/29/70	Ray Charles Lynn Anderson
33)	10/6/70	Tammy Wynette George Jones
34)	10/13/70	Marty Robbins Connie Eaton
35)	10/20/70	Roy Rogers Dale Evans Doug Kershaw
36)	10/27/70	Sonny James Peggy Little
37)	11/10/70	Tom T. Hall Jean Shepard Gunilla Hutton
38)	11/17/70	Charley Pride Susan Raye
39)	11/24/70	Tammy Wynette Ed Bruce
40)	12/1/70	Ray Charles Lynda K. Lance
41)	12/8/70	Kenny Price Linda Martell
42)	12/15/70	Waylon Jennings Diana Trask Johnny Duncan
43)	12/29/70	Roy Rogers Dale Evans
44)	1/5/71	Charley Pride Amanda Blake Mickey Mantle
45)	1/12/71	Roger Miller Peggy Little Bobby Murcer
46)	1/19/71	Marty Robbins Connie Smith
47)	1/26/71	Tammy Wynette George Jones Billy Jo Spears
48)	2/2/71	Loretta Lynn Bill Anderson

Show Number	Airdate	Guests
49)	2/9/71	Roy Rogers Dale Evans
50)	2/16/71	Hank Williams, Jr. Jody Miller
51)	2/23/71	Tom T. Hall Connie Eaton Bobby Bare Susan Raye

HEE HAW
(SYNDICATION)
BROADCAST SCHEDULE
1971–72 SEASON

Show Number	Airdate	Guests
52)	9/18/71	Roy Rogers Dale Evans
53)	9/25/71	Dale Robertson Susan Raye
54)	10/2/71	Amanda Blake Buddy Alan
55)	10/9/71	George Lindsey Kenni Huskey
56)	10/16/71	Conway Twitty Loretta Lynn
57)	10/23/71	Sammi Smith Bakersfield Brass
58)	10/30/71	Lynn Anderson Ray Sanders
59)	11/6/71	Roy Rogers Dale Evans
60)	11/13/71	Dale Robertson Kenni Huskey
61)	11/20/71	Conway Twitty Loretta Lynn
62)	11/27/71	Sammi Smith Buddy Alan

Show Number	Airdate	Guests
63)	12/4/71	Lynn Anderson
		Ray Sanders
64)	12/11/71	Buddy Alan
		Susan Raye
65)	1/8/72	Johnny Duncan
		Doug Kershaw
		Gunilla Hutton
		Buddy Alan
66)	1/15/72	Sonny James
		Jody Miller
67)	1/22/72	Tammy Wynette
		George Jones
68)	1/29/72	Bobby Goldsboro
		Susan Raye
69)	2/5/72	Jeannie C. Riley
		Buddy Alan
		Johnny Bench
70)	2/12/72	Porter Wagoner
		Dolly Parton
71)	2/19/72	Brenda Lee
		Hank Thompson
		George Lindsey
72)	2/26/72	Waylon Jennings
		Jessi Colter
		Johnny Bench
73)	3/4/72	Tom T. Hall
		Susan Raye
74)	3/11/72	Tammy Wynette
		George Jones
75)	3/18/72	Ferlin Husky
		Barbara Mandrell
76)	3/25/72	Jody Miller
		Buddy Alan
77)	4/1/72	Connie Smith
		Tommy Ambrose

HEE HAW
(SYNDICATION)
BROADCAST SCHEDULE
1972–73 SEASON

Show Number	Airdate	Guests
78)	9/16/72	Ray Stevens Arlene Harden Dizzy Dean
79)	9/23/72	Patti Page Charlie McCoy
80)	9/30/72	Mel Tillis Sherry Bryce
81)	10/7/72	Ray Price Sandy Posey
82)	10/14/72	Johnny Paycheck Ruby Davis
83)	10/21/72	Kenny Price Penny DeHaven Dizzy Dean
84)	10/28/72	Tommy Overstreet Susan Raye
85)	11/4/72	Jud Strunk Jamey Ryan
86)	11/11/72	Jeannie Seely Buddy Alan
87)	11/18/72	Bobby Bare Barbara Fairchild
88)	11/25/72	Ray Stevens Donna Fargo
89)	12/2/72	Patti Page Doyle Holly Charlie McCoy
90)	12/9/72	Hank Williams, Jr. Arlene Harden
91)	12/16/72	Barbara Mandrell Paul Richey
92)	1/6/73	George Jones Tammy Wynette Buddy Alan

Show Number	Airdate	Guests
93)	1/13/73	Tennessee Ernie Ford Sammi Smith Charlie McCoy Nashville Edition
94)	1/20/73	Loretta Lynn Conway Twitty Johnny Bench
95)	1/27/73	Johnny Paycheck Sandy Posey Ruby Davis George Lindsey
96)	2/3/73	Don Gibson Sue Thompson Demetris Tapp
97)	2/10/73	Oral Roberts Richard & Patti Roberts Frankie Laine Buddy Alan
98)	2/17/73	Jody Miller Tony Booth Doyle Holly Joe Stampley
99)	2/24/73	Donna Fargo Tommy Cash Charlie Rich Tennessee Ernie Ford
100)	3/3/73	Wanda Jackson Frankie Laine Tony Booth
101)	3/10/73	Faron Young Penny DeHaven Tennessee Ernie Ford
102)	3/17/73	George Jones Tammy Wynette Patsy Sledd
103)	3/24/73	Loretta Lynn Conway Twitty Ray Griff

HEE HAW
(SYNDICATION)
BROADCAST SCHEDULE
1973–74 SEASON

Show Number	*Airdate*	*Guests*
104)	9/15/73	Jerry Reed LaWanda Lindsey
105)	9/22/73	Johnny Rodriguez Conny Van Dyke Catherine McKinnon
106)	9/29/73	Charlie Rich Susan Raye
107)	10/6/73	Sonny James Charlie McCoy
108)	10/13/73	Tanya Tucker George Lindsey Buddy Alan
109)	10/20/73	Dottie West Billy Craddock
110)	10/27/73	Roy Acuff Diana Trask
111)	11/3/73	Tammy Wynette George Jones Johnny Bush
112)	11/10/73	Brenda Lee Buddy Alan
113)	11/17/73	Donna Fargo O. B. McClinton
114)	11/24/73	Jerry Reed Conny Van Dyke Susan Raye
115)	12/1/73	Hank Snow Diana Trask
116)	12/8/73	Jeanne Pruett Joe Stampley
117)	12/15/73	Charley Pride Susan Raye Ronnie Milsap

Show Number	Airdate	Guests
118)	1/5/74	Roy Acuff Jim Ed Brown Marcie Cates Margie Cates
119)	1/12/74	Tex Ritter Catherine McKinnon Gunilla Hutton Don Rich Bruce Bradley
120)	1/19/74	Loretta Lynn Kenny Starr Stoney Edwards Jerry Clower
121)	1/26/74	Tennessee Ernie Ford Jody Miller Tommy Overstreet Larry Scott
122)	2/2/74	Tom Hall Sunday Sharpe Charlie McCoy Johnny Bench Ralph Emery
123)	2/9/74	Charley Pride Barbara Fairchild Tony Booth Craig Scott
124)	2/16/74	Johnny Cash Jean Shepard George Lindsey
125)	2/23/74	Pat Boone Skeeter Davis Ronnie Milsap Bill Taylor
126)	3/2/74	Loretta Lynn Conway Twitty David Houston Jerry Clower
127)	3/9/74	Tennessee Ernie Ford Lawanda Lindsey Red Shipley

Show Number	Airdate	Guests
128)	3/16/74	Johnny Rodriguez
		Susan Raye
		Oak Ridge Boys
129)	3/23/74	Lester Flatt
		Hugh Hefner
		Buddy Alan
		Gunilla Hutton

HEE HAW
(SYNDICATION)
BROADCAST SCHEDULE
1974–75 SEASON

Show Number	Airdate	Guests
130)	9/14/74	Ernest Borgnine
		George Lindsey
		Lulu Roman
131)	9/21/74	Loretta Lynn
		Kenny Price
		Buddy Alan
132)	9/28/74	Freddie Hart
		Leona Williams
		Barbi Benton
133)	10/5/74	Danny Davis and the
		Nashville Brass
		Susan Raye
		Gunilla Hutton
134)	10/12/74	Jody Miller
		Pee Wee King
		Redd Stewart
135)	10/19/74	Ernest Borgnine
		Loretta Lynn
		Kenny Starr
136)	10/26/74	Bobby Bare

Show Number	Airdate	Guests
137)	11/2/74	Conny Van Dyke Faron Young LaWanda Lindsey
138)	11/9/74	Charlie McCoy Boots Randolph Mickey Gilley
139)	11/16/74	Hugh Hefner Barbi Benton Bill Anderson Susan Raye
140)	11/23/74	Nashville Edition Barbara Mandrell Buddy Alan
141)	11/30/74	Tony Booth Sonny James Johnny Carver Crystal Gayle
142)	12/7/74	Gunilla Hutton Chet Atkins Jan Howard
143)	12/14/74	George Jones Tammy Wynette
144)	12/21/74	Donna Fargo George Lindsey Tony Lovello
145)	12/28/74	Red Steagall Susan Raye Governor Winfield Dunn LaWanda Lindsey
146)	1/4/75	Mac Wiseman Tony Booth Gunilla Hutton
147)	1/11/75	Molly Bee Charlie McCoy Buddy Alan
148)	1/18/75	Bob Luman Boots Randolph Lulu Roman
149)	1/25/75	Barbi Benton Johnny Russell LaWanda Lindsey

Show Number	Airdate	Guests
150)	2/1/75	Brenda Lee
		Chet Atkins
		Johnny Carver
		Gordie Tapp
		Gunilla Hutton
151)	2/8/75	George Jones
		Tammy Wynette
		Mickey Gilley
152)	2/15/75	Dolly Parton
		Kenny Price
		Terry McMillan
		Barbi Benton
153)	2/22/75	Kitty Wells
		Freddy Weller
154)	3/1/75	Connie Smith
		Don Williams
		Buddy Alan
155)	3/8/75	Tommy Overstreet
		Susan Raye
		LaWanda Lindsey

HEE HAW
(SYNDICATION)
BROADCAST SCHEDULE
1975–76 SEASON

Show Number	Airdate	Guests
156)	9/13/75	Johnny Cash
		John Carter Cash
		Gunilla Hutton
157)	9/20/75	Loretta Lynn
		Kenny Starr
		Jana Jae
158)	9/27/75	George Gobel
		Jack Ruth
		Barbi Benton

Show Number	Airdate	Guests
159)	10/4/75	Tammy Wynette Billy Walker George Lindsey
160)	10/11/75	Ray Stevens Susan Raye Grandpa Jones
161)	10/18/75	Barbara Mandrell Doyle Holly Buck Trent
162)	10/25/75	Freddy Fender Melba Montgomery Kenny Price
163)	11/1/75	Jody Miller Little Jimmy Dickens
164)	11/8/75	Mel Tillis Sammy Jo
165)	11/15/75	Mickey Gilley LaWanda Lindsey Nashville Edition
166)	11/22/75	Barbara Fairchild Joe Stampley Lulu Roman
167)	11/29/75	Ronnie Milsap Buddy Alan Tony Lovello Gordie Tapp
168)	12/6/75	Conway Twitty Susan Raye Gunilla Hutton
169)	12/13/75	Johnny Cash La Costa
170)	12/20/75	George Gobel Tommy Ambrose
171)	1/3/76	Don Gibson Sue Thompson
172)	1/10/76	Loretta Lynn Conway Twitty
173)	1/17/76	Roy Acuff Tammy Wynette
174)	1/24/76	Cal Smith Statler Brothers LaWanda Lindsey

Show Number	Airdate	Guests
175)	1/31/76	Dottie West
		Garner Ted Armstrong
		Charles Ginnsberg
176)	2/7/76	George Jones
		Sunday Sharpe
177)	2/14/76	Tom T. Hall
		Susan Raye
178)	2/21/76	Faron Young
		Crystal Gayle
179)	2/28/76	Sonny James
		David Wills
		LaWanda Lindsey
180)	3/6/76	Kenny Rogers
		Mel Street
181)	3/13/76	Merle Travis
		Brush Arbor

HEE HAW
(SYNDICATION)
BROADCAST SCHEDULE
1976–77 SEASON

Show Number	Airdate	Guests
182)	9/18/76	Tammy Wynette
		Will Geer
		Kenny Price
183)	9/25/76	George Gobel
		Billie Jo Spears
		Grandpa Jones
184)	10/2/76	Donna Fargo
		Red Sovine
185)	10/9/76	Jimmy Dean
		Buddy Alan
		Buck Trent
		Jana Jae
186)	10/16/76	Bobby Goldsboro
		Barbi Benton
		Grandpa & Ramona Jones

Show Number	Airdate	Guests
187)	10/23/76	Ray Stevens Susan Raye Jackie Phelps Roy Clark Family
188)	10/30/76	C. W. McCall Crystal Gayle Brush Arbor
189)	11/6/76	Charley Pride Dave & Sugar
190)	11/13/76	Terry Bradshaw Barbi Benton Grandpa & Ramona Jones
191)	11/20/76	Jimmy Dean George Gobel Susan Raye Roy Clark Family
192)	11/27/76	Johnny Paycheck Mel Street
193)	12/4/76	Sonny James Narvel Felts
194)	12/11/76	Larry Gatlin Statler Brothers
195)	12/18/76	Jimmy Dean Margo Smith
196)	1/8/77	Roy Rogers Dale Evans
197)	1/15/77	Tennessee Ernie Ford Brenda Lee Merle Travis Jimmy Henley
198)	1/22/77	Jim Ed Brown Helen Cornelius Roy Clark Family
199)	1/29/77	Mel Tillis Susan Raye Grandpa & Ramona Jones
200)	2/5/77	Loretta Lynn Conway Twitty Lorne Greene Jana Jae
201)	2/12/77	Barbara Mandrell Hoyt Axton

Show Number	Airdate	Guests
202)	2/19/77	George Jones
		Tammy Wynette
		Roy Clark Family
203)	2/26/77	Ernest Tubb
		Jody Miller
204)	3/5/77	Bill Anderson
		Mary Lou Turner
		Gerald Smith
205)	3/12/77	Mickey Gilley
		Susan Raye
		Jimmy Henley
206)	3/19/77	Barbara Mandrell
		Faron Young
		Roy Clark Family
		Grandpa & Ramona Jones
207)	3/26/77	Tennessee Ernie Ford
		Connie Smith
		Merle Travis

HEE HAW
(SYNDICATION)
BROADCAST SCHEDULE
1977–78 SEASON

Show Number	Airdate	Guests
208)	9/17/77	Mel Tillis
		Susan Raye
		Thompson Brothers
		Duke of Paducah
209)	9/24/77	Roy Rogers
		Dale Evans
		Sons of the Pioneers
		Harper Twins (Bong)
		Grandpa & Ramona Jones
		Duke of Paducah

Show Number	Airdate	Guests
210)	10/1/77	Kenny Rogers Jana Jae Cathy Barton
211)	10/8/77	Jerry Reed Sammi Smith East Virginia Toadsuckers (Bong) Jimmy Henley
212)	10/15/77	Freddy Fender Dottie West Roy Clark Family
213)	10/22/77	Larry Gatlin Phelps & Riddle (Bong) Jimmy Henley
214)	10/29/77	Charley Pride David Huddleston Hank Thompson
215)	11/5/77	Loretta Lynn Sons of the Pioneers Ernest Rey Russell Knight (Bong)
216)	11/12/77	Dennis Weaver Eddie Rabbitt Jana Jae
217)	11/19/77	Sonny James Oak Ridge Boys Bob Montgomery (Bong) Kenny Price
218)	11/26/77	Tom T. Hall Sons of the Pioneers Harper Twins (Bong) Kenny & William Price
219)	12/3/77	Don Williams Dave & Sugar Grandpa, Ramona & Alisa Jones Jimmy Henley
220)	12/10/77	Floyd Cramer Kenny Roberts Thompson Brothers (Bong)

Show Number	Airdate	Guests
221)	12/17/77	Dennis Weaver
		Susan Raye
		Jimmy Henley
222)	1/7/78	Larry Gatlin
		Susan Raye
		Vernon Presley
223)	1/14/78	Billy Carter
		Barbara Mandrell
		Larry Mahan
		Roy Clark Family
		Jimmy Henley
		Grandpa & Ramona Jones
224)	1/21/78	Jeannie C. Riley
		Johnny Bench
		Tommy Lasorda
		D. J. Peterson
225)	1/28/78	Roy Rogers
		Dale Evans
		Alan King
		Jimmy Henley
226)	2/4/78	Patti Page
		Brush Arbor
		Buddy Alan
		D. J. Sarginson
227)	2/11/78	Kenny Rogers
		Joe Higgins
		The Kendalls
		Roy Clark Family
228)	2/18/78	Johnny Rodriguez
		Susan Raye
		Sheriff Katherine Crumbley
		Jimmy Henley
		C. B. Slane
		Duke of Paducah
229)	2/25/78	Ruth Buzzi
		David Houston
230)	3/4/78	Little Jimmy Dickens
		George Savalas
		Dottsy
		Harper Twins (Bong)
		Mel Jass

Show Number	Airdate	Guests
231)	3/11/78	Billy Carter
		Stuart Hamblen
		Randy Gurley
		Kenny Price
		Roy Clark Family
232)	3/18/78	Patti Page
		Danny Davis & The Nashville Brass
		Jerry Clower
		Grandpa & Ramona Jones
		Johnny Jobe
233)	3/25/78	Statler Brothers
		Linda Hargrove
		Jimmy Henley
		P. Bearer

HEE HAW
(SYNDICATION)
BROADCAST SCHEDULE
1978–79 SEASON

Show Number	Airdate	Guests
234)	9/16/78	Bill Anderson
		Mary Lou Turner
		Lonzo & Oscar
		Jana Jae
235)	9/23/78	Tennessee Ernie Ford
		Barbara Fairchild
236)	9/30/78	John Hartford
		Moe Bandy
237)	10/7/78	Oak Ridge Boys
		Bobby Goldsboro
		John Ritter
		Grandpa & Ramona Jones
238)	10/14/78	Hank Williams, Jr.
		Connie Smith

Show Number	*Airdate*	*Guests*
239)	10/21/78	Sons of the Pioneers
		Rex Allen, Jr.
		Billy Carter
		Doc Randall
		Doctor Paul Braun
240)	10/28/78	Larry Gatlin
		Ava Barber
		Joe Higgins
241)	11/4/78	Tom T. Hall
		Don Gibson
		Jimmy Henley
242)	11/11/78	Barbara Mandrell
		John Hartford
		Roy Acuff
243)	11/18/78	Mel Tillis
		Roy Head
		Gerald Smith
244)	11/25/78	Don Williams
		The Kendalls
		Tennessee Ernie Ford
245)	12/2/78	Ronnie Milsap
		Margo Smith
		Stoney Mountain Cloggers
246)	12/9/78	Sonny James
		Jim Stafford
		Jana Jae
247)	12/16/78	Tennessee Ernie Ford
		Jody Miller
		Nashville Edition
248)	1/6/79	John Hartford
		Roy Acuff
		Jimmy Henley
		Grandpa & Ramona Jones
		Gunilla Hutton
249)	1/13/79	Charley Pride
		T. G. Sheppard
		Jimmy Henley
250)	1/20/79	Mickey Gilley
		Faron Young
		Grandpa & Ramona Jones

Show Number	Airdate	Guests
251)	1/27/79	Jim Stafford Touch of Country Charlie McCoy
252)	2/3/79	Johnny Duncan Jamie Fricke Johnny Gimble Jana Jae
253)	2/10/79	Ray Price Bill Anderson Roy Acuff
254)	2/17/79	Conway Twitty Dave & Sugar Grandpa, Ramona & Alisa Jones
255)	2/24/79	Charlie Rich Mary K. Miller
256)	3/3/79	Tennessee Ernie Ford Stella Parton
257)	3/10/79	Johnny Paycheck Dickey Lee
258)	3/17/79	George Jones Eddie Rabbitt Stoney Mountain Cloggers
259)	3/24/79	Jim Stafford Zella Lehr Eddie Low

HEE HAW
(SYNDICATION)
BROADCAST SCHEDULE
1979–80 SEASON

Show Number	Airdate	Guests
260)	9/15/79	Senator Robert Byrd Hoyt Axton Con Hunley Riddle & Phelps

Show Number	Airdate	Guests
261)	9/22/79	Joe Stampley Moe Bandy Clarence Gatemouth Brown
262)	9/29/79	Rev. Dr. Billy Graham Tennessee Ernie Ford Jimmie Rodgers Michelle Rodgers Bobby Butler
263)	10/6/79	John Conlee Susie Allanson Jana Jae
264)	10/13/79	Gene Autry Statler Brothers Randy Barlow Joe Frazier
265)	10/20/79	Jim Ed Brown Helen Cornelius
266)	10/27/79	Tennessee Ernie Ford Cristy Lane Jones Family Curly & Lil Kimbler Riddle & Phelps Bud Clark
267)	11/3/79	Larry Gatlin Foster Brooks Becky Hobbs
268)	11/10/79	Senator Robert Byrd Dave & Sugar Donna Darlene Mike Edwards
269)	11/17/79	Don Williams Billy Parker Gerald Smith Riddle & Phelps
270)	11/24/79	Tennessee Ernie Ford Tammy Wynette Karel Gott Jones Family

Show Number	Airdate	Guests
271)	12/1/79	Dennis Weaver
		Clarence Gatemouth Brown
		Alan Wayne
		Kenny Price
		Lulu Roman
272)	12/8/79	Freddy Fender
		Mission Mountain Wood Band
		Stoneman Family
273)	12/15/79	Conway Twitty
		Ronnie Prophet
274)	1/5/80	Ed McMahon
		Faron Young
		Barbi Benton
		Kathy Kitchen
		Chaplain Herb McCoy
		Police Chief Joe Casey
275)	1/12/80	Hank Thompson
		Janie Fricke
		Wally Lattimer
276)	1/19/80	T. G. Sheppard
		Gene Watson
		Jed Allan
		Stoneman Family
277)	1/26/80	Dottie West
		Pat Buttram
		Jimmy C. Newman
		Lonnie Brooks
278)	2/2/80	Oak Ridge Boys
		Charly McClain
		Roy Clark Family
		Marty Sullivan
		Jones Family
279)	2/9/80	Billy Crash Craddock
		Tommy Cash
		Louise Mandrell
280)	2/16/80	Ray Stevens
		Ava Barber
		Boxcar Willie

Show Number	Airdate	Guests
281)	2/23/80	Hank Snow
		Margo Smith
		Rodney Lay
282)	3/1/80	Barbara Mandrell
		Sonny James
		Jethro Burns
283)	3/8/80	Dennis Weaver
		Randy Boone
		Dottsy
		Woody Woodbury
		Jana Jae
284)	3/15/80	Tammy Wynette
		Jimmie Rodgers
		Al Downing
		Barbi Benton
		Roy Clark Family
285)	3/22/80	Blackwood Brothers
		Ronnie McDowell
		Wendy Holcombe
		Ralph Sloan & The Tennessee Travelers

HEE HAW
(SYNDICATION)
BROADCAST SCHEDULE
1980–81 SEASON

Show Number	Airdate	Guests
286)	9/13/80	Kenny Rogers
		Ethel Merman
		Million Dollar Band
		Grandpa & Ramona Jones
287)	9/20/80	Merle Haggard
		Leona Williams
		Tennessee Moonshine Cloggers

THE *HEE HAW* BROADCAST SCHEDULE 231

Show Number	Airdate	Guests
288)	9/27/80	Norm Crosby Janie Fricke Buck White
289)	10/4/80	The Kendalls Million Dollar Band Razzy Bailey
290)	10/11/80	Ray Stevens Sylvia Susan Guttmann
291)	10/18/80	Ed McMahon Bellamy Brothers Jimmy Henley Marty Stuart
292)	10/25/80	Hoyt Axton Million Dollar Band Grandpa & Ramona Jones Joe & Rose Lee Maphis
293)	11/1/80	Tom T. Hall Jeanne Pruett Henny Youngman
294)	11/8/80	Statler Brothers Jimmi Cannon Ralph Case Dancers Nashville Edition
295)	11/15/80	Loretta Lynn Million Dollar Band Rodney Lay The Hagers Jimmy Henley
296)	11/22/80	Barbara Mandrell Roger Maris Sonny Curtis Lulu Roman
297)	11/19/80	George Jones John Anderson Susan Raye Marty Stuart
298)	12/6/80	Dennis Weaver Buddy Alan Million Dollar Band Mackenzie Colt

Show Number	Airdate	Guests
299)	12/13/80	Porter Wagoner
		Lacy J. Dalton
		The Hagers
		Joe Maphis
300)	1/3/81	Merle Haggard
		Slim Pickens
		John Conlee
		Grandpa & Ramona Jones
		Joe Talbot
301)	1/10/81	Bill Anderson
		Wayne Massey and Mary Gordon Murray
		Curly Putman
		Buddy Alan
302)	1/17/81	Mickey Gilley
		Johnny Lee
		Million Dollar Band
303)	1/24/81	Bruce Jenner
		T.G. Sheppard
		Rodney Lay
		Reba McEntire
304)	1/31/81	Paul Anka
		Sylvia
		Chubby Wise
		Ralph Case Dancers
		Gene Swindell
305)	2/7/81	Brenda Lee
		Thrasher Brothers
		Million Dollar Band
306)	2/14/81	Helen Cornelius
		Billy Grammer
		John D. Loudermilk
		Jack Worley
307)	2/21/81	Dennis Weaver
		Tom T. Hall
		Tommy Hunter
		Stacy Lynn Ries

Show Number	Airdate	Guests
308)	2/28/81	Rex Allen, Sr.
		Rex Allen, Jr.
		Eddy Raven
		Margo Smith
		Million Dollar Band
309)	3/7/81	Ray Price
		Boxcar Willie
		Kentucky Chimes
		Dancers
		Roy Clark Family
310)	3/14/81	Ray Charles
		Slim Whitman
311)	3/21/81	Slim Pickens
		Don Gibson
		Jacky Ward
		Million Dollar Band

HEE HAW
(SYNDICATION)
BROADCAST SCHEDULE
1981–82 SEASON

Show Number	Airdate	Guests
312)	9/12/81	Ed Bruce
		Gail Davies
		Wendy Holcombe
313)	9/19/81	Loretta Lynn
		Conway Twitty
		Dian Hart
		Million Dollar Band
314)	9/26/81	Jeannie C. Riley
		Big Al Downing
		Grandpa & Ramona Jones
315)	10/3/81	Audry Landers
		Earl Thomas Conley
		Willis, Carlan & Quinn

234 LIFE IN THE KORNFIELD

Show Number	Airdate	Guests
316)	10/10/81	Alabama
		Million Dollar Band
		Harlan Howard
		Carolina Kids Cloggers
		Mackenzie Colt
317)	10/17/81	Hank Williams, Jr.
		Janie Fricke
		The Niningers
318)	10/24/81	Big Bird
		Sonny James
		Billy "Crash" Craddock
319)	10/31/81	Joe Stampley
		Terri Gibbs
		Boxcar Willie
		Million Dollar Band
320)	11/7/81	Kitty Wells
		Doc Severinson
		Thrasher Brothers
		Governor Lamar Alexander
321)	11/14/81	Faron Young
		Sylvia
		Chubby Wise
322)	11/21/81	Loretta Lynn
		Conway Twitty
		Glaser Brothers
		Moonshine Cloggers
323)	11/28/81	Johnny Rodriguez
		Helen Cornelius
		Hank Cochran
324)	12/5/81	Ernest Tubb
		Billie Jo Spears
		Cheryl Handy
325)	12/12/81	David Frizzell & Shelly West
		Oscar the Grouch
		The Shoppe
		Million Dollar Band
326)	1/2/82	Jeannie Seely
		Ronnie McDowell
		Sheb Wooley
		Jerry Pate

Show Number	Airdate	Guests
327)	1/9/82	Razzy Bailey The Kendalls Little General Cloggers Leslie Nielsen Roy Clark Family
328)	1/16/82	Charly McClain Ed McMahon Sonny Shroyer Charlie McCoy & Laney Smallwood
329)	1/23/82	Bill Monroe Doc Severinson Rex Allen, Jr. Dianne Sherrill Million Dollar Band
330)	1/30/82	Bobby Bare Stoneman Family Glaser Brothers Kippi Brannon
331)	2/6/82	Mickey Gilley John Hartford Carl Smith Jimmy Henley
332)	2/13/82	Roy Acuff Brenda Lee Jimmy C. Newman Mac Wiseman
333)	2/20/82	Jimmy Dean Wilburn Brothers Cotton Ivy Roy Clark Family Charlie Lamb
334)	2/27/82	Ernest Tubb B. J. Thomas Merle Travis Stan Kann
335)	3/6/82	Don Williams John Hartford Connie Smith Danny Flowers

Show Number	Airdate	Guests
336)	3/13/82	Roy Acuff
		Margo Smith
		Steve Wariner
		Cotton Ivy
337)	3/20/82	Jacky Ward
		Reba McEntire
		Jimmy Henley
		Roy Clark Family
		Terri Merryman

HEE HAW
(SYNDICATION)
BROADCAST SCHEDULE
1982–83 SEASON

Show Number	Airdate	Guests
338)	9/11/82	Donna Fargo
		Lee Greenwood
		Real Hillbilly Band
		Moonshine Cloggers
339)	9/18/82	Ray Stevens
		Scatman Crothers
		Million Dollar Band
		Roy Clark Family
340)	9/25/82	Louise Mandrell
		R. C. Bannon
		Charlie Walker
		Ben Peters
		Grandpa & Ramona Jones
341)	10/2/82	Mickey Gilley
		Johnny Lee
		Terry Gregory
		Buckwheat Cloggers
		Connie B. Gay

Show Number	Airdate	Guests
342)	10/9/82	Jim Stafford Gail Davies Cripple Creek Band
343)	10/16/82	Sammy Davis, Jr. Eddy Raven James Bacon Georgia Peaches Grandpa & Ramona Jones
344)	10/23/82	Ed Bruce John Schneider Al Downing Felice & Boudleaux Bryant
345)	10/30/82	Mickey Gilley Johnny Lee Sylvia Sammy Jackson
346)	11/6/82	Paul Williams Charly McClain Buckwheat Cloggers Chuck Morgan
347)	11/13/82	David Frizzell Shelly West Phil Harris Kim & Karman Reid (Statlers)
348)	11/20/82	Loretta Lynn Wright Bros. Dew Drops Million Dollar Band Grandpa & Ramona Jones
349)	11/27/82	T. G. Sheppard Billy Barty Cumberland Boys Bill Caswell Buddy Killen
350)	12/4/82	Boxcar Willie Ronnie Prophet Penny DeHaven Cotton Ivy

Show Number	Airdate	Guests
351)	12/11/82	Mel Tillis Charlie Walker Darrell Waltrip Custer's Last Band
352)	12/18/82	Jim Stafford Earl Thomas Conley Million Dollar Band Merle Travis
353)	1/8/83	Oak Ridge Boys Jim Ed Brown Moonshine Cloggers Jerry Chestnut Grandpa & Ramona Jones
354)	1/15/83	Sammy Davis, Jr. Dub Taylor Barbi Benton Red Steagall
355)	1/22/83	Charley Pride Family Brown Million Dollar Band Butch Baker Gerald Smith
356)	1/29/83	Ricky Skaggs Sonny James John Hartford—Real Hillbilly Band Cindy Hurt
357)	2/5/83	Dottie West John Schneider Burrito Brothers Cotton Ivy Little General Cloggers Kenny Price & Jennifer
358)	2/12/83	Conway Twitty John Anderson Jerry Clower Wright Brothers Rodney Lay

Show Number	Airdate	Guests
359)	2/19/83	Janie Fricke
		Osmond Brothers
		Dub Taylor
		Cliffie Stone
		Beverly Cotton
360)	2/26/83	Hoyt Axton
		Gene Watson
		Irlene Mandrell
		Jack Kaenel
		Kentucky Hoedowners
361)	3/5/83	B. J. Thomas
		Helen Cornelius
		Bill Carlisle
		Dayne Puckett
362)	3/12/83	Paul Williams
		Steve Wariner
		Willard Scott
		Million Dollar Band
363)	3/19/83	Faron Young
		Leon Everette
		Dub Taylor
		Bobby Braddock

Celebrating fifteen years of Hee Haw *in 1983*

HEE HAW
(SYNDICATION)
BROADCAST SCHEDULE
1983–84 SEASON

Show Number	*Airdate*	*Guests*
364)	9/17/83	Charley Pride Razzy Bailey Jan Howard Darrell Adams Roy Clark Family Gerald Smith
365)	9/24/83	Tanya Tucker Carl Perkins Rip Taylor Million Dollar Band Moonshine Cloggers & Dewdrops
366)	10/1/83	Alabama Skiles & Henderson Big Al Downing Dub Taylor Onie Wheeler Carlock Stooksbury
367)	10/8/83	Louise Mandrell Irlene Mandrell Boxcar Willie Buddy Killen Ted Gay
368)	10/15/83	Ricky Skaggs The Whites Dub Taylor Vern Gosden Carroll Baker
369)	10/22/83	Reba McEntire Tom Wopat Del Wood Don Crawley John Garrett

Show Number	Airdate	Guests
370)	10/29/83	Tennessee Ernie Ford
		David Frizzell
		Shelly West
		Skip Stephenson
371)	11/5/83	Loretta Lynn
		Johnny Rodriguez
		Cedar Creek
		Grandpa Jones & Jones Family
		Johnson Sisters
		Steve "Shotgun Red" Hall
372)	11/12/83	Statler Brothers
		George Strait
		Aldridge Sisters
		Stoney Mountain Cloggers
		Roy Clark Family
		Steve "Shotgun Red" Hall
373)	11/19/83	Barbara Mandrell
		Ben & Butch McCain
		Chris Golden
		Jimmy Henley
		Lee Arnold

Barbara Mandrell and Roy making beautiful music together

Show Number	Airdate	Guests
374)	11/26/83	John Anderson
		Charly McClain
		Dub Taylor
		Million Dollar Band
		Grant Turner
375)	12/3/83	Ernie Ford
		Chet Atkins
		Earl Klugh
		Michael Murphy
		Gerald Goodwin
376)	12/10/83	Ricky Skaggs
		Lee Greenwood
		The Whites
		Billy Edd Wheeler
377)	12/17/83	Lynn Anderson
		Johnny Lee
		Dub Taylor
		Buster Wilson
		Moonshine Cloggers & Dewdrops
378)	12/31/83	Charley Pride
		Jack Greene
		Susan Raye
		Buster Wilson
		Grandpa Jones & Family
		Steve "Shotgun Red" Hall
379)	1/7/84	Mickey Gilley
		Charly McClain
		Tom T. Hall
		Mel McDaniel
		Tari Hensley
		David Holt
		Million Dollar Band
380)	1/14/84	T. G. Sheppard
		Gene Watson
		Vic Willis Trio
		Trilly Cole
		Leroy Troy Boswell

Show Number	Airdate	Guests
381)	1/21/84	Bobby Bare
		Jeannie C. Riley
		Skiles & Henderson
		Hee Haw Clogging Solo
		Champions (Pam
		Collins, John Hasler)
		Steve "Shotgun Red" Hall
382)	1/28/84	Ed Bruce
		James Galway
		Karen Taylor-Good
		Sonny Throckmorton
383)	2/4/84	Glen Campbell
		Mel Tillis
		Mac Wiseman
		Jerry Pate
		Kentucky Hoedowners
		Roy Clark Family
384)	2/11/84	Barbara Mandrell
		Chet Atkins
		Earl Klugh
		Johnny Tillotson
		Little Jimmy Dickens
385)	2/18/84	Larry Gatlin
		The Kendalls
		Atlanta
		Sandy Pinkard & Richard
		Bowden
		Onie Wheeler
386)	2/25/84	Tennessee Ernie Ford
		Janie Fricke
		Vaughn Horton
		High Country Cloggers
		Benny Wilson
		Million Dollar Band
		Steve "Shotgun Red" Hall
387)	3/3/84	Roger Miller
		Tom T. Hall
		Gary Morris
		Seidina Reed
388)	3/10/84	Vic Damone
		Tommy Lasorda
		Moe Bandy
		Gus Hardin

Show Number	Airdate	Guests
389)	3/17/84	Glen Campbell
		Mel Tillis
		Bill Monroe
		Steve Wariner
		Zeke Sheppard
		Red O'Donnell

HEE HAW
(SYNDICATION)
BROADCAST SCHEDULE
1984–85 SEASON

Show Number	Airdate	Guests
390)	9/22/84	Louise Mandrell
		Ronny Robbins
		Million Dollar Band
391)	9/29/84	George Jones
		Brenda Lee
		Moonshine Cloggers & Dew Drops
392)	10/6/84	Lee Greenwood
		The Judds
		Keith Whitley
		Roy Acuff
393)	10/13/84	Loretta Lynn
		Ronnie McDowell
		Sawyer Brown
394)	10/20/84	David Frizzell
		Shelly West
		Cliffie Stone
		Dale Christenson
395)	10/27/84	Porter Wagoner
		Amy Grant
		Million Dollar Band
		Twin River Cloggers

Show Number	Airdate	Guests
396)	11/3/84	Alabama Lorrie Morgan Gary Wolf Bob Murphey Len Ellis
397)	11/10/84	Dottie West Hoyt Axton Cotton Ivy & Noopey (Charles Hutson) Joe Maphis
398)	11/17/84	Osmond Brothers Stan Freese Charlene Gordon Marijane Vandivier
399)	11/24/84	John Conlee Gary Morris Donna Douglas
400)	12/1/84	Sylvia Boxcar Willie Dennis Weaver Ronnie Porter
401)	12/8/84	Louise Mandrell Con Hunley Million Dollar Band The Cannons Buddy & Kay Baines
402)	12/15/84	George Jones Kathy Mattea Lionel Cartwright
403)	12/22/84	Charley Pride Riders in the Sky Million Dollar Band Victoria Shaw
404)	12/29/84	Bill Anderson Tom & Mary Grant Sonja Shepard & Keith Brady Million Dollar Band Babcock Family

Show Number	*Airdate*	*Guests*
405)	1/5/85	Loretta Lynn
		Vern Gosdin
		David Holt
		Lloyd Lindroth
406)	1/12/85	Joe Stampley
		Lorrie Morgan
		Keith Stegall
		Jed Allan
407)	1/19/85	Statler Brothers
		The Whites
		Bobby Vinton
		Rise & Shine Cloggers
408)	1/26/85	Reba McEntire
		Billy Walker
		Dan Seals
		Kerry Gilbert
		Roy Clark Family
409)	2/2/85	Willie Nelson
		Kris Kristofferson
		Anita Bryant
		Roy Acuff
410)	2/9/85	Ricky Skaggs
		Bill Monroe
		Dobie Gray
		Million Dollar Band
411)	2/16/85	Oak Ridge Boys
		Herve Villechaize
		Eddy Raven
		Darlene Austin
412)	2/23/85	Earl Thomas Conley
		Exile
		Bill Baker
		Kimberly Chapman &
		Chip Woodall
413)	3/2/85	Tom T. Hall
		Jim Glaser
		Million Dollar Band
414)	3/9/85	Willie Nelson
		Faron Young
		Jim Stafford
		Palmetto State Cloggers
		Buddy Alan

Show Number	Airdate	Guests
415)	3/16/85	Statler Brothers
		Kieran Kane
		Stan Musial
		Victoria Hallman

HEE HAW
(SYNDICATION)
BROADCAST SCHEDULE
1985–86 SEASON

Show Number	Airdate	Guests
416)	9/21/85	Exile
		Hank Thompson
		Stan Freese
		Girlstown Band
417)	9/28/85	Reba McEntire
		Osmond Brothers
		Moonshine Cloggers
		John Hartford
418)	10/5/85	Louise Mandrell
		Steve Wariner
		Bobby Vinton
419)	10/12/85	Jerry Lee Lewis
		Bill Medley
		Million Dollar Band
420)	10/19/85	Janie Fricke
		Bobby Bare
		Ralph Emery
		Benny Wilson
421)	10/26/85	Charlie Daniels
		Eugene Fodor
		Minnesota Fats
422)	11/2/85	Mel Tillis
		George Strait
		Stan Freese
		Million Dollar Band

Show Number	Airdate	Guests
423)	11/9/85	Willie Nelson Kris Kristofferson McCain Brothers J. T. Jackson John Hartford
424)	11/16/85	Gary Morris Sonny James Don Cherry Melvin Sloan Dancers
425)	11/23/85	Loretta Lynn Mel McDaniels Patricia McKinnon John Hartford
426)	11/30/85	Marie Osmond Burl Ives Dan Seals Williams & Ree Million Dollar Band
427)	12/7/85	Ray Stevens Shelly West Ernest Borgnine
428)	12/14/85	Jerry Lee Lewis Sawyer Brown Jim Stafford
429)	12/21/85	Louise Mandrell Del Reeves Danny Darst Million Dollar Band Roy Clark Family
430)	12/28/85	Lee Greenwood Roger Miller Rockin' Sidney Blue Grass Express Cloggers Jane Robelot
431)	1/4/86	Loretta Lynn Johnny Rodriguez Boxcar Willie Million Dollar Band John Hartford

Show Number	Airdate	Guests
432)	1/11/86	Charley Pride
		Becky Hobbs
		Jim Varney
		Stonewall Jackson
433)	1/18/86	Loretta Lynn
		Helen Cornelius
		Nitty Gritty Dirt Band
		Tennessee River Boys
		John Hartford
		Ramona Jones
		Mike Snider
434)	1/25/86	Ricky Skaggs
		Connie Smith
		Tommy Hunter
		Misty Lord & Jay Ledford
		Cloggers
435)	2/1/86	Hank Williams, Jr.
		Sylvia
		Michael Johnson
		Charlie Walker
		David Holt
		Loretta Lynn
436)	2/8/86	Eddie Rabbitt
		Ray Stevens
		Forester Sisters
		Mac Wiseman
		Grant Turner
437)	2/15/86	George Jones
		Loretta Lynn
		Johnny Russell
		Million Dollar Band
		John Hartford
		Governor Lamar
		Alexander
		Alex Haley
438)	2/22/86	Roger Miller
		The Judds
		Hank Thompson
		Jim Varney
		Steele Family Cloggers
		Loretta Lynn

Show Number	Airdate	Guests
439)	3/1/86	Oak Ridge Boys Faron Young David Holt Billy Parker Loretta Lynn
440)	3/8/86	Hank Williams, Jr. Keith Whitley Merle Kilgore Rattlesnake Annie Ernest Borgnine Loretta Lynn
441)	3/15/86	Loretta Lynn Riders in the Sky Don Holst Holly Gilreath & Jon Hasler Cloggers Million Dollar Band John Hartford Ramona Jones Charlie Douglas

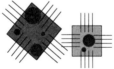

HEE HAW
(SYNDICATION)
BROADCAST SCHEDULE
1986–87 SEASON

Show Number	Airdate	Guests
442)	9/20/86	Loretta Lynn (Cohost) Exile Girls Next Door The Hagers Jake Leg and the Rum Dummies

Show Number	Airdate	Guests
443)	9/27/86	Johnny Cash & June Carter Cash (Cohosts) Gatlin Brothers Kathy Mattea Moonshine Cloggers & Dew Drops John Hartford
444)	10/4/86	Reba McEntire (Cohost) Bellamy Brothers Forester Sisters David Keith
445)	10/11/86	Mel Tillis (Cohost) Randy Travis Judy Rodman Danny White Wilful Stumble
446)	10/18/86	Jerry Reed (Cohost) Barbara Fairchild Pake McEntire David Holt
447)	10/25/86	Loretta Lynn (Cohost) Mickey Gilley The Whites George Hamilton IV Steele Family Cloggers John Hartford
448)	11/1/86	Johnny Cash & June Carter Cash (Cohosts) Dwight Yoakam Billy Grammer The Cannons Ramona Jones John Hartford
449)	11/8/86	Reba McEntire (Cohost) Tanya Tucker Tommy Hunter Kyle Petty Paul Brown Rick Hines

Show Number	Airdate	Guests
450)	11/15/86	Mel Tillis (Cohost) Louise Mandrell John Anderson George Lindsey Ramona Jones John Hartford Loretta Lynn

451)	11/22/86	Johnny Cash & June
		    Carter Cash (Cohosts)
		Gatlin Brothers
		June Carter Cash &
		    Family
		Kentucky Country
		Loretta Lynn
		Jack Clements

452)	11/29/86	Loretta Lynn (Cohost) T. Graham Brown Florence Henderson Leather & Lace Cloggers
453)	12/6/86	Jerry Reed (Cohost) Dottie West Ray Pillow David Holt Dr. Sam Faulk
454)	12/13/86	Reba McEntire (Cohost) Loretta Lynn Pat Boone Keith Stegall Clyde Foley Cummins
455)	1/3/87	George Jones (Cohost) Kenny Rogers Vince Gill Holly Dunn Million Dollar Band Roy Acuff
456)	1/10/87	Oak Ridge Boys (Cohost) Loretta Lynn Dobie Gray k.d. lang Mike Snider

Show Number	Airdate	Guests
457)	1/17/87	Glen Campbell (Cohost)
		Johnny Cash
		June Carter Cash
		Keith Whitley
		Carter Family
		Mel Tillis
		John Campbell
		Rodney Lay
458)	1/24/87	John Schneider (Cohost)
		Louise Mandrell
		New Grass Revival
		Million Dollar Band
		Loretta Lynn
459)	1/31/87	Marie Osmond (Cohost)
		Eddie Rabbitt
		Ralph Stanley & Bill Monroe
		Paul Davis
460)	2/7/87	Hank Williams, Jr. (Cohost)
		Sawyer Brown
		Sweethearts of the Rodeo
		Loretta Lynn
		M. Beeler and G. Hunter
461)	2/14/87	Glen Campbell (Cohost)
		George Jones
		Judy Rodman
		Sonja Shepard & Bobby Revis
		Mel Tillis
		John Campbell
		Roy Acuff
462)	2/21/87	John Schneider (Cohost)
		Loretta Lynn
		Gary Morris
		Riders in the Sky
		Mike Snider
		Shirley Gilbert

Show Number	Airdate	Guests
463)	2/28/87	Oak Ridge Boys (Cohost) Janie Fricke Bill Monroe Mike Williams & Michael Liter Million Dollar Band Grant Turner
464)	3/7/87	Ray Stevens (Cohost) Loretta Lynn & Ernest Lynn Mel McDaniel Southern Lawmen
465)	3/14/87	Marie Osmond (Cohost) Gene Watson Nicolette Larson & Steve Wariner Stan Freese Ramona Jones Loretta Lynn Charlie Collins
466)	3/21/87	Hank Williams, Jr. (Cohost) Marty Stuart k.d. lang Merle Kilgore David Holt
467)	3/28/87	Ray Stevens (Cohost) Loretta Lynn Steve Wariner Lyle Lovett Million Dollar Band

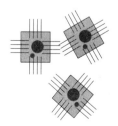

HEE HAW
(SYNDICATION)
BROADCAST SCHEDULE
1987–88 SEASON

Show Number	Airdate	Guests
468)	9/19/87	John Schneider (Cohost) Sweethearts of the Rodeo Freddy Fender Roy Clark Family
469)	9/26/87	Ralph Emery (Cohost) Ray Stevens Johnny Lee Hillbilly Jim
470)	10/3/87	Mel Tillis (Cohost) Ronnie McDowell Desert Rose John Hartford Mike Snider
471)	10/10/87	Roger Miller (Cohost) Keith Whitley Johnny Russell & David Wilkins Million Dollar Band
472)	10/17/87	Charley Pride (Cohost) Osborne Brothers Patty Loveless Roy Clark Family
473)	10/24/87	Loretta Lynn (Cohost) T. G. Sheppard Williams & Ree Sherry Glass and Bobby Revis, Jr.
474)	10/31/87	Tanya Tucker (Cohost) Roy Acuff Randy Travis Whitfield Ward Paul Davis Paul Overstreet Ramona Jones John Hartford

Show Number	Airdate	Guests
475)	11/7/87	John Schneider (Cohost) Forester Sisters Charlie Walker Million Dollar Band
476)	11/14/87	Ricky Skaggs (Cohost) Roy Acuff Ricky Van Shelton The Famous San Diego Chicken Ramona Jones John Hartford
477)	11/21/87	Loretta Lynn (Cohost) B. J. Thomas David Wills Hawkins County Hoedown Cloggers Jack Roper John Hartford Mike Snider
478)	11/28/87	Brenda Lee (Cohost) Sawyer Brown Charlie Louvin Million Dollar Band
479)	12/5/87	Mel Tillis (Cohost) Del Reeves Judy Rodman Michael Johnson
480)	12/12/87	Roger Miller (Cohost) Sylvia Jack Greene Million Dollar Band
481)	1/9/88	Louise Mandrell (Cohost) Glen Campbell Steve Wariner Billy "Crash" Craddock Steele Family Cloggers
482)	1/16/88	Hoyt Axton (Cohost) Larry Gatlin and the Gatlin Brothers K. T. Oslin Jim DePaiva David Holt

The Hee Haw *cast in the 1987-88 season*

Show Number	Airdate	Guests
483)	1/23/88	Lee Greenwood (Cohost) Kathy Mattea Highway 101 Million Dollar Band Famous San Diego Chicken
484)	1/30/88	Roy Acuff and Minnie Pearl (Cohosts) Glen Campbell Stella Parton Bill Anderson
485)	2/6/88	Barbara Mandrell (Cohost) Exile Dan Seals Hillbilly Jim
486)	2/13/88	Randy Travis (Cohost) Mel McDaniel Girls Next Door Million Dollar Band

Show Number	Airdate	Guests
487)	2/20/88	Ricky Skaggs (Cohost) The Whites Famous San Diego Chicken Ramona Jones Joe Edwards
488)	2/27/88	Statler Brothers (Cohosts) John Conlee k.d. lang Sherry Glass Burton Edwards Roy Clark Family
489)	4/23/88	Jim Stafford (Cohost) Mickey Gilley Lorrie Morgan David Holt Cliff Dumas Vicki Rae Von
490)	4/30/88	Janie Fricke (Cohost) George Jones Vince Gill Hillbilly Jim

491)	5/7/88	Barbara Mandrell
		    (Cohost)
		Larry Gatlin and the
		    Gatlin Brothers
		T. Graham Brown
		Jim DePaiva

492)	5/14/88	Tammy Wynette (Cohost) Porter Wagoner Lyle Lovett Famous San Diego Chicken
493)	5/21/88	Statler Brothers (Cohosts) Jeannie C. Riley Eddy Raven

HEE HAW
(SYNDICATION)
BROADCAST SCHEDULE
1988–89 SEASON

Show Number	Airdate	Guests
494)	10/1/88	Johnny Cash and June Carter Cash (Cohosts) Judy Rodman Carter Family Famous San Diego Chicken
495)	10/8/88	Tennessee Ernie Ford (Cohost) Oak Ridge Boys McCarter Sisters Ramona Jones John Hartford *Hee Haw* Gospel Quartet with Ernie Ford
496)	10/15/88	Porter Wagoner (Cohost) George Jones Little Jimmy Dickens Patty Loveless Grant Turner
497)	10/22/88	Brenda Lee (Cohost) Bellamy Brothers Wolfman Jack Buckles & Bows Famous San Diego Chicken
498)	10/29/88	Crook and Chase (Cohosts) Conway Twitty Highway 101 Keith Whitley
499)	11/5/88	Charlie Daniels (Cohost) Janie Frickie John Anderson

Show Number	Airdate	Guests
500)	11/12/88	Million Dollar Band Tanya Tucker (Cohost) Michael Martin Murphey Johnny Russell Famous San Diego Chicken Ryan Murphey Cowboy Quartet
501)	11/19/88	Ricky Skaggs (Cohost) The Whites Hillbilly Jim
502)	11/26/88	Johnny Cash and June Carter Cash (Cohosts) Holly Dunn Million Dollar Band Cowboy Quartet
503)	12/3/88	Gary Morris (Cohost) Asleep at the Wheel Becky Hobbs Million Dollar Band
504)	12/10/88	Jimmy Dean (Cohost) Marie Osmond Billy Joe Royal David Holt
505)	12/17/88	Mel Tillis (Cohost) Sweethearts of the Rodeo Jerry Jeff Walker Dude Mowrey
506)	1/7/89	Ray Stevens (Cohost) Forester Sisters Jennifer Powers Grant Pettingill John Hartford Ramona Jones
507)	1/14/89	Brenda Lee (Cohost) Ricky Van Shelton Mel Tillis Steele Family Million Dollar Band

Show Number	Airdate	Guests
508)	1/21/89	Charley Pride (Cohost)
		Sawyer Brown
		Mary-Chapin Carpenter
		Jerry Jeff Walker
		Famous San Diego Chicken
		Hoyt Axton
		Bobby Rose
		Rick Biddle (WOWL-TV)
509)	1/28/89	Roger Miller (Cohost)
		Glen Campbell
		Kathy Mattea
		Ricky Skaggs and Sharon White
		Big Al Downing
510)	2/4/89	Waylon Jennings (Cohost)
		Louise Mandrell
		Mac Wiseman
		Ralph Emery
		David Holt
511)	2/11/89	Reba McEntire (Cohost)
		Gene Watson
		Canyon
		Susie Luchsinger
512)	2/18/89	Merle Haggard (Cohost)
		Randy Travis
		The McCarters
		Cale Yarborough
		Famous San Diego Chicken
513)	2/25/89	Loretta Lynn (Cohost)
		John Denver
		Telia Summy
		Misty Carter
		Brent Montgomery
		Cowboy Quartet
		Mike Snider and Gerald Smith

Show Number	Airdate	Guests
514)	4/29/89	Waylon Jennings (Cohost) Tammy Wynette T. Graham Brown Richard Petty Kyle Petty Million Dollar Band
515)	5/6/89	Reba McEntire (Cohost) Kitty Wells Lyle Lovett Louis Nye Famous San Diego Chicken
516)	5/13/89	Glen Campbell (Cohost) Alabama Burch Sisters Ace Cannon
517)	5/20/89	Loretta Lynn (Cohost) Vern Gosdin Jo-El Sonnier Ken Kercheval Million Dollar Band Billy Holt Roy Acuff

HEE HAW
(SYNDICATION)
BROADCAST SCHEDULE
1989–90 SEASON

Show Number	Airdate	Guests
518)	9/16/89	Barbara Mandrell (Cohost) Larry Gatlin and the Gatlin Brothers Williams & Ree Jim DePaiva

Show Number	Airdate	Guests
519)	9/23/89	Jimmy Dean (Cohost)
		Lorrie Morgan
		Skip Ewing
520)	9/30/89	Steve Wariner (Cohost)
		Forester Sisters
		Big Al Downing
		John Hartford
		Ramona Jones
521)	10/7/89	Holly Dunn (Cohost)
		Kenny Rogers
		Carl Perkins
		Drema Hinton
		Chuck Gifford
522)	10/14/89	Roy Rogers and Dale Evans (Cohosts)
		Riders in the Sky
		Big Al Downing
523)	10/21/89	George Jones (Cohost)
		Patty Loveless
		Leather & Lace
		Roy Acuff and George Jones
524)	10/28/89	Robin Leach (Cohost)
		Don Williams
		Highway 101
		David Holt
		Lulu Roman–Roy Acuff Song
525)	11/4/89	Barbara Mandrell (Cohost)
		Baillie & the Boys
		Sherry Glass and Bobby Revis
		Lloyd Wells and Ernie Ford
526)	11/11/89	Kathy Mattea (Cohost)
		Restless Heart
		Clint Black
		Williams & Ree
		John Hartford
		Ramona Jones

Show Number	Airdate	Guests
527)	11/18/89	Ray Stevens (Cohost) Lacy J. Dalton David Holt
528)	11/25/89	George Jones (Cohost) Nitty Gritty Dirt Band Steele Family Cloggers Tommy Lasorda
529)	12/2/89	Regis Philbin and Kathie Lee Gifford (Cohosts) The Judds Shenandoah
530)	12/9/89	Roger Miller (Cohost) Foster & Lloyd Suzy Bogguss
531)	1/13/90	Tanya Tucker (Cohost) Garth Brooks LaCosta Vicki Bird
532)	1/20/90	Orville Redenbacher (Cohost) Charley Pride Daniele Alexander Stan Freese
533)	1/27/90	Crystal Gayle (Cohost) David Ball
534)	2/3/90	Waylon Jennings (special guest) Connie Smith David Holt
535)	2/10/90	Ricky Van Shelton (Cohost) Desert Rose Band Roni Stoneman John Hartford Ramona Jones
536)	2/17/90	Charlie Daniels (Cohost) John Hiatt Vicki Bird
537)	2/24/90	Oak Ridge Boys (Cohosts) Moe Bandy Roni and Donna Stoneman

THE *HEE HAW* BROADCAST SCHEDULE

Show Number	Airdate	Guests
538)	3/3/90	Lionel Cartwright (Cohost) / Janie Fricke / David Holt
539)	3/10/90	Waylon Jennings (Cohost) / Sawyer Brown / Jessi Colter
540)	3/17/90	T. Graham Brown (Cohost) / Jennifer McCarter & The McCarter Sisters
541)	3/24/90	Hank Thompson (Cohost) / Glen Campbell

HEE HAW (SYNDICATION) BROADCAST SCHEDULE 1990–91 SEASON

Show Number	Airdate	Guests
542)	9/15/90	Garth Brooks / Suzy Bogguss
543)	9/22/90	Glen Campbell / Alan Jackson / David Holt
544)	9/29/90	Barbara Mandrell / Jo-el Sonnier / Magnum Cloggers
545)	10/6/90	Vern Gosdin / Baillie & the Boys / *Hee Haw* Cowboy Quartet
546)	10/13/90	Eddie Rabbitt / Jann Browne
547)	10/20/90	Hoyt Axton / Holly Dunn / Kentucky Country
548)	10/27/90	Lee Greenwood / Wild Rose

Show Number	Airdate	Guests
549)	11/3/90	Conway Twitty
		Sweethearts of the Rodeo
		Jim DePaiva
550)	11/10/90	Tanya Tucker
		Paul Overstreet
551)	11/17/90	Patty Loveless
		Mark Collie
		David Holt
552)	11/24/90	Ricky Skaggs
		The Whites
		Merlin Olsen
553)	12/1/90	Lorrie Morgan
		Travis Tritt
		Moonshine Cloggers
554)	12/8/90	Loretta Lynn
		Jim & Jesse
		Henry Cannon
		Grant Turner
555)	12/15/90	Louise Mandrell
		Canyon
		Charlie Nagatani
556)	1/5/91	Ray Stevens
		Forester Sisters
		David Holt
557)	1/12/91	Marie Osmond
		Asleep at the Wheel
		Mac Wiseman
558)	1/19/91	Glen Campbell
		T. Graham Brown
		Ramona and Alisa Jones
559)	1/26/91	Lionel Cartwright
		Shelby Lynne
		David Holt
560)	2/2/91	Tony Orlando
		Charley Pride
561)	2/9/91	Reba McEntire
		Aaron Tippin
		Mac Wiseman
562)	2/16/91	Oak Ridge Boys
		Alison Krauss and Union Station

Show Number	Airdate	Guests
563)	2/23/91	Tammy Wynette Steve Wariner

HEE HAW
(SYNDICATION)
BROADCAST SCHEDULE
1991–92 SEASON

Show Number	Airdate	Guests
564)	1/4/92	Barbara Mandrell Vern Gosdin Joe Diffie
565)	1/11/92	Merle Haggard Alison Krauss and Union Station Les Taylor
566)	1/18/92	Garth Brooks Trisha Yearwood Diamond Rio
567)	1/25/92	Lorrie Morgan Desert Rose Band
568)	2/1/92	Ronnie Milsap Highway 101 Aaron Tippin
569)	2/8/92	Alabama Pam Tillis Brooks & Dunn
570)	2/15/92	Patty Loveless Doug Stone The Dillards
571)	2/22/92	Garth Brooks Louise Mandrell Billy Dean
572)	2/29/92	Alan Jackson Kathie Baillie & The Boys Matraca Berg

Show Number	Airdate	Guests
573)	3/7/92	Barbara Mandrell
		Sawyer Brown
		B. B. Watson
574)	3/14/92	Oak Ridge Boys
		T. Graham Brown
		Robin Lee
575)	3/21/92	Forester Sisters
		Mark Collie
576)	3/28/92	Ricky Skaggs
		Jim & Jesse
		Clinton Gregory
577)	4/4/92	Holly Dunn
		Mark Chesnutt
		Gold City
578)	4/11/92	Lionel Cartwright
		Marty Stuart
		The Remingtons
579)	4/18/92	Marie Osmond
		Ronnie Milsap
		Eddie London

Show Number	Airdate	Guests
580)	4/25/92	Lee Greenwood Linda Davis Marty Brown
581)	5/2/92	Brenda Lee Exile Jim & Jesse
582)	5/9/92	Merle Haggard Steve Wariner Donna Ulisse
583)	5/16/92	Asleep at the Wheel Shelby Lynne Dude Mowrey
584)	5/23/92	Eddie Rabbitt Suzy Bogguss Rob Crosby
585)	5/30/92	Gary Morris Sweethearts of the Rodeo Hal Ketchum

ACKNOWLEDGMENTS

THE IDEA for this book began when I received a telephone call in 1992 from Marc Eliot, who at the time was working with Roy Clark on his autobiography. Marc wanted to check some facts regarding Roy's long involvement with *Hee Haw*. We spoke several times, and during one of our conversations, Marc asked if I'd ever thought about telling the whole story of *Hee Haw*. The more I thought about it, the more I realized the time had come to put down all that I remembered from what had been one of the most privileged times of my life—my quarter-century involvement with one of the great phenomena of television. *Hee Haw* was truly unique—there will never be another show like it. The times, the business, the nature of country music, and the intermingling of personalities—all this happens once in a lifetime. I feel blessed to have been a part of the history of *Hee Haw*.

I'm delighted to say that my relationship with Marc, a brilliant writer, extraordinary musicologist and chronicler of our popular culture, was and continues to be a source of pleasure. In spite of the long hours of reserach, discussion, contemplation, and recall, we never "lost our cool." Quite the contrary: we often found ourselves laughing over incidents related both to *Hee Haw* and to our own lives. For more than a year, Marc was my partner on this project, and if nothing else, proved himself worthy by being able to put up with my "Samisms."

Our agent, Mel Berger, of the William Morris Agency, proved crucial in putting us together with another inveterate *Hee Haw* fan, Gary Goldstein of The Berkley Publishing Group. Working with the team of Mel, Gary, and Marc made me feel as if I'd just won an Emmy.

I also wish to thank Lara Robbins for her valuable production contributions. I feel I owe many thanks to a lot of people who have been a part of the show and my life these past twenty-five years. It's important for me to tell you that in many places where I write about "I", I mean to include all those who, in spirit and in reality were the true "we" of *Hee Haw*. I hope I've included everybody, but if there are some who slip through the ever-widening rungs of memories—agents, managers, PR people, record label executives, sponsors, and advertisers—I hope they'll understand. My collective thanks to them all.

I wish to especially thank the following:

Jonathan Winters, a genius and, I'm proud to say, a personal friend. It was on Jonathan's show that I gained my first introduction to TV production.

Perry Lafferty, the CBS executive who kick-started *Hee Haw* in 1969 and who through the stormy years, always considered me a loyal employee.

Frank Peppiatt and John Aylesworth, the creative team who taught me how to handle writers and deal with talent.

Nick Vanoff, my Buffaloian friend and top producer who trusted my pencil and pushed me to the top of the show business world.

Bill Harbach, Nick's partner, who dubbed my special way of speaking "Samisms" ("Call ASCAP", "There's a bird in the studio!").

My office buddy Alan Courtney, a champion salesman who guided me in my dealings with TV stations and advertisers. Alan's assistant, Dottie Delaplain, who had that sweet and precious voice when talking to station programmers, which helped convince them to air *Hee Haw*.

My directors—Bill Davis, my first partner whose great eye made the *Hee Haw* Honeys prettier and prettier; Bob Boatman, a trusted friend who went from lighting to directing more than four hundred shows before his tragic death; Steve Schepman, whose sheer ability earned him the job.

Gene McAvoy and Bill Camden, who designed the sets and gave *Hee Haw* its cartoon look, which their successors, Jim Stanley and Chris Tibbott, maintained to the very end.

My writers, all of whom put up with my endless changes and always made me look good.

Marcia Minor, my right arm from CBS who protected and nurtured me through the highs and lows. Sandy Liles, who made my job easier by staying one step ahead of me.

What can I say? The cast of *Hee Haw* became my family. I thank them all, and especially:

Buck Owens, the businessman of the music industry who, with his manager, Jack McFadden, selected the right talent needed when we first began.

Roy Clark, whose many contributions to country music and comedy helped make our show so unique. He was always great to work with, and no matter what we asked for, never said no.

I consider Minnie Pearl, Grandpa Jones and Roy Acuff my mentors. They kept me and the show straight and traditional.

All my friends at the Grand Ole Opry, Hal Durham, Jerry Stobel and Debbie Logue. We worked together so well and shared the same problems. We sure had many laughs and lots of fun.

Archie Campbell and Gordie Tapp, who took me away from the city and made me "country."

I wish to give a great big *Hee Haw Sa-loot!* to the following, who made me shine with pride, and whom I shall never forget:

Don Harron, Jeanine Riley, Stringbean, Grady Nutt, Junior Samples, Lulu Roman, Cathy Baker, The Buckaroos with Don Rich, Wild West Fanci with Rodney Lay, The Nashville Edition (Joe, Dolores, Wendy and Herschel), Gunilla Hutton, The Hagers, Lisa Todd, Jackie Phelps, Jimmy Riddle, Barbi Benton, Misty Rowe, Marianne Rodgers, Roni Stoneman, Gailard Sartain, Buck Trent, Kenny Price, John Henry Faulk, Mackenzie Colt, Diana Goldman, Nancy Traylor, Slim Pickens, Victoria Hallman, Kelly Billingsley, Irlene Mandrell, Jeff Smith, Jackie Waddell, Linda Thompson, Dub Taylor, Charlie McCoy and the *Hee Haw* Band, and George "Goober" Lindsey. Put them all together, they spell *Hee Haw.*

No variety show ever can excel without guests. There wasn't a guest on the show who didn't become my friend. Whether or not they had a song on the charts, our guests always came on for Sam. They, too, shall not be forgotten by me.

Heartfelt thanks to the following folks at Channel 5, our Nashville home when we first started in 1969: the late Tom Baker, Roy Smith, Harold Crump, Tom Irwin, and their secretaries, Joyce Thomas and Vicki (Elliot) Freedle.

I am grateful also for the support I received from Ed and Thelma Gaylord, the entire Gaylord family and their administrative assistant, Thelis Clark, for keeping the show going an additional ten years after it was sold by Yongestreet to the Gaylords. I thank the late Jim Terrell and also Glen Stinchcomb for helping to make the acquisition happen. Bud Wendell and his executive staff, especially the folks in accounting for their support, understanding, and trust. I must not forget good ol' George Cooper, who was then president of the AFM (American Federation of Musicians) Nashville local and had the wisdom to work with me in helping to introduce what was considered revolutionary taping techniques in 1969.

My thanks to all the city officials and government executives of Nashville, and the Country Music Association who stood by us when the critics nearly dismantled *Hee Haw* our first year.

Finally, there is, of course, my family. My in-laws, Poppy and

Clem Massell, who prayed for my health and safety when I was away (as I so often was) from my Los Angeles home. My parents, both now deceased, my dad Anthony, who did not get to see a *Hee Haw* show, and my mother, Louise, who saw many and lived to witness my success. She was so proud of me, she called me Mr. *Hee Haw.*

My lovely family almost grew up without me, because of the amount of time I inevitably had to spend in Nashville. I thank my lovely wife Grace who stood by me and understood my love for *Hee Haw* and country music. I so admire her courage and strength for raising our four lovely children, Linda, Lisa, Tony and Torey. I want to tell them now I'm sorry I may have missed a few birthdays, hugs and kisses—but at least I never missed a Little League game! I also want to thank the newer members of my family: Linda's husband, Brendan; my grandchildren Matthew and Katie; and Torey's wife, Lynn, and their son, Dominic.

In closing, my heart says in a most humble way, thanks to you all out there for sharing the most precious years of my life.

That's all. God Bless.

With love,
Sam Lovullo
Los Angeles
September 1996

That's All-l-l-l-l!

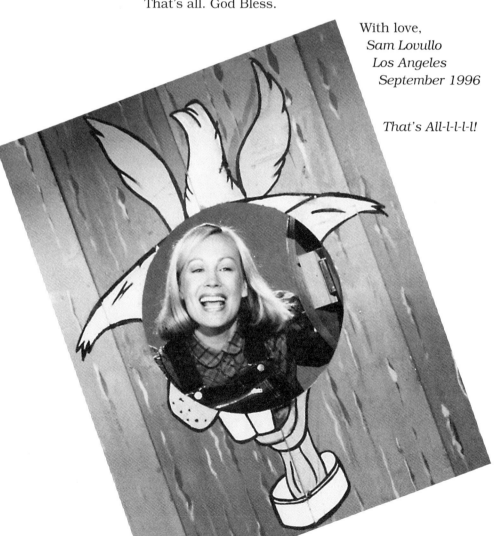